CW00734919

CONFESSIONS
of a
SENSITIVE
MAN

An Unconventional Defense
of Sensitive Men

WILLIAM ALLEN

ISBN (Print): 978-1-09832-516-9

ISBN (eBook): 978-1-09832-517-6

I dedicate this book to my mother for without whom this would not have been possible. Often the best mother for a sensitive male is a sensitive woman. Like myself, she is a highly sensitive person, struggling from time to time to find meaning and place with her sensitivity. Her golden heart and delicate Southern ways belie the relentless strength that lies below. Like water shapes the rock, she has shaped me gently over my years and made me the proud, highly sensitive man that I am today. This book is for you, Mom. Thank you for the one constant in my life—your love and support.

Confessions of a Sensitive Man takes us on a journey that is, at once, personal, poignant, and ultimately validating for sensitive men and the people who love them. Deeply introspective, Bill has gifted us with the wisdom he has attained that only comes with long reflection on life's many challenges as sensitive men.

—Tracy Cooper, Ph.,D. author of *Empowering the Sensitive Male Soul*

William Allen has provided a timely and encouraging guidebook for the highly sensitive man who has yet to realize the gift of his capacities. In these turbulent times, may every wholehearted, compassionate man read this book and recognize themselves as the heroes we need.

—Bev Martin, Coach, Facilitator of Insight and Change
www.bevmartin.com

"William Allen's book is academic, progressive as well as offering readers a practical education. It is well supported with facts and resources and is well articulated. It contains a good blend of lecture and facts followed up by his personal observations about his own life as an HSP male. "

—Linda Nichole Carrington, Ph.D, author of *The Heart of Your Power, Playful Guidelines for Awakening your Inner Wisdom*

I wrote this book for every man or boy who was told they were too sensitive or too emotional; that they weren't man enough or masculine enough simply because they feel more, sense more, and experience a broader range of emotions. For every man or boy who needs more alone time to process these feelings, who needs to think more consciously, and as a result, is more cautious and deliberate in action, this is for you. For all of you males out there representing twenty percent of the male population who are highly sensitive, or as I like to put, highly sensing, I wrote this book for you.

This book is not a clinical tome designed to give you the latest updated information on Highly Sensitive People. I am not a psychologist or a therapist or medical doctor. I am a man in my sixties who has been highly sensitive for the entirety of my life. I have carried this personality trait with me everywhere I go. Most of my life, I did not even know this trait had a name. It was not until the late nineties when I read Elaine Aron's book, *The Highly Sensitive Person*, that I knew it was a personality characteristic that was quite normal, although not predominant.

When I found out I was relieved and from that point forward devoured anything I could read on the subject. I became an evangelist for high sensitivity. I saw it in people I worked with, my family and friends, in people in public life, celebrities; everywhere I looked it seemed I could easily pick out HSPs. Instead of feeling alone and isolated, I realized I was part of a larger family of highly sensing people. Psychologists estimate that twenty percent of the human population has this feature, male and female.

Several years ago, I started writing a blog called The Sensitive Man (www.thesensitiveman.com). As I wrote, I became aware of the myriad questions I had about being a highly sensitive male. These questions were not the kind you find in a typical clinical book on highly sensitive people. My life experiences were the genesis of these questions. My childhood, my education, my adult working life, and raising a family of HSPs drove the questions. It was in many ways a "boots on the ground" blog about living life through the lens of an HSP male. The blog was filled with my experiences, questions, and what I realize now—my wisdom accumulated through trial-and-error living life as an HSP.

Not long after writing a few blog articles it dawned on me that this could make a useful and unique book. The purpose of the book was to educate about the trait in laymen's terms, to validate through experience and opinion the value of the attribute, and to provide questions about the trait that would appeal to further research. Based upon Dr. Aron's proposition that high sensitivity is a necessary evolutionary trait to protect and aid the species, I promoted throughout the book the value and purpose of the unique cultural and social value that HSPs offer and particularly HSP males.

I could see that what I was suggesting was something more than just encouraging HSP males, but also proposing a new model for men. We are living in a time where the term *toxic masculinity* has become part of the popular vernacular. The label is not as some men imagine a war on masculinity but rather a battle against a distortion of masculinity technically called *hegemonic masculinity*. The book repeatedly speaks about how this has affected women, children, and men over the centuries. Most of the world's pressing problems today have, at some point, their origins in this poisonous role model for men.

I see a job for HSP males in a needed transformation of male roles. We HSMs can be thought leaders and mentors for restoring balance to men. We can help men become more human and less toxic, healing long-buried emotional distress caused by archaic cultural and familial norms. Part of the book focuses on this idea.

The book is lightly researched in keeping with the theme of offering my accumulated learning, yet throughout, I do have a good bit of supportive references. The references were useful in proposing ideas and thoughts on high sensitivity that were somewhat unconventional and to reference other research that would suggest this line of thinking would be productive. There are many great books out there for those purists who insist that books about psychology can only be written by psychologists or researchers. The older I get, the more I appreciate the notion of the wisdom of the tribes or elders. I suppose vanity keeps me from identifying with the term elder, but the years instruct me that the descriptor fits. It was, after all, my life that led me to write this book. My confessions are now my admissions.

In many ways, this book was written by my older self for my younger self. It is with that hope that I offer this book to highly sensitive boys and men younger than I. In some ways, it is the campfire book where the older man, the storyteller, tells illustrative and instructive stories about life to the younger men gathered about the crackling fire. It is about the accumulated experience that life rolls out to each of us, where the only evidence is the memory deep within. There is value in that.

As you read the book, you will note there are sections in the chapters about my personal experiences. I try to illustrate through my life how sensitivity has impacted me. Many of my proposals are my observations that have occurred throughout my life. This is not to be construed as evidence-based fact one might receive from a therapist or doctor, but rather the little gems that you get from your grandparents or experienced progenitors. I have also suggested further studies in areas I found lacking research and hope as the years go by that these will be addressed.

Although high sensitivity has been around humans throughout history, we are just coming to grips with researching the trait—there is much still to learn. Typically, in each chapter, there is a suggestion or tips section that is relevant to the topics. I wish I would have had something like this to read when I was a young man. It would have been instructive and helpful and could have helped me make better decisions growing up.

I want to thank those who have been leaders in the research on high sensitivity. Dr. Elaine Aron is a pioneer and perhaps the godmother of this trait. All of us who write on this topic owe her a great deal of gratitude. Her work was seminal and built the framework on high sensitivity. Reading her works has given validation in many ways on who I am and how this characteristic has shaped my life.

The late Dr. Ted Zeff was one of the first to home in on the sensitive male, in particular the sensitive boy. His work has been instrumental in acknowledging the proper way to nurture and raise sensitive young males. It is sad that he is no longer with us.

Dr. Tracy Cooper has written many books on HSMs that are professionally researched and enlightening for anyone interested in high sensitivity in men. He is a leader on the concept of high sensation seeking HSMs, something that I think deserves a lot more attention. He is a thought leader on HSMs, and I do appreciate his work.

I want to thank my editor, Jami Carpenter, who, with her help and guidance, has helped me to take a rambling collection of thoughts, words, and blog articles and help me shape and form them into a readable book. A great editor is gold to any writer.

I want to thank my wise woman counsel: JH, RS, LC, NS, BM, MH, BP, MS, and YJ. These women have been my muses and served in different capacities in my life. This group is a collection of friends, partners, mentors and confidants who, over the years, have encouraged my indulgence in writing. You know who you are. I want to thank my love, Donna, for her support and inspiration and teaching me everyday how to be a better man.

And, finally to my children, Hayley, Fletch, Bax, and Jody. Hey kids, I did it. 'Nuff said.

Table of Contents

Chapter 1

What ... me, Sensitive?

Growing up, I knew I was different. I was different from all the other boys in the neighborhood. I was taller, skinnier, and more sensitive. Yeah, sensitive. At the time I didn't know what sensitivity was all about. Growing up in South Carolina in the fifties and sixties, the profile for boys was rough-and-tumble, getting dirty, getting into fights, and letting all criticism roll right off your back.

The last thing I wanted to be was a sensitive boy.

Back then, every boy was subject to the code: boys were expected to be little men. They had to be tough, unemotional, and above all, not like little girls.

It was easy to fail this code if you were a sensitive type. I saw things differently; I experienced life through a different lens and filter than most boys. It was harder for me to "just get over" life's bumps and bruises. I took them to heart and ruminated ferociously the mistakes I made, whether real or imagined. I felt alone most of the time, the only boy in a family of girls. My father was distant and somewhat disaffected. He was an HSP (a highly sensitive person) himself but didn't know it. I don't know whether he was trying to whip me into code or if he knew it would be easier for me if I simply conformed. Eventually, I got the message and created a self-image through sports.

I was a fairly good athlete, rangy and quick, but not with supreme athletic ability. It was enough to make me slightly above average. This went over well with my male friends. I knew this because I was generally picked in the top five for things like kickball, softball, and especially basketball. Being tall made it easy not to be missed for early selection. You can't teach tall.

I loved football but hated the contact. My dad played football in high school. He was voted most athletic in the school, so there was some pressure for me to be athletic, although I admit, it wasn't a fanatical expectation. I put more pressure on myself than anyone. This was a proving ground. This was a way I could prove I was a man.

Before high school, there were Dixie Youth Baseball and Pop Warner football. I never was talented enough or motivated enough to play baseball. That was a miss on my part. Wearing your baseball cap on game day to school was a sign that you had arrived as a little man.

I tried out later for Pop Warner, and the coaches pretty much sealed my fate. They must have been ex-Marine Corp drill instructors because they wore our butts out in the first practice. Kids were falling out all over the field. I was one of them. I was beyond sore. The pain was excruciating, and I knew that football was probably not for me.

Back then, there was no organized basketball for kids, so I just played around the neighborhood. We developed our own neighborhood teams and played other kids in the surrounding neighborhoods. Games could last all night, and best of all, there were no coaches to screw it up for us. I didn't mind contact, and that was a good thing as I was generally picked to play center. As my skills improved, respect began to come.

I was on the eighth-grade team for a brief time but hated the coach. He yelled constantly; sometimes, I thought, simply to yell. I didn't like that. He was an ass. I quit the team, even as the varsity coach, a neighbor, was talking to me about moving me up to the high school team. This is a place where being sensitive really hurt me. I got nervous about the "promotion" to varsity and was overwhelmed with fear. I quit before my basketball career could begin, succumbing to my fears.

This continued throughout high school. I had trouble with relationships. On the one hand, I was a pretty shy guy in the public eye, but quite gregarious around close friends. It was difficult for me to ask girls out on dates. I was like most teenage boys, pretty awkward with talking to the opposite sex. Not like the more popular boys who seemed to have a personality trait that made them calm and debonair. I assumed it was a lack of masculine magnetism on my part. Again, another place I failed to meet the boy/man code. Of course, it never helped my cause to always be in pursuit of girls who had no interest in me.

I got used to dealing with a lot of emotional highs and lows, the angst of adolescence. For the most part, I dealt with it alone. The feelings I had didn't seem manly enough to discuss with my parents or friends. I learned to be my own best friend.

As I got into the upper grades of high school, I started underachieving. I was an honor student up until my junior year of high school when I met my first crush, a senior girl, in yearbook staff. She was different. This was the early seventies, and by all definitions she was a hippie chick. I was from a conservative and devoutly Christian family. Our meeting was like the meeting of matter and anti-matter, and it changed my world. Everything I had learned to that point, I never questioned. I may not have liked it, but I was not positioned to oppose the values that I had been brought up with. She opened my mind to a new way of looking at things, and I began my long journey to accepting and embracing who I was.

My life was altered. I questioned everything and allowed myself to go with the flow wherever it took me. At times, I felt as though being the sensitive man I was made me a freak or failure. I found the openness of the sixties and early seventies opened my thinking to new ideas, some of which made more sense to me than those I was taught as a child. It felt right to my sensibilities. I thank my first crush for that important bit of insight.

Throughout my adult life, through two marriages and three children, three stepchildren, and a career in corporate America, I found myself still feeling inadequate, underachieving, and a bit of an outcast. I read voraciously to find some hint about what it was that made me different. In college, I majored in psychology, hoping to find clues about myself. There were no easy explanations or answers. I kept looking.

In the mid to late nineties, I found a book that finally explained who I was. Dr. Elaine Aron wrote her seminal work on Sensory Processing Sensitivity, called *The Highly Sensitive Person*. It was the book that quite literally helped me to reframe my life. It was more than an explanation for my sensitivity; it was a validation for it. I knew when I read the book that it was going to have an impact on my vocational direction. At the time, I was still working for a large financial concern as an IT Manager. I still had about fifteen years more to work in that job, but at some point it became apparent that I needed to leave and pursue interests that were more in line with my personality.

Recognizing and acknowledging my sensitivity has been a lifelong endeavor. It has been a journey and a transformational experience. I continue to learn every day the value of this trait, a trait that is called Sensory Processing Sensitivity (SPS).

What the Hell is SPS?

Sensory Processing Sensitivity sounds like something no one wants to have. It almost sounds like a disorder of some sort. Actually, it's not. It's a personality trait where increased sensitivity in the central nervous system, coupled with deeper cognitive processing of social and emotional stimuli, allows for perceptually greater awareness of environmental cues.

This awareness can lead individuals to be able to sense things in the environment not easily perceived by most individuals. The key to this processing is not actually in the sensory organs, but rather in the brain and how the inputs are processed. People with SPS have low perceptual thresholds and deeper thought-processing ability. It tends to spawn cautious behavior and low-risk taking.[1]

Those with SPS are prone to overwhelm, share deep empathy for others, and have greater emotional reactivity.[2] The trait can lead to giftedness. With higher perception levels, inventiveness, greater imagination skills, and creativity can subsequently occur. The primary characteristics associated with the trait and tendencies lead to high sensory processing, high sensory perception, introversion, high emotional reactivity, submissive behavior, and high levels of inhibition.[3] Introversion is not a given with this trait as a small percentage of people with SPS are extroverts.

The important distinction about SPS is that it is not a disorder and should not be confused with high functioning autism, post-traumatic stress disorder, or schizophrenia.[4] It is now being regarded as an important survival trait. The cautious nature of the SPS population is desirable for protection of the species, providing important 'canary in the coal mine' information to the larger non-SPS population. The awareness displayed by many SPS individuals is often gleaned from the environment that is missed or not recognized by the larger group. The SPS quality has been observed in over one hundred non-human species.[5] I find this comforting to know that I am helping the species to survive, even though sometimes I feel hardly capable of surviving a rough day of life.

People with SPS can be quite adapted to their environments. With the proper early childhood upbringing, SPS children can grow up to be confident and emotionally stable adults. However, if the childhood experience is negative and non-supportive, with parents ignoring the needs of SPS children, the effects can create a negative adulthood experience, leading to high anxiety and depression. This is especially true for males. About one-third of the SPS population is estimated to have had negative childhood experiences.[6]

The Godmother of Sensitivity – Elaine Aron

Dr. Elaine Aron is a research psychologist and psychotherapist. Her 1996 book, *The Highly Sensitive Person* identified the personality trait for Sensory Processing Sensitivity. She also coined the term, which has become the de facto moniker for SPS individuals – Highly Sensitive Persons, more commonly known as HSPs.

Along with her husband, Arthur Aron, Elaine has performed many of the early studies on HSPs and their characteristics. She is an HSP herself, which certainly was a driver in her pursuit of this research. Both Dr. Arons have done important research on the psychology of love and have incorporated additional specialized research on love and the HSP.[7] Her 2001 book entitled, *The Highly Sensitive Person in Love,* elaborates on her research with her husband on the complicated and emotional aspects of highly sensitive people and romantic relationships.

Dr. Aron's work has opened the minds of many individuals, who like me, have been looking for answers about our sensitive personality temperament. She has provided guidance, illumination on the subject, and literally opened the topic up for discussion and debate for the estimated one billion humans on the planet with this characteristic. Her work has defined the characteristic to many as being normal and even essential to human survival. No book on sensitivity could legitimately ignore her contribution and not offer some thanks for her work.

Are you tough enough?

Hidden within our cultural norms are the codes that men have to maintain. Men are expected to be tough, to be able to handle all situations in an unemotional and logical way–always. Part of this code requires the compartmentalization of emotions, the suppression of so-called feminine emotions (i.e., fear, anxiousness, uncertainty, overreaction, hysteria), and to supplant those with certainty, calmness, a show of strength, and courage. This is code for never showing vulnerability or weakness. This expectation applies to boys as well.

The indoctrination begins early in life for boys. As early as they talk and walk, they hear the beat of the masculine drum. It is a slow, steady march through boyhood to adolescence to adulthood. If a boy fails to measure up, he is immediately corrected and told to toughen up. It is a Marine drill sergeant mantra. It is beaten into every one of us both figuratively and—and sometimes literally— from birth. Do not be sensitive!

But what does tough really mean? Does it mean resilient, does it mean thoughtful, does it mean understanding your emotions and dealing with them? No, it means single-minded robotic behavior, shaped by the group of dominant males where weakness is death and strength comes from intimidation, where emotions are suppressed, where peer pressure reigns and adherence and allegiance to this Neanderthal, knuckle-dragging man code means acceptance to the man club. It is 'welcome to the hunt' or relegation to staying behind with the woman folk.

It is all very primal. It reflects a time in human history so different from our current milieu. It does not reflect the currency of our culture today. It is archaic and backward. It exploits as human weakness characteristics of nurturing of caring, of sharing deep emotion. It disallows the right of every man and boy to display for all to see, the emotion that lies within.

Being tough means not being human in present-day jargon. Being tough means playing the ubiquitous movie leading man role, a hard-driven, callous, scarred by life, manbot who wins in the end in spite of his lack of humanity. Being tough does not allow for being soft and vulnerable, compassionate or nurturing, qualities all humans can and should express. Being tough often means not really being able to express manhood in a myriad of ways. Being tough means a rigid and inflexible code that in the end is toxic for everyone.

What about sensitivity? Can sensitivity and toughness swim in the same pool? Can a man be tough and sensitive? Yes, if tough means resilient, resolute, and confident. Yes, if sensitive means compassionate, thoughtful, in touch with feelings, and expressive of those feelings. Sensitivity can dilute the toxic toughness we witness with our outdated man code. Not to wipe it out, but to redefine what toughness means. Perhaps we need a new word, a word that combines the two into a new ideal for men and boys to aspire.

I know in my life, whenever I showed the inappropriate emotions in front of my male authority figures, the words 'toughen up' would chastise and steer me back into the fold. My dad often said, "Are you a man or mouse?" as if to imply that showing tears or fears or uncertainty was a weakness. He could only think of the mouse as the meekest of creatures. It was to tell me that I wasn't measuring up, that I wasn't a man, that I had work to do. Quickly, I would suck up my tears, lift my head, and pretend that my feelings didn't matter. Because, well, they didn't.

The worst thing a young boy could be called was a sissy. Being a sissy meant that you had fallen so far from the male ideal that you now were in jeopardy of having your penis fall off. Just like that, the words were as effective as a switchblade. Castrated without recourse. Cast out from the boy/man club, ostracized from your peer group, all because you weren't tough enough.

As I got older, the word 'sensitive' and its perfect companion, 'too,' became the pejorative 'too sensitive,' and began to surface. Now it wasn't just male peers or male authority figures; girls began to wield this blade as well. "You're too sensitive!" often came out of a female's mouth with the velocity of a bullet at close range. It was bad enough to be called sensitive by males, but to have a female call me that was more painful, more immediate, resonating at my core, and attacking my manhood. As I grew up, 'sensitive' was a word I learned to hate.

What's Wrong with the Word Sensitive?

The word sensitive in our culture does not always have pleasant connotations. Yes, it can describe a sensitive artist, a sensitive poet, a delicate female, or someone who has intuitive skills that are considered above and beyond the norm but rarely is it seen in a positive light in reference to men. To be sensitive is to be too frail for the world, especially the world that men frequent.

It is seen as a female trait, all scrambled emotion wrapped in a bow. Those men who are sensitive are often seen as drama kings (or queens), devoid of self-control, and lacking in the discipline a real man possesses. Sensitivity is rampant emotion, reactionary emotion, illogical emotion, not the prescription for the ideal male. No self-control according to the code; it leads to bad decisions, bad planning, and bad living. Sensitivity is feeling and seeing things that are superfluous to living a life in command of one's destiny. There is no escaping it. Humans are sensitive creatures. And men are humans. The logic is impeccable. We need to return as men to our human roots.

What does sensitivity or high sensitivity mean? Simply stated, sensitivity is about the ability to take environmental cues, see the nuances in that information, and process it at a deep and thoughtful level, extracting emotional content almost automatically to derive deep and meaningful insight. Sometimes this content is simply overwhelming for those with SPS and the overwhelm that appears to the outside world is just irrational emotionalism. I like to think it's releasing the copious amount of data or even the extraneous data, much like a pressure cooker releases steam. It's not drama; it's a process to an end.

In lieu of this simple reframing of sensitivity, don't you think we ought to look again at how we define this word and what emotional meaning we attach to it? Today with the advent of an HSP movement, there is momentum building towards seeing the word sensitive in a positive light. Perhaps pulling back and looking at a broader perspective, seeing the emotion often associated with sensitivity as just a part of the process of being highly sensing, a term which I like to describe the brain function used by SPS individuals.

Lighten up, Francis – On Being a Sensitive Male

Sometimes I think we HSP males are the hardest on ourselves. We are conditioned to believe that we don't measure to expected cultural norms for masculinity, simply because we are more emotional, more likely to be overwhelmed with stimuli, more observant, and more cautious.

This internal recognition that we HSP males are not measuring up often leads to avoidance behaviors that deny true self-identity, creates conflict between our internal maps and those of the culture, and often ensures contact avoidance with other males who are not HSP and likely to threaten our identity. This makes coping difficult. Part of the solution is educating those around us to understand our worldview. That will take time.

Many HSPs have become some of our greatest leaders, our leading artists (in all media), philosophers, religious/spiritual leaders, and provide great counsel to the other 80 percent of the population.

And because HSP traits (sensitivity, etc.) are seen as female characteristics, it is no wonder that HSP females tend to be more highly regarded than HSP males, which puts undue pressure on men with this personality type.

Being an HSP male makes one more vulnerable to criticism, humil-iation, bullying, and ostracization. Trying to fit into the larger culture of males can be a source of self-doubt and loathing, which is only amplified by the HSP trait of enhanced internal sensing. This is not a good model for a happy, well-adjusted individual.

Now, this is not to say that all HSP males are destined to a depressing, lonely life of self-loathing, but while we are just now getting a handle on the trait and its expression in men, the much-needed support is often spotty and limited.

An observation of mine came to light at the death of comedian Robin Williams. As Williams was one of the most innovative and original comics of my generation, I naturally followed his career in TV, standup, and film. There was always a nervous uneasiness about Williams that I sensed came from an underlying sensitivity that belied his external persona.

In interviews, he seemed to use his comedy to mask his true feelings and like a magician, use humor as sleight-of-hand. He was masterful at this, and of course, audiences loved it. I believed, however, something deep and insecure was below the surface.

His dramatic depiction of real humans, with real feelings in *Good Will Hunting, Dead Poets Society, What Dreams May Come*, and others, showed a brilliant, if not tragic, representative of what an HSP male can become.

The world needs more HSP males to rise and own their highly valued traits. As the late Dr. Ted Zeff said, HSP males need to empower them-selves and help save this planet from a runaway warrior class of non-HSP male-dominated leaders who rarely take counsel from the priests, artists, philosophers, and thoughtful people who are here to guide and moderate. We need to retake our emotions, our feelings, and our powerful observa-tions and present them in ever-changing ways before it's too late.

This book is about how I learned to cope with my sensitivity and to embrace it as the unique gift that it is.

CHAPTER 2:

What Defines a Sensitive Man?

What a Sensitive Man is Not

From a cultural perspective, we define sensitive men in the negative. It's not a trait that most men want to associate with their masculinity. And those of us who are sensitive men are often caught apologetically explaining away our sensitive characteristics as aberrations and passing emotions.

A particularly negative trait for sensitive men is high emotionalism. Any emotion other than abject joy or righteous anger is not permitted in any demonstrable way for 'real' men in our culture. Emotions are a sign of weakness. High emotions lead to problems for men. Men with high emotions are considered effeminate and unstable—high emotions lead to bad decisions and unclear thinking, or so says the prevailing attitude. Highly Sensitive Men (HSMs) are typically more expressive with their emotions, but learn early on that expressing too much emotion is not a good thing.

Because we register more emotion does not signal that we are weak or more effeminate; it simply means we are allowing more of our human side to show through. I see this as example-setting behavior.

Another characteristic often attributed to HSMs is the inability to make quick decisions. Many believe that having the ability to generate quick decisions is a sign of masculine decisiveness. Deliberation and deep thinking seem to be absent from this definition of how a man makes decisions. Impulsive, irrational, and often reckless decision-making—or somehow devining the correct decision in nanoseconds—is considered the norm. Because of our capacity to think through all options deeply, HSMs are deliberate decision-makers. In order to process the various trajectories and come to a decision, one must think thoroughly, and that takes time. The outcome generally is a good, well thought out and, logical decision, which appears to some non-HSP males as indecisiveness.

Overwhelm does not conjure up a battlefield general facing overwhelming odds. Many HSPs face overwhelm because of sensory overload. This is not a weakness, yet it is portrayed as a lack of courage or capacity to handle an onslaught of inputs. Overwhelm for most HSMs generally means the need to retreat and regroup. This is a human trait and one in which most HSPs don't have the luxury of bypassing. Though it often leads to poor decisions with dire consequences, Non-HSPs' ability to plow ahead is considered a sign of leadership or manliness. Overwhelm means—I'm full. I've reached capacity and need to release and reprocess. That's all.

Because some characteristics of HSMs mirror characteristics that females are encouraged to exhibit, men who express these same feelings— are nurturing, empathetic, or gentle—are often seen as lacking testosterone and are somehow deficient as men. How ridiculous is this? All the above characteristics are human in origin and are native to both genders. The idea that men can express these feelings, emotions or actions, means that HSMs are more comfortable in their humanity than most traditional males.

Any expression of what we consider culturally to be feminine traits, such as empathy or nurturing, or softer qualities, almost automatically makes a man suspect of being "gay or bi." The logic is that if you are effeminate or show feminine qualities, or deviate from the norm, you must be gay. How often do boys hear this among their peers? Feminine qualities are attributed to being less of a man, even though gay men are no less masculine than straight men. What makes you a man is what dangles between your legs. Period. The rest is cultural bias and arbitrary definition.

Common Traits and Characteristics

What of these Highly Sensitive Men? What are they made of? What makes them different, special, or extraordinary?

Highly Sensitive Men have the ability to intuitively understand another's point of view, the trait most associated with empathy. This makes HSMs more likely to be kind and understanding, and in fact, explains why so many HSPs are clergy, counselors, advisors, or teachers, both male and female.

The ability to process information more deeply leads to greater cognition and perception, which leads to clearer thinking, better decision-making, and greater overall intelligence. Now whether HSPs are innately more intelligent or whether they gather, store, and process information better, and because of this have better access to more information outputs, is something that may need more research. However, the result is a smarter individual, brought there by keen observation and perception skills.

Being more cautious, less prone to risk-taking, and making decisions more slowly may make the typical HSM seem more passive. Taking deliberate steps toward action is not being passive. And while some HSMs or HSPs may actually act passively—socialized to believe that any action they take is incorrect—slow movement to action is not a sign of passivity. HSMs may buck the prototype for male decision-making processes, but nevertheless, their cautious nature makes their decisions more probable for positive outcomes.

Sensitive people are often creative and imaginative. They live so much of their lives in their heads, and because of the deep processing capacity of their brains, they can use their insight and intuition to look at things in a creative light. This makes HSMs likely candidates for creative outlets as artists, writers, actors, and thinkers. Because HSPs have this extra ability for deep thinking they can draw on nuanced problem-solving skills that might be overlooked by non-HSP individuals.

Always looking for meaning in everything, HSPs are naturally drawn to spiritual matters. They tend toward more esoteric religious models, seeming to gravitate from one existential problem to another. Having a spiritual framework helps them to organize and put meaning to things that might seem random, cruel, or unjust, to understand the complexities of life.

In addition, HSMs are compassionate leaders; when given a chance to lead, they are dreamers and visionaries, environmental harbingers (since the environment is so important to HSPs), are thoughtful and conscientious lovers and partners, and can be good close friends to a select few, but lousy superficial friends for convenience sake.

Some HSPs are prone, believe it or not, to seek high sensation activities, but not in a reckless and thoughtless way. Their unique wiring requires that at times they seek high stimulation and then return to low stimulation scenarios for recovery. It's like driving a drag car, instead of a stock car, a short burst of speed and danger, then back to normal life. It's not about endurance; it's about sensation.

HSMs generally are good fathers, husbands, make great employees in the right environment, and can be trusted and counted to deliver. HSMs tend to hold themselves accountable in the highest light because their idealistic and perfectionist natures will not allow them to be immoral for any length of time.

Labels and Alphabet Soup

Have you noticed lately that we have a label for everything and anyone these days? We have become acronym obsessed. Our acronyms have become our new coat of arms. Every disenfranchised group, every subset of a group, now has its own special alphabet soup label to identify themselves.

But really, what is the purpose of labeling each other? Is it to say, "I'm included in this group and you're not," followed by launching a website, printing some signs, scheduling a protest, raising awareness, gain recognition; then what? All this to point out how different we are from everyone else, how special we are, rules for how to engage us, how to deal with us, and how we deal with you. I understand this sounds a bit cynical because I believe in diversity and inclusion and celebrating our uniqueness, but I wonder, are we all getting a little bit overboard here? Let's dig into this some.

Some labels are pejorative, meant to hurt, segregate, and outcast a group. I don't want to focus on them. I'm more curious about labels that people place on themselves. Doesn't that create animosity, promote diversity or bitterness, resentment, and hatred? Some argue that it's divisive, and frankly many are getting tired of the long and growing list of social labels. I'm not sure that rejecting diversity is the answer, but I think maybe we can all be a little more judicious about adding to this growing list. So, where does all this labeling come from?

Labeling theory[8] promotes the idea that self-identity can be formed, influenced by, or determined by the terms we use to describe or classify ourselves. There are lots of elements at play with this theory, including the effects of stigmatization attached to the label and how that affects identity, or the effects of feedback from the labeled group regarding group norms and conformity, and self-policing standards regarding deviation from the label norms and how that influences behavior.

Labeling can lead to self-fulfilling prophecies for the labeler and the labeled.[9] Labels categorize sets of characteristics and sometimes may seem arbitrary, yet can carry much power over the individual because of the perceptions associated with the labels. In some cases, joining certain labeled groups can even carry some cachet. In other words, it's the "fit in" mojo that drives us to either create or join labeled groups.

Our self-identity is heavily influenced by feedback from others. The ego identifies with the labels, and the labels become our perimeter boundaries wherein we live our lives.[10] This over-identification with labels can inhibit us from living life fully and freely. Our true self, the essence beneath the subjugating ego, is in a constant state of flux throughout our lives. It is not static.

The ego clings to the labels it self-identifies with and confines us and forces us to remain with the labels we create and accept as *us*. Yet we have a level of awareness that can rise above the labels, let go of the incessant feedback loop of opinions, boundaries, and herd mentality that keeps us from experiencing our uniqueness, nested and protected within a labeled group. No one is immune to this.

We are all searching for individual congruence and constantly trying to match our changing identity to our long held labeled identity and trying to find resonance and authenticity.[11] Being aware of our own personal evolution can help make the trap of over-identification with a label less of a sticking point, as well as recognizing some labels we accumulate are temporary, and more importantly, not who we are as individuals.

So what about HSPs and HSMs? With so many underrepresented groups of people, race, gender, sexual preference, and religious groups out there, does it help our cause to educate about being an HSP individual by choosing to jump into the alphabet soup, holding our three-letter acronym up proudly? And are we a minority group? Even though our numbers are smaller than the population at large, does this qualify us for protected group status? Since we have only relatively recently been labeled and are just now beginning to get some recognition as a personality group, what can we expect as far as empathy from the larger population?

I think we are a unique case. HSPs have been around as long as humans have been around. We are not something recently evolved. We show up culturally, ethnically, racially, and evenly along gender lines, and our reach is quite extensive. If you ask people and explain what it is to be sensitive in personality terms, everyone seems to know someone who is an HSP. I have often found that when asked about the HSP in their lives, most people recall qualities that are often seen in a favorable light. We don't buck religious beliefs, we don't offend sexual tastes, we don't have unique physical characteristics, and we straddle all cultures. To be sure, we fit in nicely; even though we often feel we don't fit in, as a group we are quite adept at fitting in. We get along, help others, don't make waves. Sound familiar?

I have noticed that I am beginning to identify with the label HSP. It gets broached more and more in conversation, especially when I sense other HSPs are present. Within minutes, if they are not aware of the label, they begin to identify with it via conversations with me. I have become an evangelist for high sensitivity, a recruiter, if you will, for those who can identify with the characteristics of the group. I'm doing my part in educating others, even non-HSPs who seem to want mightily to correct this 'condition' at one extreme or at least understand it at the other extreme.

Perhaps the folly of this is that like any personality characteristic, there is much diversity within the HSP community, and with our heightened sensitivity, the variations are large and wide. Like sexual preferences, we cover a large territory and a broad range on the sensitivity map.

A commenter on my blog, The Sensitive Man (www.thesensitiveman. com), seemed to be all flushed about the need to add still another group acronym to the alphabet soup bowl. "Why can't we just all get along," the reader commented. Although in principle I agree that we should all get along, sometimes theory is harder in practice. What, then, can we do to promote awareness of high sensitivity without creating a victim stigma to our community and the world? Although we have nothing to apologize for, by creating more dialogue, I think we all win. Especially among HSPs who are not yet aware of the gift they possess.

Here are some tips for recognition and integration:

- We are all the spear tip of this movement and must lead the effort for education and understanding. Because we are not an ethnic group, we can use the diversity within our ranks to deeply penetrate the culture at multiple levels. Look for opportunities to talk about sensitivity, especially with males in your sphere of influence. Spread the word.

- I'm not sure we are 'cause' per se, any more than redheaded people with freckles or blue-eyed Africans. We can promote understanding and express who we are, but I'm not sure we are at a place or need to demand any rights. We are a different type of human being for sure, but by modeling who we are, we can affect change. I don't see an HSP march on Washington in the near future. Helping people who are unaware they are HSP is a better goal.

- First thing, let's start at the start. That means educating and working with kids. Especially young boys, who may have the hardest time with their sensitivity because of cultural expectations. The generations to come will benefit the most from this effort, as will society at large in subtle ways by empowering these young men to utilize the gift of sensitivity for the greater good.

- Understand that today many people are frustrated with the alphabet soup of various groups demanding rights. Some of the groups certainly deserve recognition and acceptance, and I will always advocate for that. Others may be grandstanding for attention, but who's to say. Be patient, be kind, and gently educate. Since we straddle all levels of society, we are in a unique position to show some universality of this personality trait.

- Finally, one of the great things about living in our times is recognizing the great diversity within the human race. Instead of a great mass of homogeneity, we are now blossoming as a culture by recognizing our individuality. Some people see this as complicating our world, a world that should have uniformity and sameness, which seems safe and secure to them. But our diversity is our strength, recognizing that we are all humans unified with many of the same characteristics, yet elegant in our differences. Uniformity is boring; ask any former Catholic school kid. As HSM/HSPs, we are part of that diversity. Fundamentally, we all need to know that what we are is alright. Being an individual is cool. When diversity is the norm, the death knell will toll for bullying, and maybe someone will spill the bowl of alphabet soup.

Embracing our Eccentricities

We are a peculiar bunch, we HSPs. Some might even say we are a bit eccentric. This is especially true for Highly Sensitive Males. We HSMs are a small percentage of a small percentage of the human population, and we don't meet, for the most part, the stereotypes of the modern western male. But ... eccentric?

Dictionary.com[12] defines eccentric as *adj.*: deviating from the recognized or customary character, practice, etc., irregular erratic, peculiar, odd. *Noun*: A person who has an unusual, peculiar, or odd personality, set of beliefs, or behavior patterns. The word has its roots from the (Medieval Latin) *eccentricus* and from the Greek *ekkentr(os),* which is to be out of the center. It is used in geometry and astronomy to describe something that is out of center or not concentric. In other words, something that lies on the outside.

Eccentricity is often tolerated or even revered in those who are very wealthy or are celebrities. Their odd ways and behaviors can become fashionable among the masses, and are sometimes talked about as if these eccentrics are geniuses or acceptable outliers. In that regard, eccentricity can be a favorable quality, making one a leader or a trendsetter by walking a different path.

But what makes us HSMs seem eccentric to others? Is it the emotional aspects of our personalities, our broad accepting worldview, or our internal conflicts about our masculinity? What about our aversion to overstimulation, the hermitic deep processing of our experiences, or the masculine/feminine polarity that many HSM men wrestle with? Are we too moody, too quiet, too sensitive to criticism, too introverted? We can be too empathetic, too observational, and too persnickety to environmental changes, but are we that different? Do we appear to the outside world to be outliers, strange, hard to figure out, and hard to live with? In some cases, do people want to throw up their hands and give up on us because we are too much work?

But does that make us eccentric? Maybe. Eccentricity, also known as quirkiness, is not necessarily a maladaptive behavior. But, yes, we can be a bit off-center from mainstream personalities and behaviors. Many HSPs have intellectual giftedness and curiosity, and a propensity for original and creative thought. We see things differently via our peculiar and unique perceptive lens. But are we eccentric?

The psychologist David Meeks states that eccentrics are less prone to mental illness than the general population.[13] Doesn't that seem odd? Perhaps if you look at some of the other defining characteristics of eccentrics, it makes more sense. Eccentrics have an enduring propensity for non-conformity, are creative (sound familiar?), have a strongly motivated curiosity (and I would add observational skills), an enduring sense of differentness, and embrace this wonderful idealism that drives them to want to make the world a better place to live. Besides, eccentrics are intelligent, outspoken, and have a quirky, mischievous sense of humor. With that battery of personality characteristics, it seems eccentrics are well armed for survival in uncertain times, does it not?

Because we HSPs have increased awareness and sensitivity to our environment and we process very deeply and thoughtfully, it makes sense that to the majority of the non-HSP world we may seem to be a bit different. And what about our tendency toward overwhelm—how we can so easily be affected by others' moods or emotions, then retreat to our voluntary isolation, our emotional caves. We are prone to unrealistic perfectionism at times, which sometimes causes us to live out of sync with our environment and the people around us. So with our enhanced qualities of sensory detail, nuanced expression, and meaning, our emotional awareness, which leads us to greater empathy and an expression of creativity, can we not be seen as eccentric?

Think about this: the following people have been associated with the quality of high sensitivity or Sensory Processing Sensitivity:[14] Woody Allen, Steve Martin, Orson Welles, Edgar Allan Poe, Salvador Dali, Picasso, Stephen Spielberg, George Lucas, Nicole Kidman, Katherine Hepburn, John Lennon, Elton John, Alanis Morissette, Neil Young, and Dolly Parton. And my personal favorite, Robin Williams. That's a pretty quirky bunch, wouldn't you say?

Eccentric … well, yes, in a lot of ways. But they turned that eccentricity into beautiful art. They are beloved by millions. And perhaps their sensitivity played heavily into their creative process. For some, it might have been a way to mask and protect themselves; for others, it might have been a way to reach out and find common ground with the world. But for all of them, they risked being called eccentric to rise above criticism and be themselves.

So, if we HSPs are that quirky, strange, or weird, what do we do about it? Is some eccentricity good for HSPs? I mean, is eccentricity really simply being different? But wait, we are different. We already know that. Instead, how do we embrace our eccentricity, so we can stop worrying about what others think about us? Should we promote and socialize our uniqueness? As people learn more about our nature, our personality, our SPS secret, maybe will they better understand us, and with that, begin to normalize us.

Here are some things to think about concerning our "eccentricity":

1. Accept that eccentricity is not a bad thing. Perhaps embracing our uniqueness is a better way of looking at it. Let's come out of the shadows and into the light and accept that we, regardless of how different we may seem, are neither good nor bad. We just are.

2. As HSPs, we need to all work to promote and create awareness of this personality trait. In spite of the publicity and great work of Dr. Elaine Aron and others who continue discussing and researching this trait, many, many people still do not know they have this trait and others aren't aware of the trait at all. Write a blog, give a talk, introduce yourself as an HSP, explain what it is, and offer your insights into how this has impacted your life. Embrace the differences. Be proud of who you are.

3. Help those who are willing to understand us with tools to understand us. Refer them to Dr. Aron's site, www.hsperson.com. For those who will not understand or don't want to understand, accept that they are going to see us as eccentric.

4. And finally, please, teach other HSPs and especially our HSM boys that they are okay as they are. Give them skills and tools to live a fulfilling life in a world that may be difficult and challenging for them. They need our support, maybe more than any subset of the HSP population.

My Experiences

As a child, my grandfather, the only living grandfather I had then, avoided having any contact with me. He much rather enjoyed being with my cousin, a much more typical boy, than spend time with me. He saw me as a 'momma's boy' and chided my mother for making me into a sissy.

He saw traits in me, such as me outwardly showing emotion, my aversion to aggression, and my quiet and contemplative nature as being a weakness. I must admit I didn't like the man. He was gruff and insensitive and an alcoholic.

No interaction was a good interaction for him. I could have used his attention. He could have taught me to fish, one of his passions. He could have let me sit down and watch him in his workshop, make furniture or craft artistic expressions out of wood. He could have, but he didn't.

Almost in spite, he warned me to stay away from his workshop. He told me that snakes and spiders were in there, and they would bite me if I dared brave going in the door. It was a mystery to me what lay behind that faded grey wood door. I'll never know.

It was an opportunity wasted for both him and me. He could have given a little boy confidence, confidence I so sorely needed. He could have made a change in my life by just showing up and modeling a few masculine behaviors.

Later on, long after he had passed, I had several defining conversations with my uncle, his oldest son. His interactions with his father were similar, yet more stern. As I listened to him talk, I could sense that my grandfather was a man in pain, a man who suffered from a cancerous and swollen pituitary gland that pressed on his brain and caused him to have severe headaches.

He was a country boy on the surface, yet he had a visionary's mind. He was a genius at inventing things but lacked the business savvy to bring them to market. He was a talented artist and painted portraits. Buried deep within him was a gentle man, a sensitive man he would not let out.

He saw in me the same and was repulsed by it. Our culture defined him. He could not be what he was, because it would not present to the world the prototype of masculinity. It would have been weak, and that former Marine was not going to be weak.

My loss was his loss.

When I was about nine-years-old, my family took a weekend trip to Gulfport, Mississippi, to visit the beach with family friends. One of the families had a boy who was a few years older than I. He was bigger and stronger than I and was a bit of a bully. I wasn't too keen on having to play with him, but my parents were pressuring me to hang out with him, so I did. That evening the men went out to do some crabbing on the dock and left the kids and women back at the beach house.

The boy and I were getting bored, and this kid decided he wanted to wrestle me. He didn't ask; he just grabbed me and threw me to the ground. As I wasn't prepared for the takedown, he pinned me quickly . Once on the ground, he proceeded to put me in a scissor hold—his legs wrapped around my midsection. He was fairly strong and squeezed down hard around my diaphragm. The harder he squeezed, the more air was pushed out of my lungs. It hurt. I was beginning to gasp for air. I squirmed to get loose, but the more I moved, the more tightly he bore down. It was like a boa constrictor.

There were other kids around, some younger boys and I think some girls. They all just stared at me, not offering any help. I have a high tolerance for pain, but this was starting to get to me. I was totally defeated—abject humiliation. I felt tears welling up in my eyes, not from the pain; it was the idea that I was going to be defeated by this older boy. In front of the other kids, I was made to be submissive, to give in and give up—cry, Uncle. I suppose the noise attracted the attention of the mothers who came in and broke up the exhibition.

The older boy gloated over me. That look of dominance added to the humiliation. The boy pleaded that we were just wrestling (a typical boy thing), and the mothers glossed it over. My mother came to me and put her arm around me.

About that time, the men came in from the porch. I was still sniffling when my dad came in. The boy explained to the men what had happened. My head was hanging low; I looked slowly up to see my dad's face. He had a look that could cut through blue steel. It was a quick glance, laser-like that could eat at my insides. He was not happy. I could feel the disappointment from across the room. I always got it when I disappointed him. He would take his black horn-rimmed glasses off, hold them by the rim in one hand and shake his head, expelling air, in an exasperated way. That let me know I failed him. I failed the boy code.

CHAPTER 3:

Being Different Growing Up

Quiet and Alone

I was a shy child and introverted. One of my earliest recollections was around the age of four. My parents had switched churches, and I can clearly remember the first Sunday we attended the new church. I was taken to a rather large room divided into sections. My mother and father knew I wasn't going to go lightly into this strange place. The minute I knew I was being sent off to be with complete strangers, the waterworks began. I can remember screaming and kicking. I felt abandoned as I watched my parents exit the room and disappear down the hall.

At some point, I calmed down. To be fair, the Sunday School teachers were nice people, but I didn't feel right. I know I didn't want to be there. Some might say it was a good lesson for me. I needed to allow my parents to go do adult things, like going to the Adult Sunday School class, but I was not used to being out of my element. It was a process I experienced over and over again in the first ten years of my life.

We moved several times in my young life. Probably not as much as a military family, but it was enough for me. Moving was hard; essentially, it meant I had to start over again. Not just meet new friends, but rediscovering my new baseline, find the new comfort zone. This was not an easy process for me. I was very aware of my surroundings. To be comfortable, I had to know who were friends, who were enemies, or folks I had to watch out for. By the time I was nine-years-old I had moved four times, each as difficult as the previous one. I had changed schools four times before fourth grade, in some cases bouncing from one state to another. Of course, there seldom was continuity in the educational systems in the sixties. I was in the South, at one point going from a state last in education to one just a couple notches above.

My nearest sibling was female, four years younger than me. She was hardly relatable to me during this time. I felt alone and isolated. No one understood how I was dealing with this. I was traveling a path that presented many obstacles and challenges to a shy, insecure, introverted, sensitive young boy.

I never thought of myself as bookish. I didn't care to read Hardy Boy mysteries or books for young fiction readers. I was a more practical information enthusiast. In 1964 my parents invested in a set of World Book Encyclopedias. To me this was a fabulous gift. It had pictures and tables, lists and articles, the likes I had never seen before. I devoured the set, cover to cover book to book, from A to Z. I spent hours with a single encyclopedia reading about everything, everyplace, learning things I'd never heard of in school. It was the Internet version 0.1. And I loved it. It was then, at that tender age, that I became an information freak.

I loved it so much I faked being sick so that I could get out of going outside and playing with my friends. I had more stomach aches, more headaches in one summer than any child should have had. Yet, my friends never got wise to the fact that I was ditching them for the M or S encyclopedia. I soon learned to take concepts, say tracing the lineage of the British monarchy from Alfred the Great to Queen Elizabeth, and then researching from one king or queen to another. I learned to use these tools to research and learn concepts and ideas, and I spent hours doing that alone in my room.

My room was my castle, my refuge, my sanctuary. I spent many hours playing with toy soldiers, cheap little plastic K-Mart soldiers. I didn't play with them like a normal boy, no; I created scenes from a movie with dialogue, action and in the end, no one got killed. I didn't shoot my soldiers up with BBs or throw rocks at them to knock them down. No one ever was blown up, but within my head was a deep orchestration of these plastic actors on a stage of bunkbed mountains, battlefields made of carpet, bunkers behind tables or chairs, and lakes and rivers made of throw rugs. Sometimes it took hours to set up the scene, long convoys of troops, tanks, and jeeps. It all played out in my head. There was a rich world of possibilities between my ears.

As I got older, approaching fifth or sixth grade, I discovered how easily I became embarrassed. Unfortunately, for me, the kids in class found that out, too. They could make me turn beet red by simply directing some unwanted attention my way. Some kid would fart and then point at me, chastising me for the rude breach of etiquette. I knew it wasn't me, but because I was embarrassed, I blushed. Blushing is the equivalent of an admission of guilt for eleven-year-olds.

If a girl in the class ever took a liking to me, well, the same embarrassment bullies would announce to the class that this young lady was in love with me and that at semester end we were getting married. I was a goner the minute our two lives were linked. I'd turn a deeper shade of red than normal, especially if I liked her back. It was uncontrollable, like truth serum; my deep inner feelings, which I normally hid, sprang forth onto my crimson face. It was transparency at its worst. Some of these pranks, in hindsight, were good-natured, not spiteful or mean, but some kids get off on a fractured sense of control. And, honestly, it was painful enough that some days, I faked a stomach ache just not to go back and face the humiliation. Again, I felt alone and isolated.

I developed a pattern of avoidance behaviors. I was sensitive to scratchy clothes or odd food consistencies if a plate was too hot or too cold. Even as a young child, I was terrified of loud noises. We vacationed one year near the Myrtle Beach Air Force base. The jets flew low to the ground where we were staying, approaching the runway or taking off to veer skyward over the beach. They always came when I least expected and scared me half to death.

But I grew out of these fears. As I got older I avoided social interactions, the coed birthday parties, the swim parties, the chances for serious embarrassment, or in my mind, humiliation. Any opportunity where I would be out in public around peers or adults or frankly, anyone, I found myself avoiding. I shied away from Little League, because every game was a venue for rabid, trash-talking parents and spectators who became invariably attached to a team. I wasn't very good at baseball, so the opportunity for humiliation was great.

This sounds over the top, but to me, humiliation was something that needed to be avoided at all costs. My shaky young man's ego was not framed to handle the onslaught of criticism or mockery that screwing something up provided. It was sad that my ideas about myself and self-image were so hinged on my inner world. There was never outward confirmation because the only place I could get that was in the outside world. And sadly no one was pushing me gently to test the waters. It formed a lifelong habit of avoidance that I am just learning to overcome.

Living in the Shadows

A lot of the avoidance was predicated on avoiding criticism and my fear of criticism. I believe this fear arose from the lack of support I had from the key adult male authority figures in my life. These men, primarily my father and my maternal grandfather, found a lot to criticize in me. They could be harsh at times. Harsh for a sensitive boy may seem mild to others, but as a conscientious child who wished to please or least garner favor with my male role models, criticism was tantamount to attacks on my fragile ego.

My mother's youngest brother was the notable exception. My uncle often made time for me and let me ride with him in his cool British sports car. He talked to me as if it mattered and showed me the respect or at least attention I so desperately needed. This was rare, though, to find a model for me what a man could be: kind, supportive, a teacher of sorts who used laughter, instead of harsh words, to motivate. Somehow, he understood me. He appreciated the child I was.

Otherwise, from Boy Scout scoutmasters to pastors or coaches or any adult male family members, I was socialized to accept the prevailing norm for male role behavior. Which in so many words, is to be a man in the nineteen sixties, World War II definition. Conform or be rejected. This binary choice did not make room for kids who didn't fit that model.

What I learned was what I didn't learn. I didn't learn how to be confident in myself or who I was becoming. I never learned to deal with my sharp emotions, how to let them flow over me, immerse and release them, and not hold on to them. I struggled internally with those feelings and never felt the guidance of an older, wiser man. There was no one to steer me through the difficult process of expressing my emotions, my fears, and my constant worries about the external world. My only dialogue was with myself, and that internal dialogue was often corrupted by my negative impressions of the outside world. I didn't know how to be masculine, especially coupled with my sensitive nature. I had to learn almost entirely on my own. My only feedback came from a select few male friends as I got older. It was a hit or miss process. Mostly miss.

Without the confidence of experience or the wisdom of elders, I could not stand alone on my own. I felt helpless and defenseless. Not knowing where to turn, I leaned on my mother.

When I was five-years-old, there was a homework assignment for the boys to outline their father's handprint on a piece of art construction paper. The girls were to outline their mother's handprints. My father was out of town for work, as was usually the case. I panicked. When I realized he wasn't coming home that night, I knew I couldn't complete the assignment.

My mother proposed an idea. She let me trace her hand on the paper. She told me to tell the teacher about my father and that I used her hand instead. The next day at school, I lied and said it was the hand of my father. When the teacher showed our pictures around the class, it became clear to a lot of the boys that my father's hand was a lot smaller than other fathers. Of course, I was embarrassed and a bit ashamed that I had lied. Instant Karma. Somehow an important lesson was learned that day. I couldn't count on my father to be there for me. But my mother would be.

This pattern continued throughout my childhood. I suspect many boys felt the same about their fathers. What made it worse for me was that I was an only boy and I was sensitive. Not standing up for me or being present for me made it hard for me to stand up for myself.

In confrontations, I found ways to avoid direct contact. I never learned how to walk with confidence. I never learned to defend myself. I avoided fighting. I avoided confrontation. I learned to withhold my opinions and not stand boldly in my truth. I ran away from fights, mostly after getting my ass kicked a few times. It was a behavior that followed me into adulthood.

The South, where I spent most of my formative years, has always been built around the military model—of behavior, of conduct, of honor, of obligation, of manhood. It's the only place in the country with military colleges that are not nationally sanctioned. Men send their sons there to become men. Many come out broken or scarred for life. The ones who graduate perpetuate that model to the next generation. And so it goes.

Then the sixties came and slapped the rest of the country directly in the face. A large part of the country woke up to the realization that it was time for things to change. The South slapped back and never looked twice. The mythos of manhood in that region has hardly changed in four hundred years. That myth is like a statue. It stands tall with the green patina of age. It commemorates an ideal of the past, an ideal that's time has come and gone. Yet it still stands in the town square—a reminder to everyone that change only happens when ideals change. I grew up in that shadow.

Rising to the Top

As was often the case with me, I didn't fit in well. I tried hard to conform outwardly, but never quite managed to internalize those changes. I felt I lived the life of an imposter. There was much incongruity of who I was and what I presented to the world.

Around friends, the neighborhood kids, I was much more confident. These interactions were more one-on-one, and I selected my friends carefully. As my family settled in to the neighborhood in South Carolina, where I grew up, I gained a newfound sense of confidence in who I was. I found that I was a natural leader and organizer.

Our neighborhood was almost a frame right out of *The Little Rascals*. We organized baseball, football, and basketball games with other neighborhoods. I found myself being the one everyone came to find out what was going on. We built campgrounds in the woods, organized campouts with the neighbor kids, and generally had idyllic summers. I was the one doing the organizing, and I liked that role.

At one point, I decided to create a neighborhood newsletter and received a student style typewriter where I crafted stories. The next-door neighbor's mother was a school teacher, who mimeographed the newsletter so we could distribute them.

Yes, in the right circumstances and with a certain comfort level, I could easily rise to the top. I was a likable, smart kid and believed in the team concept, yet appreciated my friends as individuals. I was well organized and great planner for the neighborhood. I never realized that these characteristics were natural talents. I just never received the right feedback.

In school plays, I was always chosen to be the play's narrator, usually the first kid out in costume, reciting my lines nervously, but flawlessly. If the costumes were dorky, I got the first laugh, which, of course, was embarrassing for me. One year, we performed a play about George Washington and the founding fathers. I walked out in front of the curtain to start the show, with a quick narration about the subject matter, sporting a concocted wig made of cotton balls that, by the time the play had started was beginning to disintegrate. I was tall and skinny and must have looked ridiculous because the audience burst out in laughter when I walked to center stage. Yet, somehow, I managed to execute on my lines and exit red-faced but relieved. My good memory and my conscientiousness were showing. Perhaps that was why I landed the same part every year.

I had a very good sense of humor, a family trait, one that my father shared with us. When I was around familiar company, I could do some spot-on impressions, voices, and characters that made my friends laugh. This was very encouraging. I had a knack for parody and loved to watch comedians on television. My favorites—and inspirations—were Jonathan Winters, George Carlin, and Bill Cosby (before the troubles). I loved to watch oddball shows like *Get Smart* and *Green Acres*; it seemed the more absurdist the comedy, the better for me. When *Laugh-In* came on in the late sixties, it was the sole reason I never went beyond First Class Scout. I quit going to Scout meetings because they were in the same time slot as *Laugh-In*.

There is much to be said for a good sense of humor. I think it can be one of the best redeeming qualities for a sensitive boy/man. Our keen sense of observation can aid us in adding layers of texture to our humor. I believe the best comedians are all sensitive people. There is some ironic and dramatic underlying reason that HSPs put themselves out there for criticism, just to present their quirky view of life. Brave souls, all of them.

Risky Business

As I started to reach adolescence, my proclivity for mischief began to emerge. I was clever about the mischief I got into but smart enough not to get caught. On the surface this does not sound much like an HSP trait, but if you think about if you were planning a mischievous caper, you might want an HSP along to provide some cautionary counseling. There was risk-taking but with the caveat of not going too far, of pushing the envelope, but not tearing it, of dancing around the edge of danger, without tripping into the abyss.

Now most of this risky business was not much more than what you might expect of an adolescent boy—smoking, drinking, some minor shenanigans, like setting siege to a neighbor boy's house with cherry bombs, egging a few cars, putting beer cans at the bottom of a steep hill and watching cars smash over them, or harassing a friend who needed to be reminded of his place in the pecking order. Much of this behavior belied my sensitive nature.

It was a call to seek out high sensation activity, even for just a brief time. It was part of my emerging personality, something I later found out is a characteristic of a segment of the HSP population, High Sensation Seeking. The characteristic never led to any serious trouble, but in hindsight was pretty stupid and in some cases, reckless. I was lucky I didn't get into more trouble. I was a good kid, but bored.

Another behavior I considered risky was that early in life I got into a bad habit of not finishing things I started. First, it was swim lessons when I was about eight-years-old. I had never taken swimming lessons before, so I was immediately placed in the beginner's class with all the little kids, some as young as four or five. This embarrassed me, as my peers were all in intermediate or advanced classes. I took to instruction well, and before the class concluded, the instructor wanted me to perform the graduation exercise, which was to swim a lap doing the American crawl. I was nervous and got worked up over this test. The nervousness overwhelmed me. I couldn't go back and do the thing that would have gotten me into the intermediate class. I lied to my mother, concocting some story about my stomach being upset and after strong protest, I won out. I never went back.

It was a dangerous precedent. It taught me a negative lesson about not facing my fears. It taught me if I was afraid of something, I could find a way to avoid it. This simple little failure in my life would be compounded over and over again. As an HSP, I have had more than my share of fears crop up in my life, some that most non-HSPs do not see as anything to block forward progress on achieving a goal.

But the lesson I learned that day in Mississippi in 1963 was that if you are clever enough—and I was—you can avoid anything that might cause you pain or discomfort. So many things I should have and could have done, but because of the lack of perseverance and drive and the emphasis on pain avoidance, I never learned a martial art, never learned to play guitar, never played organized sports, and never became an Eagle Scout.

If this sounds like sour grapes, it is. Much of what we learn as children carries on through adult life. The good behaviors build confidence and poise; the bad behaviors rob us of life's richness. Yes, we can change them as we get older, and yes, ultimately we are the captains of our own souls, but now I know that especially for highly sensitive boys, confidence needs to be instilled early. For many of us HSPs we navigate life with one foot on the gas and the other on the brake. How liberating it is to take the foot off the brake and just drive.

CHAPTER 4:

Common Traits and Characteristics
of Highly Sensitive Males

A s with any personality type, certain characteristics are associated with that personality type. With High Sensitivity, Elaine Aron [15] devised a model that is a broad umbrella of four main traits that all HSPs display. She denoted an acronym for these characteristics called DOES, which stands for Depth of Processing, Overstimulation, Emotional reactivity/empathy, and Sensing subtleties.

Each of these personality characteristics is fairly broad in scope but describes the main behaviors most often seen in highly sensitive people. In this chapter, I will flesh them out a bit and relate them to Highly Sensitive Males and share my own experiences. As an HSP or HSM, you may have other personality characteristics that may be shared with other HSPs but not necessarily denoted here. It is a matter of putting a fine point on a rather broad definition because it's difficult to account for all the variations of sensitivity and individual differences. As research continues on the topic of sensitivity, there will no doubt be additions and branches of this personality that will be more clearly defined by further research.

These characteristics are not defined by gender, so there is no more or less of the characteristic in males or females. They are all indicative of high sensitivity. The main difference is how society or the prevailing culture regarding masculinity perceives these traits in comparison to acceptable male behaviors. This is where the rubber meets the road. Many of these traits are perceived as non-masculine by many Western cultures and will affect the HSM living in that culture. I will also discuss that briefly and touch on it again in later chapters.

D: Depth of Processing

Depth of processing is an interesting concept that deals with the way sensory input is processed within the brain of highly sensitive people. There are many implications for processing at the level and detail HSPs do when presented with data inputs. Studies have shown that when given inputs that require determination of subtleties, HSPs tend to use more of those parts of the brain associated with deep processing. They also are more prone to incorporate the use of a part of the brain known as the Insula, which is used to integrate various sources of brain inputs from external sources to emotional inputs to body movements to garner subtleties within the environment.[16]

HSPs tend to use stored memories to relate meaning to disparate pieces of information. The use of emotional encoding of memories enhances this process as it makes the memory more likely to be retrieved when needed. The ability to access deeply stored data, retrieve that data, and bring it into the current context, gives HSPs the ability to present more options for problem-solving compared to options in present moment mode. This tendency to present options with analysis often makes decision-making for HSPs more time-intensive than may be usual for non-HSP thinkers.

The ability to draw down on unconscious resources to tap into memories or emotions from the past allows HSPs to be more intuitive in problem-solving than most of the general population. The ability to analyze at a deep level makes the HSPs good at analyzing all options to a problem before coming to a conclusion. The drawback to this is the time and effort required to process this much data.

The ability to connect the dots comes with a price. Because HSPs are thorough thinkers, exploring all options, and generally being more cautious about drawing quick conclusions, HSPs are often slow to make decisions. In a culture where quick and impulsive decisions are rewarded and expected, this can be a drawback. For males, this idea of being slow and cautious in coming to conclusions generally means that in a time-crunched world, this type of thinking is perceived to be overthinking, or worse yet, shows a lack of decision-making ability, which can have implications for job assignment or promotion. This can affect self-confidence in the workplace and earning power.

To complicate matters, if HSPs are in high-pressure situations, where quick and sometimes rash decisions are demanded, the whole depth of processing mechanism can be shut down because of the stress of having to perform under demanding conditions.

This is not an option for HSMs. This process is part and parcel of being highly sensitive, not something turned off or turned on when needed. This is what we do with our sensory and environmental input; we absorb it and then drive it down with deep thinking tendencies. This is not necessarily a bad trait; in fact, I suggest that it may be one of our most valuable traits as it gives us insights often overlooked by others.

Because these conclusions don't come at lightning speed does not diminish their value to the workplace or society. The ability to survey a vast amount of data inputs, process them against prior experiences, and come to new insights or conclusions, takes some time. I think that HSPs, being very cautious about announcing a conclusion, require some internal vetting to ensure that the resolution or conclusion is solid and has merit.

HSPs are often criticism averse and don't want to make a decision before it has properly been thought through. This tendency to be cautious about decision-making actually falls well within the evolutionary guidelines provided by nature in equipping a portion of the population to thoroughly and cautiously analyze the environment. It is a species survival trait that aids the general population in advising for good decisions about the health and wellbeing of the group.

The use of this trait can lead to thought fatigue within HSPs. HSPs are designed to do this type of processing for periods that do not exhaust the individual's resources. At times this processing can lead to thought loops that can be even more exhaustive, recursive thinking that exhausts the individual both from a physical and emotional standpoint. When this happens, overstimulation occurs.

O: Overstimulation

Overwhelm, overwhelm, and overwhelm—the seeming natural state of the HSP. When too many stimuli, too much processing, and too high of expectations, whether internal or external, highly sensitive people tend to end up in the condition of overload. This seems to be a universal quality of all highly sensing people. It's not so much that we HSPs receive more data inputs than the rest of the population, but what we receive we filter less and process more. And because our brains tend toward deep processing of information, we can easily get caught up with too much to process and too little time to do it.

This quality of what I term high conscientiousness pushes many sensitive people to perfectionism, which leads eventually to the landfill of overload mental activity. Now some of us pride ourselves on being able to multi-task and problem-solve, but when the conditions are continuous, and the expectations are impossible, then overload-overwhelm-overstimulation happens. Sometimes it's not just the need to process, but the need to process perfectly, which sets us into overdrive. Credibility means something to

HSPs, and delivering reliable and vetted outputs, conclusions, and decisions can be taxing on our systems.

I don't like to look at this as being a problem because we have delicate systems that must be constantly balanced in order to function, but rather a problem of throttling. As HSMs, we need to know our limitations and work within them, moderating and modulating the inputs and processing to reflect the need for periodic rest and downtime.

Sometimes I believe we HSPs tend to run sprints in marathon races, where pacing is more important than racing. Why does this happen with people who do not thrive on exhilaration, but in fact shun high-pressure situations? Well, it could be the mirror neurons it appears we possess that allow us to mirror behaviors of those around us. We learn by being like the persons we are near. When we work in stressful work environments or are around people who tax our resources, we still find ourselves emulating them to get along and to be accepted. Where does this lead us? It drives us to overstimulation and ultimately to fatigue and shutdown.

Since caution is one of our behavioral drivers, we often find there is both internal and external conflict to our cautionary nature when confronted with expectations to hurry up, whether making decisions or in giving feedback before we are ready to do so. This also creates stress and leads to overwhelm.

When overstimulation sets in, the only productive thing for an HSP to do is to find a way to create some down time. Rest, relax, release are the antidote to overstimulation. Get out of the way of the runaway train—get off the track and live to fight again another time. Non-HSPs may be able to get away with avoiding overwhelm, or they may be able to ride out the stress storm, but HSPs will not do that well. It quickly escalates into a health concern, when constant overstimulation is not addressed.

Where this affects HSMs is that the prevailing cultural norm for masculine behavior under fire is to stay the course, gut it out, and find peace later.

Highly Sensitive Males operate with a different system that requires that they take the time to decompress to function at a high level once again. There is little mercy from the larger macho non-HSP culture for HSP males who become overstimulated and need a reprieve.

Overstimulation happens; it happens to non-HSPs as well. The fact that it happens more frequently to highly sensitive people should serve as a warning to the general population about the state of stress in our society. In many ways, HSPs are the canary in the coal mine, an early warning system that should be a wakeup call to everyone when stress gets to be too much in the culture, the workplace, or at home.

Not all HSPs suffer overstimulation to the same degree. Some are easily overstimulated, and others can handle more input and stress. HSPs are not clones of each other, but with as many individual differences as any personality type or group. Yet even those in the lower threshold of overstimulation within HSPs are generally still higher than the non-HSP population. When all the characteristics are taken together, they interact with each other and on each other to create a highly sensitive personality type. This dynamic makes us HSPs one of the most interesting personality groupings in the human population.

E: Emotional Reactivity/ Empathy

HSP brains are wired differently. We utilize areas of the brain—such as the mirror neuron systems that allow us to act in conjunction with someone else to mirror their neuronal firing—which aids in driving empathy with others. In addition, the firing in mirror fashion with someone else allows us to learn to follow that behavior or activity. These moments of empathetic learning are generally seen where a positive outcome is anticipated, or that there are positive emotions associated with the individual we are following.[17]

HSP research is showing that the more positive the emotional situation, the more strongly we encode the learning. The fact that HSPs are more strongly emotional or process emotions more strongly than non-HSPs may mean that we learn best under emotional circumstances. It has been said this emotional encoding aids us in retaining the information needed to grow, even if the information is negative feedback.

We more easily retain that we failed to complete a task properly, and because of the emotions associated with the task, we more powerfully encode the memory of what went wrong and are more determined to perform the task correctly in the future. The caveat is that the feedback must provide the correct response and be offered as corrective criticism. It is hard to imagine—as sensitive as most HSPs are—that negative feedback offered with negative emotion and severe criticism would inspire an HSP to move toward correcting the behavior. I suspect that under this circumstance, the opposite occurs. Rumination sets in, and the HSP individual registers the pain and sting of the criticism and recoils from trying to perform the task again. A painful memory, a poor result.

As with non-HSPs, but even more so, HSPs thrive when there is positive feedback, even if corrective, and in an environment that fosters positive outcomes. Our natural emotional reactivity to continued performance improvement could be inhibited if the main thing remembered was a negative emotional environment. Studies are bearing that out, and the suggestion is that HSPs will thrive in environments that are deemed to be positive and supportive.[18]

I have to emphasize that as an HSM I'm tired of hearing from primarily non-HSPs that because I easily show and display emotion, somehow that makes me a "drama king." Outward displays of emotions are not necessarily a bad thing. True that sometimes there are those who use emotional displays to manipulate and maneuver to get what they want. Showing more overt emotion does not necessarily qualify for that moniker, and I for one am sick of hearing it.

It's clear to me that those who scream of over-dramatization are often the ones most likely to show it in conflict situations. HSPs caught in that crossfire will naturally show emotional reactions, but are doing essentially what comes naturally to them. If life is drama or drama is life, then one thing is certain: drama requires conflict to exist. And conflict comes with an emotional price tag. HSPs get unfairly labeled as overly emotional, especially men who are HSPs, who are required by Western masculine regulation to abstain from all emotion, save anger. This is an unnatural state for all humans and is especially egregious for HSMs.

Where does empathy come in to play? HSPs and HSMs are naturally empathetic. This desire to connect with others at a level that goes beyond mere sympathy, but reaches down to feel the same experience of the person being empathized, is very common in highly sensitive people. Our ability to use mirror neurons not only aids in learning but creates an environment of empathetic reach, embracing the other, by feeling the same emotions. Humans are social animals; the need to reach out to others is a part of our survival strategy.

It has been suggested many times by Dr. Aron that HSPs are evolutionarily designed to aid in the survival of the species. Our ability to sense subtleties certainly comes from paying attention to environmental cues but also to surmise the emotional cues offered by our fellows. The empathetic nature of HSPs makes us ideal as advisors because of our intuition, our insights, and our internal compass. Empathy plays a large part in that.

This empathy we experience affects our behaviors, too. Where many non-HSPs may feel less connected to others, their behavior might reflect a lack of compassion, nurturing, or disconnection from others. HSPs are quite the opposite. We feel connected by an emotional umbilical cord to those around us, and therefore, this empathetic connection affects our behaviors toward others.

The downside often is sublimating our desires to satisfy the needs of others. This feeling of empathy can be so strong as to affect the language chosen in talking with others, knowing that our words can affect their feelings. While this is nice and polite, perhaps, it can delay delivering a harsher message if that is necessary for the other person to receive proper feedback. For highly sensitive men, this can mean a label of being called too nice and not direct and forthright in delivering messages.

S: Sensory Subtleties

HSPs are often labeled as sensitives, those who can gain nuanced information from the environment simply by showing up and paying attention. But what exactly does that mean? Think back to the idea of the depth of processing. The sensory information that HSPs receive is largely the same data input as anyone else, HSP or not. Our eyes aren't bigger, our ears aren't better receivers, our skin doesn't have more sensory cells, our taste buds aren't fatter, our noses aren't olfactory blessed. We receive the same inputs as the general population does.

The deciding factor is the way this data gets filtered and processed. Our brains are wired to take data inputs and process them more thoroughly, passing many times through a process that gleans the maximum amount of information per packet. Our eyes don't see any better than others, but our brain processes the small fly on the wall that no one else notices. Body language is processed through sight and memory to discern that someone is not happy, but is not revealed in their outward demeanor.

We smell the strong perfumed woman in the room twenty feet away, because we register the annoyance of the strength of the application of the perfume. We detect the music is too loud, because our processing of sound does not allow us to filter out the exceeding thumping of the bass line in the music. You could surmise that our filters are triggered at a lower threshold than others. If so, then we notice more in a quick cursory scan of the environment. The subtle taste of too much salt in an hors d'oeuvre that offends our tongue may go unnoticed by another who simply ignores the discrepancy. The scratchiness of the starched shirt we are wearing becomes annoying over time because we can't easily shut off the sensory processing.

This does not mean we suffer from over sensory input or hypersensitivity, but that our processing of the sensory input gets processed over and over to the point where it can become an annoyance. Even so, that ability to process deeply the information we receive can be a source of intuition and insight. Seeing the nuanced or noticing the subtle makes it easy to infer the detail of a situation and see things that others don't. This is the source of much creativity and why so many creative people are highly sensitive people.

The effects on emotions and intelligence can be profound. A mood can change in a flash, simply because of noticing something in the environment that is irritating or troubling. The subtle texture of our world can be a source of newfound inspiration or the source of emotional pain. To see the subtle aspects, the fine details of the world, can certainly enhance the intelligence of the individual, especially if there is an emotional charge to what is seen. I think this is why so many HSPs are perceived as being more intelligent.

It isn't about raw processing power or the ability to discern logical solutions to problems, but rather a way of sensing one's way around the environment, picking clean the leftovers that others pass by, the small details that in some cases can be life or death. It then becomes encoding and storing the knowledge for later use. It is with the deep processing that this stored data becomes valuable at a later date. Good memory aided by strong emotional coding.

This is where the value add is for this characteristic; the ability to learn from the subtleties of life and not leave behind any useful data, to gather every stone and turn them until they are polished nuggets of knowledge. This is a very slow, deliberate process. This is why HSPs are not quick decision-makers. The decisions they make are often full of insight and provide a big-picture vision that detail decision-making with its raw churning of information may miss.

Now I don't want to paint a brushstroke so broad that it appears all HSPs are intuitive gurus who are always accurate about conclusions. They are not. Intuition can only go so far, and sometimes internal biases can color the outcome regardless of the input. Energized emotion or fatigue can factor into discoloring the insights, perhaps distorting the obvious, with personal prejudices. As always, our senses can fool us, and regardless of how sure we processed the input accurately, we can be off the mark as much as non-HSPs. Being the conscientious creatures we are, we may back off with our intuitions if they are proven to be inaccurate. Confidence can wane without some reinforcement from the external world.

I see this trait as a valuable part of the HSP profile. It should be encouraged, not discouraged. When there is inaccuracy, we should chalk it up to the absolute uncertainty of any thought outcome, and that our conclusions are either inaccurate for the moment, spot-on, or ahead of our time. Coming to conclusions is often an iterative process; each stroke of the wheel brings you closer to accuracy; one conclusion leads to another until a consensus is gained.

Many HSPs don't recognize the value of this nonstandard intelligence we possess. It is complementary to the logical, deductive reasoning of the twenty-first century, which is focused on the following of a specific format and hard grinding out of solutions. HSPs tend to snatch things out of the blue and place them in order, creating new thoughts and patterns. It is a process that allows us to look up from the desk and see out the window, sensing and feeling our way to intuitive solutions, ones that can never be seen without lifting one's head.

What the World Sees: the Perceived Traits

What the world sees when they view an HSM is generally a large body of traits and characteristics that are considered over-generalizations and categorized based on those generalizations. For HSP males, this can be particularly vexing as the tendency is to gender fix certain traits as being feminine and un-masculine. This obsession that the world has on fixed and assigned gender roles is arbitrary and in many ways, unnatural. Humans have a wide range of behaviors, and limiting these behaviors can stultify human personality growth. This training begins at a very early age.

In the West, HSMs are often seen as being uncharacteristically emotional. This can be displayed as showing tears in public, publicly displaying fear, expressing love and nurturing behaviors, showing empathy, being moved by a performance or artwork, or even talking about intuitive insights, especially those not seen as logical or following the evidence.

When things turn argumentative, HSMs are seen to be overly dramatic, and they can and often do display emotion overtly. This, in Western eyes, is a feminine trait and diminishes the group view of HSMs as being effeminate and not manly. The paradigm that is offended by these traits is the one that locks men into only being able to display certain emotions like anger or joy.

Generally, fathers or male authority figures who indoctrinate these young males correct any notions about the proper manly emotional states that are permitted. These men wrongly tell young boys that these emotions will emasculate them and should be avoided at all costs. The price of that advice lingers throughout a man's life. It leads to emotional isolation and helplessness, both places where no human should tread.

As men, HSMs who process with the typical thoroughness of HSPs are often seen as wishy-washy, unable to make snap battlefield decisions, and when you throw in the wild card of intuition—illogical. The stereotype is that we think like females, which of course, is another derogatory gross generalization about female intelligence that is not only insulting to females but the HSM population.

I have heard this nonsense time and time again from males, subtle and not so subtle put-downs of women that helps perpetuate myths about gender roles and capabilities. To feel the sting of this as a male only makes us more mindful of the limitations of Western male gender definitions and the burdens that women have felt for millennia.

Most HSPs are introverts; in fact, approximately 70 percent of the HSP population is considered introverted. This doesn't make us the most social of creatures. We try, make an effort, but generally find solace alone or with a close coterie of friends or family. By nature, we are not party animals, and often eschew the bright lights and loud noises of social gatherings. Since most of the world is extroverted, and we live in a culture where extroversion is celebrated and embraced, it once again makes us seem like outcasts. In men, the idea of being loud and boisterous, of being a party animal and prancing around like a territorial ape, is a good sign of being an alpha male. Of course, the aspiration of most men who embrace that cultural myth is to be the big dog, the primary, the alpha.

The soft-spoken, mostly quiet, introverted male simply doesn't make the cut. There's something very beta about that, of course; it means weak, effeminate, submissive. The perceived trait is that we, as highly sensitive people, are not social enough, and at the very least, we should cut loose and be loud and impulsive, like the rest of the pack.

As has been noted by Dr. Aron who suggests that HSPs have an evolutionary role to play as the cautious advisors and counselors to the rest of the world, I ask you, would you rather get your spiritual, intuitive advice from a person who spends large quantities of time being loud and obnoxious, trashing bars late at night, getting in fights, or from someone who sits quietly in a cave and is contemplative, spiritual, and intuitive? I guess that depends on the type of advice you're looking for, but I'd put my money on the quiet guy.

Of course, a lot of this is about generalization, generalizations about HSMs, and generalizations about the rest of the world. Not all HSPs are the same; not all are introverted or supremely quiet. Not all introverts are HSPs; not all non-HSP males are assholes. But the point of this book and the underlying message is that we live in a world full of polarities. Sides get picked at the extremes, and people live and die by those extreme messages. As a result, people are often boxed off into arbitrary categories, labeled and shucked for whether we provide value or not—depending on the prevailing attitude. You don't shake up attitudes by being entirely reasonable. To see the underlying truths, sometimes you have to uncover the lies that blanket them and are willing to burn those blankets.

In the end, it's the old argument about the internal view versus the external view. The world sees the external view and loves everything externalized. To live outside of your head, live outside of your thoughts is where the world will reward you. But HSPs live primarily internally. Our internal view is the true view in our minds. It is hard for us to break the invisible barrier that often keeps us safe and secure within our thoughts and emotions. It is our challenge to live in the external world, while still being authentic to our internal worlds. Unfortunately, we have to live with the world view of us, which for HSMs is not always fair.

My Experiences

I have always overthought things. Every argument lost, every decision not made, every heartbreak, every time I felt I made a bad decision I rehash and ruminate for a long time afterward. I always find a way to procrastinate a decision. For some reason being able to put off until tomorrow a decision I could make today gives me some comfort. I don't know if I drop it down in the subconscious and hope for more processing time, or whether the idea of having to make a decision immediately bothers me, but invariably I put the decision off if I can.

For years I worked in a corporate environment as a middle manager. This type of decision-making style doesn't often go over very well, because the immediacy of some senior manager needing decisions made yesterday isn't very forgiving for those of us who need time to think first. This, in my opinion, is an epidemic problem in corporate America. It is reflective of our masculine culture, where thinking is often an afterthought (no pun intended). Decisions are made on impulse and sometimes raw emotion. The shit storm created by senior management is often tended to and cleaned up by middle managers below. Needless to say, I wasn't happy working in that world.

I am an emotional guy. There, I said it. Things move me, and then I'm emotional. A work of art, a movie, a song, a piece of literature, the admission of love to someone, the receipt of love unexpected—all move me to tears. Not an outburst of tears, just the watering of the eyes kind of tears, the kind of tears guys say, "Why, there must be some dust in the room." But, yes, that's what I do. I used to be apologetic about it, but not anymore. If I get labeled as the emotional guy in the room, so be it. I don't care anymore. I am learning to quit trying to by the cultural norm. Things move me; I now allow myself to experience that aspect of life. And you know, it's wonderful. It adds dimension and depth. So, I'm an emotional guy.

I used to question my masculinity a lot. The feedback I received growing up was that my masculinity was questionable. I remember once, in a psychologist's office, I was given a Rorschach inkblot test. I thought the answers I gave were pretty creative, pretty intelligent, without too much reading into them. The evaluation I received was that I had issues about my sexuality and gender identification. *Really?*

At the time, I was put off by that evaluation, but in hindsight, I think I could see where some of that might have come. I don't put much credence into the Rorschach; I don't think it's used that much anymore. It's largely an interpretive test and depends largely on the evaluator. Yet, I think that psychologist may have hit on something I was projecting, maybe not onto the test, but in the way I delivered my answers. It simply reinforced a misconception I had about masculinity, about being a man.

I don't feel that way so much anymore. I'm learning; I'm allowing myself to grow as a man, an HSP male. I hear the arguments against bucking the masculine model, but I don't care anymore. That's not me. And I have found there are a lot of men who don't buy into it anymore. It's the beginning of a movement well overdue.

Yes, I get overwhelmed. Still. That is part of who I am. I don't shut down as much as in the past. I have learned techniques, ways to deal with the overstimulation. An obvious one is to avoid overstimulation altogether. Avoid the hassles, the energy drains, the situations that cause overwhelm. I have learned to moderate my responses and detox and decompress when I need it. I let go of trying to control everything. But it still hits me from time to time, situational things, things I can't control—life. Yet I'm learning that my unique system, my brain, my body, my personality all need special handling. I've learned to do that for myself and to educate those around me about how I am. It works.

I am very empathetic and intuitive. It's not like the kind of empaths you see on the Internet. I'm not able to discern your thoughts or your emotions, but I can read a person pretty well where strong emotions are concerned. And even if I am not clairvoyant, I can sense in the other person, pain, love, heartache, joy. I don't have to stand over a special energy field or hold a crystal or talisman to do that; it just happens naturally. The intuition is not divination; it's filling in the tiny gaps in information from the environment. Many of these gaps come from small bits of data that my subconscious picks up—very nuanced information. My brain is designed to bring this information into a big picture, which forms as intuition. It is really just seeing the obvious in small grains of sand. Sometimes, I'll "just know." This is something we HSPs tend to do more than others.

Think of a fortune teller or psychic. Do you see male or female? Most likely a female. The intuitive trait is not one which we in the West often ascribe to males. Again, going against type. That's what we HSMs do. But it's okay, we're revising the model.

CHAPTER 5:

What is Sensory Processing Sensitivity?

T he trait that defines the Highly Sensitive Person personality is called Sensory Processing Sensitivity—SPS. This trait, part of a larger category of traits and theories about environmental sensitivity, pertains to how organisms, in this case, human organisms, adapt to the environment by way of sensory inputs and adaptations to move toward or away from change or stimuli in order to survive.

Sensory Processing Sensitivity involves increased sensitivity of the central nervous system and deeper cognitive processing of emotional, physical, and social stimuli.[19] It is estimated that 15 to 20 percent of the human population has this characteristic and supports the idea of its evolutionary value because in order for the characteristic to retain value it must be utilized by a small portion of the population. Its utility diminishes the larger the numbers of individuals within a population have this trait. This is known as negative dependency frequency.[20]

First popularized in her book, *The Highly Sensitive Person,* Dr. Aron was instrumental in classifying this characteristic as a trait and not a disorder, and that this trait can be positive and evolutionarily significant. She and her husband developed a standardized measurement scale, known as the Highly Sensitive Person Scale, and for children, the Highly Sensitive Child Scale, which has become the benchmark for measuring an individual's tendencies toward high sensitivity. In addition, this trait has been observed in over one hundred non-human species of animals.[21]

The work has been built on earlier work by Eysenck and his views on introversion, Pavlov's work on overstimulation, Gray's work on Reinforcement Sensitivity Theory, and Jung's work on Introversion and Extroversion.[22] All of these personality antecedents relate in some way to how the individual reacts to stimuli in the environment.

Early studies looked at this sensitivity, which focused on childhood temperaments, Thomas and Chess (1977) and Mehrabian developed a self-reporting tool that measured something akin to sensitivity.

Aron believes that the innate characteristic within SPS is the reaction to environmental cues and a pause-and-check processing, especially in novel situations.[23] This has important implications for the survival skills of the species where certain individuals are more cautious and contemplative when presented with new environmental cues. This is a hallmark for the cautious nature of HSPs.

Introversion studies led to the Sensory Processing Sensitivity theory, where the marker for sensory stimuli was seen to be lower in introverts than extroverts. This, coupled with the addition of a depth of processing component and the importance of emotional reactivity in learning, and the tendency toward overstimulation rounded out the parameters of the SPS theory. The emphasis here is on learning and adaptability.

A real issue comes down to accurate decision-making. The emotional reactivity component of SPS that aids in evaluating a situation correctly, without the need for conscious thought, turns out to be the quickest and most efficient form of decision-making, according to Aron.[24] The ability to analyze and decide based on emotional reactivity, memory, and unconscious learned processes appears to make the SPS individual ideally suited for analyzing a situation and making an efficient decision, which plays against type.

Increasingly, the Sensory Processing Sensitivity theory is gaining traction as part of a collection of adaptive personality models that focus on individual abilities to process environmental stimuli within the Environmental Sensitivity model. As its credibility rises, it is taking a larger portion of that model and may be the central theme within how individuals react in the world.

There is now some conjecture that SPS is part of a continuum that includes all members of the population, allowing it to be more broadly defined in personality theory. The idea is that there are essentially three groups of SPS types within the larger community. Those who have low SPS (also known as Daisies), comprise 20 to 25 percent of the population, those in the mid-range 45 to 50 percent of the population (the Tulips) and those most associated with this trait, the high-end SPS individuals (known as Orchids) at approximately 20 to 25 percent. The flower metaphor illustrates the environmental requirements of each of the flower species, Daisies being most environmentally adaptable with the least amount of effort/nurturing and the Orchids being the most demanding of the environment with higher requirements. This illustrates the necessity of a positive development environment on high SPS individuals, where the correlation between thriving, positive, supportive, and nurturing environments is extremely high.

Sensory Processing Sensitivity Traits

People with SPS are considered highly sensitive individuals. A myriad of traits are associated with this personality, many of which have to do with a rich and complex internal life. SPS individuals are generally very conscientious and diligent, tend to be more spiritual, and are moved more easily by the arts and being in nature. HSPs display more empathy and sympathy to those less fortunate or to helpless animals or creatures in need of aid.

Sensitive individuals show more creativity and can be quite innovative thinkers, if not under pressure or are being watched.

Studies show that HSPs have increased activation in the reward centers of the brain, flourishing in positive environments, where there is support, nurturing, and ample time to perform expected tasks. They often experience feelings of awe and satisfaction because of increased deep thinking functioning and sensory awareness. In addition, a study has shown that SPS individuals are more likely to report mystical phenomena in sensory deprivation tanks than the general population.[25]

The downside of SPS borders on neuroticism. Feelings of depression, anxiety, and stress, internalizing problems too much, lower levels of happiness in life, poor stress management strategies—and in the wrong environments, lower work satisfaction. The environment is everything to an SPS individual. Since HSPs are more sensitive to the environment, picking up subtle and not so subtle cues can create situations of overwhelm and stress. If consistent and persistent these moments can lead to self-devaluation and depression. There will be more focus on this later in the book, but suffice it to say that a bad environment for sensitives is chaotic, unpredictable, with ambiguous expectations, lack of support and empathy, loud, with high-pressure demands, and inability to process and think.

Future Research and Criticism of Theory

The history of Sensory Processing Sensitivity is barely thirty-years-old. A good percentage of that time has been spent building validity to the theory. SPS has moved from being considered a disorder to—in the right circumstance—a positive and useful personality trait.

Nevertheless, the current body of research for SPS, although growing, is severely lacking. There is a need for more biological based research, more studies under different research criteria utilizing fMRI technology to map reactivity to stimuli in various brain areas to characteristics for SPS individuals and compare those to the rest of the population. Studies are now showing genetic markers to dopamine and serotonin systems, but more studies are needed to bear out the genetic component of this trait.[26]

Research needs to question the stability of the trait across time based on environmental factors. More research needs to be done at creating ideal environments in which to raise SPS children and how to gain optimal usage of the key traits that positive environments seem to nurture in HSPs.

The testing needs to be more refined for identifying the SPS positive characteristics and less framing in a negative or avoidance light. The testing needs to be culturally neutral, so that cultural biases do not interfere with test results. If SPS is truly a continuum, then perhaps a more refined test can determine the level at which any individual might be placed. Throughout the remainder of the book, there will be suggestions as to other areas where a researcher may want to focus, perhaps in a more social psychology area.

More research is needed in developing the best strategies for HSPs to deal with stressful environments, overwhelm/overstimulation, best therapeutic strategies, developing better work environments for HSPs, and life coping skills. This research needs to focus on childhood strategies for SPS individuals to teach proper use of this trait for better life skills.

My thoughts in this area of psychology and personality theory certainly support the idea that research in Sensory Processing Sensitivity is lacking. So many areas to cover, but in writing my blog, *The Sensitive Man*, I often found that I had an idea or my own personal theory about something related to sensitivity and could not find any relevant research. As this concept of sensitivity takes hold, and perhaps even with the expansion of this definition to include a continuum of all humans, further research will explore not only the physiology of sensitivity but the psychology and the sociology of sensitivity impact on culture. As we continue challenging our definition of masculinity, perhaps valuable lessons can be learned from understanding how sensitivity affects manhood and if this can be seen as simply an aberration or more likely an evolutionary step forward.

An area I personally would like to see explored is the effects of personal growth, learning and experience, and accumulated wisdom on SPS over time at the individual level. Do they heighten the sensitivity, dull it, or allow us to mold into something malleable and adaptable, creating greater experience and increasing coping skills as we age? I know I have adapted to change and age. I have learned to silence some emotional responses and explore areas of my creativity, sometimes pushing the boundaries of my comfort zone. I consider this to be valuable, not only for me but for something all HSPs and HSMs, in particular, should explore. Growth comes with change, and change can create discomfort and sometimes pain. The pain often bears new fruit, bringing in the seed of more change and growth.

CHAPTER 6:

Deep Processing and Overthinking

Deep Thinking, Overthinking

One of the four main attributes of Highly Sensitive People is that HSPs routinely process emotional and environmental content more deeply than others and dwell on a topic for a longer period of time. We HSPs are often prone to deep thinking to what others may term as extreme lengths, which requires alone and quiet time.

HSPs use parts of the brain that are associated with deep processing and higher use of the part of the brain called the Insula—an integration tool that connects more of the brain in synchronicity.[27] The myth that we are slower thinkers is not supported. Research shows that HSPs have stronger, faster reaction times exhibiting our faster brain processing.[28] Our natural startle reflex supports that idea. The fact that we often process more data than non-HSPs may give the outward appearance we process at slower rates, but in fact, we are processing more data at higher rates with more outcome options analyzed.

What is deep thinking? Is it something only intelligent, philosophical types do? Is it complex thinking? Or is it simple thinking that is overly processed? Most deep thinkers display characteristics that seem good fits to what we consider HSP traits. They often are introverted, observant, humorous (albeit quirky), voracious readers, forgetful, curious, planners, problem solvers, socially awkward, and independent.[29]

A lot of the psychological studies involving deep thinking suggest it is a part of the definition of levels of thinking. A lot of this relates to how memory works: the deeper the encoding, the deeper the processing.[30] That makes sense; much like a hard drive on a computer stores data for later retrieval, deeper encoding makes data available for later processing. Shallow encoding leads to more short-term processing, which effectively comes and goes quickly.

Another factor for enabling deep processing—the more emotional the content, the stronger the encoding. Most HSPs are emotionally charged creatures. Much of our input is likely highly charged and stored effectively in long-term memory, where it can be drawn upon and processed for longer periods. Because deep processing often involves the use of semantics, language helps to encourage the analytics of deep thinking.[31]

Many of the brain areas associated with memory and depth of processing—the hippocampus, amygdala, and neocortex—are areas often associated with HSP brain processing.[32] Whether HSPs as a whole have more powerful hippocampal areas (memory) or a more active amygdalae (emotion) might give additional credence to the idea that we are naturally wired for this type of processing. Since the Sensory Processing Sensitivity characteristics seem to occur across species, not just humans, you have to wonder if this quality is not evolutionarily ordained and functionally important for survival.[33]

But when does deep processing become overthinking? Overthinking is not considered to be a positive attribute. In fact, there are distinct health consequences for persistent overthinking.[34] Two main outcomes of over-thinking are rumination and worrying, both having stress consequences.

Rumination is a process where the past is relentlessly rehashed with no productive outcome. Sometimes rumination involves circular recursive logic that leaves the individual feeling helpless and hopeless. Worrying, the projection of rumination, involves deriving negative predictions about the future—utilizing previous unsuccessful outcomes as input.[35]

Neither strategy leads to positive outcomes and can drive negative thought patterns down deeper. An infusion of emotions almost always energizes this exercise and can lead to anxiety, stress, and depression. If you find yourself stuck in this thinking and recognize it, then challenge your thoughts, focus on active problem-solving. Give yourself time for neutral reflection and mindfulness. Or, give yourself a consuming distraction to break the cycle, and if that fails to work, seek help.

The consequences of overthinking are much different than deep processing.[36] I'm not sure that deep processing can spawn overthinking, regardless of what non-HSPs may think, but it behooves us HSPs to be mindful of where our deep processing is leading us. Overthinking can lead to real mental health issues—anxiety and depression. It certainly can inhibit the benefits of your deep processing ability by causing analysis paralysis, and with that, added stress can contribute to sleep disturbances.

Our HSP ability to rely on deep processing of inputs is certainly one of our shining characteristics. It doesn't lend us to making hasty decisions or staccato-like shotgun decision-making. But our ability to deeply process and forecast outcomes is what makes us good advisors, counselors, and teachers. At some point, we have to accept our conclusions and go with them by taking action or risk treading into the realm of overthinking. We need to trust our gut; as an HSP, our instincts are generally right, in large part because of our deep thinking capabilities.

When Deep Thinking Does Not Serve Us Well

Overthinking is a problem that many HSMs have, but may not recognize as such. Our thinking is that *this is the way I am, everybody tells me*

I overthink things, but no one says, "Hey, you are such a thorough and conscientious thinker." Nah, that doesn't happen.

People who overthink take deep thinking beyond just heavy processing; there is something obsessive about overthinking. Overthinkers seem to get caught in an endless loop of options, choices, and decisions. The nature of most HSPs is to be correct, especially in thought. The idea of criticism bristles even the hardiest of sensitive people. Being wrong, being hasty, or coming to an incomplete decision is like the obsessive student looking to score a perfect score on every test.

The result of overthinking is to delay decision-making while pondering, if just a bit more processing is needed to arrive at a conclusion that resonates with the entire body and mind. This is fine if we HSPs lived in a cocoon with our decisions only affecting us and no one else. The real world is not like that.

One of the problems is that most HSPs don't get any training to learn to prioritize our thinking process. Decisions are generally made to minimize risk outcomes and to maximize rewards. It's about knowing when to take the risk and when not to short change the process. It's about knowing when it's okay to be wrong, to expedite the decision, knowing those wrong decisions can often be corrected and learned from, with the idea of making better decisions, and when needed, faster decisions. How often in the workplace does this happen? How often in life does this happen?

Of course, with our 'ability' to ruminate or worry, we play these two obsessions like broken records, coming back to the same spot in our heads over and over again. This creates a tendency toward catastrophizing outcomes before they occur, leading to this even more obsessive overthinking. If HSPs are not confident decision-makers and have a history of being criticized for decisions or have made bad decisions, many of these come with emotional consequences. We have bad outcome anxiety. Can you say sleepless nights?

This is why it is so important for HSPs to have supportive environments in which they work, live, play, and are raised. The point is that deep thinking is not the problem.

In fact, it is a very positive characteristic of SPS; it is when the decision process becomes obsessive because of poor thinking strategies or because the HSP is not confident in his or her decision capabilities that we have the obsessive overthinking problem. It's more about knowing when to take deep dives in thinking versus relying on memory and previous learning for quicker decisions and to understand the risk implications of the decision.

Imagine a decision tree that first evaluates the priority of the decisions, then places the decision into the appropriate bucket—deep thinking versus quick thinking. Next comes the ranking of risk in the decision and assigning an allowable risk for that decision that makes the criteria for evaluation easier to determine. Is this a high risk-high reward situation, or low risk-low reward scenario, and can the risk assigned be tolerated? If so, do the appropriate processing, then stop and make a decision. I realize this all sounds "flowcharty" like computer programming, but having a workable heuristic model would make decision-making faster, and I think easier for those prone to overthinking. Accept the risk, take a chance, make a decision.

Of course, this does not apply to all decisions, and yes, many decisions need careful consideration. As HSPs are cautious thinkers by nature, we should exercise that cautiousness when appropriate. That's one of our strengths. But we should also recognize that all decisions don't need the same level of processing and should be relegated to shorter, easier methods when outcomes are not as critical.

This gives us options. Confident HSP thinkers seem to know that. They realize that every decision isn't life and death, and don't hold themselves accountable for every decision for some absolute correctness of thought that no human can reach. Confidence breeds trust in our instincts and intuition, which is the vast store of experiences, memory, and past decisions residing in our unconscious mind. Trusting our gut is often hard for HSPs, but not trusting can have painful consequences, too.

How often do conscientious, sensitive persons find themselves in a situation where a bad decision or mistake (and this is relative) causes them not to allow for self-forgiveness about the decision. Preventing self-forgiveness is a learned punishment strategy that perpetuates the continued process of overthinking. It facilitates loop thinking, which is simply a way of delaying a decision or not making one. Again, overthinking is learned, deep processing is innate.

Deep Thinking Advantages

I have great regard for the deep thinking attribute that SPS banner carriers have. It allows us to process more detail in our thinking, which expands the options of the outcome of the thinking process. I believe that deep processing capabilities make HSPs great solitary thinkers. Solitary thinkers rely less on other external inputs, say from friends, family, or colleagues, and can allow for free play with ideas within their internal framework. To be certain, there are indeed external inputs, but most of those have been previously processed, categorized, and stored and are used in the thinking process in novel ways.

This allows SPS thinkers to be more creative and individualistic in their thinking. This is great for creative problem solving, creating works of art, proposing new, untested ideas, and generally contributing different perspectives on old lines of thinking. Besides, our use of emotional reactivity in decision-making might provide for dredging deeply encoded information that had a similar emotion associated with it during memory encoding. As stated previously, emotional reactivity has been associated with better learning outcomes. All of this facilitates deep thinking, which I believe is the greatest value SPS individuals bring to bear in society.

If HSPs trust their intuition and insights more, coupled with their deep thinking process, I believe more HSPs would be more confident in their decisions and contribute more to solving society's problems. There seems to be a strong bias in science and our culture against the use of intuition, although, if you examine the history of science, and especially the moments in science when breakthroughs occur, intuition often is the determining factor.

Since HSP intuition is a strong suit in our thinking process, encouraging and rewarding HSPs for reaching out a bit might facilitate better ideas in business, education, government, religion, the arts, and sciences. This could lead to more breakthrough thinking, more innovation, more thought-provoking considerations, and less reckless, short-sided, one-dimensional thinking.

Intuition is often considered emotional thinking, but emotional thinking is not always a bad thing. Sometimes it adds an urgency, importance, and priority to decisions. It always adds a bit of humanity to thinking, which we sorely lack now. Decisions are often made for the expediency of greed, politics, or unfortunate inflexible scientific dogma.

Thoughtful decision-making is a lost art these days. The world is based on machine speed thinking rather than careful and cautious deliberation. For the moment, our brains can still out process any machine on the planet. We have a group of people, within the human population that is, at least as is being proposed, who have an evolutionary purpose, adding measured thought and ideas into the vast kettle of impulsive world thought. It's time to wake up to that.

My Experiences

As an HSM, I am often confronted with the admonition that I over-think everything. Always striving to get to the most attractive and favorable decision is my objective, although many have told me that I am too slow and deliberate in making decisions. Yes, it does take me longer to make important decisions, but I am always looking at the alternatives, weighing them, and trying to put them in some priority order. This is no more evident in my thinking process for relationships.

At the beginning of any dating relationship, there is a period of uncertainty. Does the person really like me? Is she going to be able to satisfy my needs? Am I good enough for the other person? Most of these questions are a product of self-doubt and lack of confidence. As an HSM, I certainly have been subject to this line of thinking. Because I am always over evaluating things that are new and unknown, I tend to go through a three or four-month ritual of great scrutiny and evaluation with any new relationship . Depending on the individual I am dating, the uncertainty can range from mild to extreme.

A great deal of worrying always takes place. At my age, everyone I meet has some baggage they carry with them—family, exes, friends, etc.—which adds to complicate matters. It is rare at this time in my life to find anyone with little or no emotional baggage, perfectly well adjusted, and without the element of doubt. This doubt often takes the form of not knowing if former relationships will come back to haunt them or me. The worrying thought pattern is usually my imagination running wild. I see myself vesting my emotions into a relationship only to find the object of my affection retreats to a former love, or, worse yet, finds someone else.

You can see the pattern of lack of confidence, but also the pattern of incorrect thinking. Stated plainly, it's overthinking the situation. So, for three or four months, everything said, every action taken is evaluated. Instead of enjoying the present, I find myself almost automatically living in an imagined future, looking for unexpected and negative outcomes.

The flipside of this is rumination. Thinking about everything I have said or done in the new relationship, evaluating my behaviors, my thoughts, my words, my choices, looking for a pattern either good or bad. This is overthinking at its worst. This habit was formed young and engrained over the years. It is a product of a lack of self-confidence or self-worth and enhanced by the ability to think deeply. It is a self-inflicted hell, trying to find homeostasis and balance.

The clear problem is that I fail to enjoy the new relationship for what it is, a chance to learn about someone new and myself. This cautionary thought process does not allow me to experience the sometimes turbulent beginnings of a new relationship easily. I am working on this, learning to experience the moment.

Some see this as over obsessing about an outcome that can't fully be determined. Some might see this as controlling or even manipulative if used to maneuver another person to be something he or she is not. Regardless of the point of view, it is not healthy if it takes on an emotional track that is uncomfortable. There is a type of torture overthinkers experience because of a need to protect themselves from pain and control their environment. In the end, it's a losing strategy.

It's not inherently necessary for HSPs; however, I think the potential is higher because of our capacity to evaluate our environments so deeply. If the HSP has had previous crushing relationships, the tendency could be exacerbated. In my case, it's an amplification of deep-rooted fears of non-acceptance, abandonment, and lost love.

This theme of self-image weighs heavily on many of the HSPs I know. This is particularly true for HSMs. We are different, we act and think differently, and we feel and intuit emotions much more strongly than non-HSP males. I once told a former lover the thing that makes me an attractive partner (the romance, the flowers, the poems, and the thoughtfulness) also produces the worry, the uncertainty, and the lack of confidence. The two don't always go hand in hand, but depending on the individual, they can. The emotional polarity can be maddening.

Another area for overthinking occurs in confrontational situations, such as heated disagreement or argument. Arguments tend to be highly emotional, volatile, and rapid-fire. For those quick-witted souls who can make logical or cohesive arguments under such conditions, my hat is off to you. I, for one, cannot. My overthinking and tendency toward overwhelm sabotage any effort on my part to make a cohesive argument or rebuttal. As the accusations or emotions fly, my brain used to tracking things in a manageable way, receives each remark, and not only does it try to process it quickly, it begins the endless evaluative loop. As one thing comes, then another, then another, and my brain quickly overloads. The ability to single thread multiple verbal assaults is lost on overthinking. The evaluation of each argument quickly devolves into emotional outbursts that are sometimes incoherent and haphazard.

Of course, the day after, I begin the rumination process, followed shortly after that by the worrying process. Twenty-four hours after the argument, when time has allowed the transcript of the confrontation to set in, I come up with some pretty astute comebacks, but alas, they are too little … too late. This is where overwhelm and overthinking overlap. The two add up to a one-two punch that makes me less than a formidable debater under fire. Perhaps my tendency to avoid confrontations comes from my experiences in losing arguments. But unless I have a Zen moment of utter clarity, I cannot verbally and cohesively argue back.

Both of these examples are painful reminders of my sensitivity. They remind me that I am different, and to successfully navigate life, I am going to have to find different ways to approach these situations that fit my personality and my temperament. Later in the book, I'll be talking about some of these strategies.

CHAPTER 7:

Behavioral Quirkiness

Passive-Aggressive Behavior

Passive-aggressive is a label often meted out by non-experts to cubbyhole people who may be moody or not willing to talk the straight talk, people who are quiet and not assertive, or even as a way to manipulate others by placing a derogatory label on them. As an HSM, I have been called passive-aggressive by those who think my thoughtful and deliberate approach to things is manipulative. Not so.

What is passive-aggressive behavior, anyway? The classical definition describes this as a group of manipulative behaviors used to provide resistance to another or others, mired in moodiness, sarcasm, stubbornness, learned helplessness, blaming, backhanded compliments, or in some way to mask hidden anger.[37] The gist of this seems to be about an inability to process anger in a straightforward and positive, assertive way. Repressed anger, lack of assertiveness; sound familiar, HSMs?

Passive-aggressive behavior is learned at home. Children are made to feel that anger is something not to be expressed, find ways to allow the inner turmoil to seep out, and passive-aggressive behavior is one way to do that. It also occurs in families where any honest, straightforward emotional display is discouraged, and again, the child learns coping strategies that help relieve the internal pressure cooker.

Passive-aggressive behavior in the extreme is defined by the Diagnostic and Statistical Manual (DSM-V) as a disorder needing therapy. In its lesser forms, passive-aggressive behavior is more of a failed coping strategy that is a distorted approach to getting your point across. It's childish behavior, it's manipulative, and it's catty.

The root of passive-aggressive behavior most often stems from anger, disappointment, or hurt feelings. The motive for passive-aggressive behavior is a subtle type of revenge that is manipulative but not aggressive.

Not surprisingly, men and women process anger differently. Men are taught to be more visual, external, and aggressive, while women are taught to suppress their anger and vent in more subtle and diffused ways.[38] You might think the perfect candidates for passive-aggressive behavior are women. But this does not seem to be the case. Because women verbalize more than men about their emotions, they can find suitable outlets of expression that don't lead to aggressive behavior. Conversely, men aren't always allowed to express aggressive anger, repress the feelings, and find passive-aggressiveness as a way to cope with anger.

But what about HSMs? Because we tend to be less assertive and certainly less aggressive, are we better candidates for passive-aggressive behavior? On the surface that seems logical, but thinking about one of the hallmarks of HSPs—empathy—it seems less likely that this behavior would be implemented.

Empathy is a powerful force in its own right. Manipulation of another stems largely from a lack of empathy toward the other. Having the sensitivity to react to others' reactions makes us more likely to consider the outcomes before implementation, and our empathetic and sensitive nature makes it unlikely that we would feel good about this strategy.

With that said, it is not impossible to imagine an HSP using passive-aggressive tactics in desperation, but as a long-range strategy, it just doesn't feel right. It requires some disconnection from the "what I say" and "what I do" to react passive-aggressively. And this would be the point where HSMs would struggle.

Let's dig a little deeper into the HSM personality that might lead others to label HSPs as passive-aggressive. Because HSMs tend to be more connected to their emotional state and are aware of the emotions of those around them, do we tend to get more defensive when emotions run hot? The answer is a resounding yes. We are very sensitive to criticism, and as a result, this often leads to people-pleasing behaviors, some of which are inauthentic. This becomes a point of incongruity for our internal compass.

This can become a disconnect in our communication with others as we pursue an often idealistic goal of continual peace and harmony with the world. As Dr. Elaine Aron states, "...(HSPs) are naturally more influenced by feedback, and it may even be why we are more emotional generally."[39] We take that feedback to heart, process it, and at some point take action. The time lag may appear to others to be a form of passive-aggressive behavior (shutdown reaction, quiet, not saying what we feel, etc.).

We hurt more easily, too. HSPs are not angels. We have a dark side as well. As men, we still have the drive to act aggressively, even if it is not our nature. Can we formulate strategies to react less aggressively, but still show passivity and milder aggressiveness? Perhaps, we show signs of hypercritical evaluation, self-flagellation, indecisiveness, irritability, moodiness, need for solitude, naiveté, and eccentricity, but taken as a whole, is this passive-aggressive? I can understand where the non-HSP world could see that. But it's not, and the key is the motive. Manipulation and revenge are key motives of passive-aggressive behavior and are not major drivers for HSPs.[40]

Dr. Aron points out, "Generally, the research does not point out or show increased activation in HSPs in areas of the brain related to 'primitive emotion'[41] ... Rather than 'getting all stirred up' more than others, we tend to process emotional experiences more in 'higher' parts of the brain, the ones designed precisely for emotional regulation." Anger, a swift-moving emotion, helps us to set boundaries and protect our rights.

For HSPs, this highly charged emotion can leave us in a processing overload. Our reaction is not often swift enough, and hence boundaries can be lost. This is upsetting even for HSPs and can lead to coping strategies that may not be best for our personality type. Sometimes, the non-HSP world sees this as passive-aggressive without truly understanding what that term means.

Slow to anger does not mean the anger is not present. Because we HSMs tend to suppress some of the aggressiveness of anger, we still have to process our reaction to anger. At some point, it will come out. Assertiveness training is helpful, and the use of assertiveness strategies is in alignment with HSP values. Most of us never get this type of education. This is unfortunate. I know for myself at some point an eruption point occurs, and like a volcano, the anger explodes unexpectedly — bad strategy, and for that, we get bad labeling.

So what can we do? If you show passive-aggressive tendencies or what the non-HSP world describes as such, here are some ways to deal with that:

1. Be up front with your feelings. Understand that it's okay to disagree or be in opposition to another's opinion. Say what you mean—the more direct, the better—without incessant elaboration. If this is difficult, consider assertiveness training.

2. Don't get into melodramatic gunfights with gunslingers. Why? They will attack you before you can even draw your gun. They shoot first, process later—opposite from us. Instead, let your inner radar direct you away from the drama and feel glad that you avoided the fray. And take note, a passive-aggressive type shot over the head will not work with them anyway. See the duel scene in Kubrick's, *Barry Lyndon*. It's not about winning a battle; it's somebody else's problem.

3. Be mindful of the will for aggressive retaliation if you sense that. What button got pushed, why did it affect you, and is it worth pursuing another way? Generally not, but being mindful keeps you in charge.

4. If you find that you are in a passive-aggressive moment, ask yourself if you are trying to manipulate your adversary. Is this a subtle issue of control or lack thereof? How does this make you feel? It's like beating a dead horse that died throwing you out of the saddle. Weird and unproductive.

5. The real issue here may be that a rude person hurt your feelings. Separate the feelings from the person. Put the feelings in a box for self-examination later, deal with the person now. Are they your ally or are they your foe? If they are the latter, dismiss them and move on. Moving on for HSPs is a big deal. We hold on to things too long, lingering, ruminating, digesting, then regurgitate and repeat. Sometimes that is useful to our work, our being; other times it's just wasted time and emotion. That's why I say jettison the detritus and learn to move on. Some people don't deserve your deep consideration.

Emotion Junkies

Did you ever feel like an emotional junky, sometimes like a slave to your emotional patterns? Brain chemistry drives our emotions, and the subsequent addiction to those brain chemicals can lead to repetitive and habitual behaviors that may be feeding a circle of "junk" behavior. As we all know, HSPs commonly deeply experience emotions. We react to the stimulus and because of the deep processing mechanisms we process and reprocess the emotion attempting to make sense of those feelings. This repetitiveness is what intensifies the emotional reaction. Within HSPs this leads us, at an unconscious level, to seek out more intense emotions, which may seem contrary to our need for moderation of emotional experiences.

What makes this happen? Emotions occur at the unconscious level and are driven by peptides released by the hypothalamus.[42] These peptides proteins are then released into the body and attach to cells with corresponding receptors. When attached, they produce the desired effect in the cell, which corresponds with a bodily function associated with that emotion. The process is largely unconscious, yet experienced and felt at the conscious level. The feelings may drive more of the same emotion, creating an addictive cycle of stimulation based on our experiences.[43]

In other words, addiction drives the experience. Of course, there are other brain chemicals involved, but the basic process lends itself to a model of possible addiction. It stands to reason that HSPs, more so than the general population, might be subject to this type of addiction because of their increased ability to experience sensory information and most importantly, the ability to hyper-process that information.

In its simplest form it looks like this: 1) thoughts created in neurons networked together, 2) trigger a chemical release from the hypothalamus, peptides, which 3) release to the cells and attach at receptors on the cell creating 4) a visceral reaction, which is recognized 5) via consciousness resulting in a feeling. The emotion spoken of earlier is largely automatic and unconscious and driven by brain/body chemistry. The feeling is what we recognize consciously. It is simply emotion wrapped in thought.[44]

Addictions by most definitions are largely automatic behaviors driven by unconscious emotion or memory or association. And the operative word here is repetition. This is why addiction is so difficult to treat and deal with consciously. The neural patterns are so reinforced that they occur without thought. It is only when we recognize the pattern that we can affect an interruption in the behavior.

Now, how does all of this affect HSMs? Highly sensitive people are, by definition, people who experience sensations, feelings, and emotions more intensely than the general population. Could it be that because of this ability we as highly sensitives can become eventually more habituated or desensitized to emotion?

If the nature of emotion is largely addictive (perhaps for survival purposes), then this addiction to emotion could lead to an ever-increasing need to experience more intense emotions to satisfy the addiction. The more highly charged the emotion, the more repetitive the emotion, the more likely the receiver cells will need to create more and more receptor sites to handle the incoming data, thus allowing the whole experience to grow more intense.

A subgroup of HSPs are sensation seekers. Sensation seekers tend to look for experiences that provide novel experiences, adventure, and thrill-seeking rushes, splashes into social activities that may be unconventional, and are prone to boredom susceptibility.[45] HSPs who are also sensation seekers may exhibit a less driven desire for over-the-top experiences, but need to break the monotony of HSPs' careful and cautious behavior. Could this not include seeking highly charged emotional sensations as a way of producing a high?

This may be truer in HSMs, because of our cultural expectations for men, in general, to be more daring, bold, and adventurous. We find ourselves taking the bait and falling into the trap of sensation seeking. Sometimes, we HSMs need not venture much farther outside of our craniums to get that rush experience. A good heartbreak can seem like bungee jumping.

Maybe HSPs fall in love more often and fall harder in love just for the adrenaline rush. Or we moderate our emotions, smoothing out the intensity by avoidance, thus interrupting the process before intensity becomes too strong. In reverse, could this lead to a state of emotional anorexia? Does being an HSP come with an automatic regulation system that prevents overstimulation by shutting down input and requiring emotional time-outs? If so, that could make us less likely to become subject to emotional addiction. Interesting to think about. We, as a group could be emotional junkies and not even be fully consciously aware of that addiction.

Here are some thoughts on how to deal with high-intensity emotions if you are an HSM:

1. At some point, you have to acknowledge that you are experiencing emotions and feelings more intensely than the general population. Some emotions are naturally more intense than others. You will experience love and pain, sadness, and rejection much more intensely. Not surprising, the high emotions of joy and love, etc., can be just as difficult to deal with as the low ones such as pain or sadness. Buckle up when you know these are coming, but don't mindlessly ride the roller coaster. Mindfulness can interrupt the patterns.

2. Don't avoid intense emotions to keep some imaginary status quo or level playing field. Part of why we are here and configured the way we are is to experience things at a much deeper level. Maybe this is spiritual, maybe it is evolutionary, or maybe there is just some simple life lesson to learn from each experience through the eyes of an HSP. Go with it and if it gets too intense, then gather your trusted tribe members around you and find your cave.

3. Take some time to examine and see if historically, you have sought out intense emotional situations. For example, do you always find yourself in difficult love situations, complete with roller-coaster emotions? Do you choose to experience sad novels, films, or works of art to feel the pain deeply? Not so much as a self-inflicted wound but to kick start your emotional machinery. If so, you might be an emotional junkie. When dealing with powerful brain chemicals,

it's not farfetched to believe that one can become addicted to the coursing flow of emotional juice.

4. For each of us, the real key is how to come down from the high wire. No one can live balanced precariously between high and low all the time. Some return to neutral activity is needed for all of us. Find a practice of meditation, yoga, Tai Chi, mindfulness or brain training that will help you fly neutral for a while to process and recharge. You'll need it.

5. This area (emotional intensity in HSPs) needs to be researched further. HSPs everywhere can benefit from learning more about how emotions affect us differently than non-HSPs. This goes way beyond learned behavior patterns from childhood but rather deals with brain chemistry and the subtle workings of our pleasure centers and how they shape our emotional life, like an endless cycle, back and back again to the sensation.

Honoring the Anima for Men

Hey gents, for those of you who slept through high school biology class, here's a little news flash for you: we all start out as females.[46] So when I mention honoring the anima, Jung's delineation of the unconscious female mind in all men, then you realize that perhaps a biological component played a part in creating that facet of men. You see, when the fetus is about nine weeks, testosterone kicks in for males, and it just keeps kicking in throughout our lives. Even when the hormone dries up, the after-effects of all those years of raging aggressive hormones leaves its residue on our psyches.

For thousands of years of human history, the male domination of culture, religion, politics, and civilization has left the planet exhausted and nearing depletion. It's an unsustainable path, with no room for escape. And Gaia will revolt if we don't alter our course.

We must all embrace the role of the feminine energy that permeates all of life on this planet. We are cut off from our sacred creative core when we only follow the destructive path of unbalanced masculine energy. Without the calming, nurturing, and creative alliance with the feminine, we are on a one-way ticket to hell. Balancing the aggressive yang energy with calming, life-giving yin energy means we all must embrace that side in us that brings healing. This includes men accepting and encouraging feminine energy within and outside of themselves.

This means honoring the feminine energy in all things. As HSP males, we are perhaps perfectly suited to usher in what appears to be an impending era of female leadership and feminine spirit. As males who are often more in touch with our emotions, we unconsciously embrace both the masculine and feminine. We are in tune with the subtle differences between the two and can aid in leading this movement forward in conjunction with wise female leaders. We know of the anima within and must learn to accept the gift that it brings.

Yet, this movement requires more than just HSP males to champion the transition. Highly sensing males must aid other men to acknowledge and promote the critical need we have at this juncture in our history to restore the ancient wisdom of feminine inspired leadership. The need for a feminine influenced direction is dire as we witness the destruction of our planet, our human values, and the decency of nurturing our planet back to its point of equilibrium.

Embracing the feminine does not mean that men have to become female. It is not about vanquishing masculine energy either. It has and always will be about balance.

HSP males are going to have to put themselves out there. This is not a comfortable position for most sensitive men. We need to push back on an aggressive and powerful force that has long been entrenched in our culture. We will need to convince not only males, many who have profited from this current era of male dominance, but females who are still entrenched in the old male authoritarian model. Many women need to be educated and liberated from this antiquated philosophy, and some may only listen to male figures, rejecting the advice of their feminine peers. This is a place where HSP males might be quite useful. Our sensitivity and compassion, coupled with our male personas, might help with these females' transitions.

So how can we men embrace the anima within and facilitate the change to the divine sacred feminine?

1. Acknowledge and own your emotional self. If you want to cry, then cry, damn it. If you want to laugh and feel joy, do it. If you want to be angry, don't hold it back. Open yourselves up, men.

2. Acknowledge and own your nurturing side. A great place to do this is at home. If you are a parent, get in there and help your partner with the kids. If you are not a parent, then look for the need around you: an elderly parent, someone in need, a daily act of kindness. Nurturing changes you. And the changes I speak of must come from within.

3. Acknowledge and own your intuitive side. This means paying attention to your gut, listen to your heart, be quiet sometimes, and let the wise inner self help you.

4. Acknowledge and own your creative and spiritual side. If you follow the third point, this should become easier and easier. Creativity and spirituality come from within but is sourced from a greater place than you. I'll leave it at that, mainly because there are a billion interpretations of where that is, but you can be sure there is a there somewhere.

5. Acknowledge that there is strength in feminine energy. Think about this for one minute. We have a long history of the human species

on this planet. There has been a female involved with every person who ever existed. Without that foundation, nothing exists. Thank the divine Mom in every woman. There is incredible strength in feminine nature. You see it every day. Never forget that.

6.   Acknowledge and own the masculine within. There is boldness and action in the masculine. This energy will be needed, too. Embrace your masculine energy, balance it with the anima, and you can become a nuclear fusion of loving change.

7.   Finally, participate in the revolution to the sacred feminine. It's really an evolutionary cycle, and like a wave, you can ride it, or you can get swept away by it; either way, you wind up on the shore.

Positive Disintegration Theory

In the early sixties, Polish psychiatrist Kazimierz Dabrowski developed the Positive Disintegration Theory,[47] a personality development framework that emphasizes personality evolution via overexcitability (OE) crises of the individual, which amounts to a heightened experience of stimulus via increased neuronal sensitivities. This experience places the individual into crises, which expands the boundaries of personality and allows for growth. Individuals progress through levels of development spurred by these existential sensory excitements, eventually achieving a creative, altruistic state that optimizes human potential.

It seems a perfect developmental model for Highly Sensitive People, with our highly sensitive natures. We are well equipped to experience these catalysts for growth that could lead us to become highly advanced personalities per this model. But do our unique personality characteristics make us better designed to evolve to a higher level of human personality, and if so, for what purpose?

Let's look at the theory. Some of the main tenets of the theory are: 1) tension and anxiety are necessary for personal growth, 2) personality is not innate but must be learned, 3) developmental potential (DP), a key component, is a result of the overexcitability (OE) factor as well as the drive for autonomy, 4) the disintegration component refers to the breakdown of our primary integration, which is a more reptilian early life personality focused on selfish drives and survival. This basic personality is formed as a result of primal instincts and socialization and must dissolve for developmental growth to occur.[48]

Emotional reactions create the development of individual values, different and individuated from societal norms. Decisions are then made about the individual essence (which I read as the core of the person), and then existential choices allow expression of the higher self and inhibition of the lower self as measured against these newfound values.

The levels of development occur along five stages. The developmental potential for each individual derives from various genetic features expressed through interaction with the environment. Through various mechanisms including overexcitability (OE), specific abilities and talents, and a strong desire for autonomous growth, this potential is realized. There are five aspects to (OE), which include: psychomotor (excessive physical energy, impulsivity), sensual (expression through the senses), imaginational (visualization in the mind), intellectual (voracious learners), and emotional (empathy).

For those with high levels of OE, which is expected for HSPs, the road to development is not an easy one. Many highs and lows make navigating through development difficult. People with high developmental potential have a strong compulsion to work through and walk their path. I find that in my contacts with HSPs this seems to be a common theme.

As Dabrowski mentioned, we all start at the same place—the primary integration level. Many people stay at this level their whole lives, never advancing, focusing on self-centered objectives and survival strategies at all costs. This has nothing to do with intelligence. It is about the emotional development of the individual. Many intelligent, powerful people stay locked here, their success predicated on fulfilling their basest desires. Others live there to follow and conform, never fully developing a strong sense of self. There is great social and peer pressure to conform, a robotic and rote existence.

The next level, Unilevel Disintegration, occurs as a result of brief periods of crisis, followed by existential despair and then transformation. An example might be adolescence, a financial crisis, or the death of a loved one. Generally, these crises are horizontal—right/wrong, forward/backward types of decisions. This is a transitional stage. Many people pass through this level, as life presents many challenges. However, the transition eludes some, and they regress to Level One, an easier state of being. Those who utilize the opportunity grow and begin to see the formation of individual values and beliefs.

At the third level, named Spontaneous Multilevel Disintegration, many either progress or regress to lower levels. The key question is, "Do I follow my instincts, my teachings, or my heart?" Following the heart is the realization of the awakening of the third level. Relying on personal values developed over the previous stages and individual and unique perspectives allows for breaking the mold and standing alone. This is a vertical choice level, involving many options spanning over many disparate levels, much like three-dimensional chess. There is an expansion of thinking outside of the box, exercising the individual's own beliefs and values. This level is a gateway to higher levels for those who embrace the work. Many never move beyond, and some even regress; even fewer move forward.

Level Four is called Directed Multilevel Disintegration. The process of disintegration of the primary integration continues. At this level, more conscious and deliberate choices are made by the individual. The growth becomes centered externally, seeing beyond self, and taking a more prosocial stance. It is a movement toward mammalian thinking—what is good for the herd, what is good for the group, more empathy, and more expansion. The individual begins to think in terms of what is the right thing to do over more selfish interests.

Finally, at Level Five comes the Secondary Integration, which is guided by conscious choices based on personal values. Shedding the primary integration, the individual awakens to his or her potential as a fully functioning human. Now distinct and separate from simply surviving and self-centered obsessiveness or obligation to conform to a societal norm that no longer seems relevant, the person is free to exercise free will. Choices are now made on the personal values honed over the various levels. True creativity, originality, and a higher level of being occurs. At this level, the primary integration is replaced by the unique integration of the individual.

How do HSPs fit into this developmental model? At what level do HSPs seem to gravitate? Do we experience OE more often than most non-HSPs, and does this move us forward in development faster than others?

This seems to make sense considering our innate sensory sensitivities and our capacity for deep, reflective processing. With the exception that some HSPs might find retreating to a lower level more comfortable, albeit for temporary rest and reflection. As a group, we largely move forward without much conscious effort.

All HSPs should be encouraged to pushing boundaries, for this is where crisis meets learning opportunity and growth ensues. Most of the individuals Dabrowski studied to develop this theory were at their peak creatively and spiritually. Level Five sounds a lot like a high functioning HSP and could represent a good model for HSPs to adopt.

Do the various levels equate in some way to various spiritual levels? The qualities of each level suggest traveling from base instincts to a more altruistic and spiritual peak at Level Five. Could HSPs, then, be more prone to being spiritually "enlightened?" It seems so, but only for the ones who push forward, rising above the crises of life, learning, retaining, discovering the value of their unique personality.

Yet, can we break free of our obsessiveness with OE and fully see crisis as a tool for higher evolvement? Facing existential moments in life head-on with confidence in spite of the pain moves us to higher levels of being human. With that, I believe we can live our lives with our full potential and help the planet evolve. It's an interesting thought and an even more interesting theory.

Confusing Psychological Disorders with High Sensitivity Autism

High sensitivity is sometimes confused with autism, especially in children. Although on the surface there may be some similarities, autism and sensitivity are distinctly different. The main features of autism surround the individual's inability to process sensory input, which causes confusion, lack of interest in developing social connections, and communication issues.[49]

Those on the spectrum seem to mimic the inward processing of HSPs: the need for quiet and alone time and the lack of need for high social interaction. HSPs, however, do not have problems with processing sensory input or get confused on these inputs. There is no jumbling of signals within HSPs; however, because the processing is internal, to an observer it can appear there are problems attendant to the deep contemplation HSPs perform. Nevertheless, High Sensitivity is not the same as autism.

Sensory Processing Disorder

Another disorder that is confused with high sensitivity is Sensory Processing Disorder (SPD). SPD is a neurological disorder with two features that deal with the degree that sensory input is processed.[50] One, hyposensitivity is a lack of sensory stimulus processing in the brain, which tends to dull information coming from the senses and leads to confusion in processing this input. Two, hypersensitivity, is overstimulation of sensory input via brain processing, much like with HSPs; however, in SPD, this information leads to confused and distorted results.

With HSPs, the processing is more clear and focused as if enhanced, providing more sensory data than non-HSPs. Although with some HSPs this overload of information can be overwhelming, it does not lead to distortion or confusion. This appears to vary among HSPs, with some individuals highly sensitive to stimuli and others less so, but still more so than the general population.

My Experiences

I have been described at times as being passive-aggressive, sometimes baiting people to get an expected result. This often plays out in romantic situations, where sometimes rule books go out the door. Because I have avoided confrontational situations, it has developed into an almost guerrilla strategy for me to dance around the edges of confrontation without totally being engaged.

It masks my true feelings and is admittedly manipulative. Because of my HSP traits, it has developed in me as a self-defense mechanism, one that I am working on eliminating. As I have gotten older, I'm learning to be more authentic and express my feelings outwardly, honestly, and straightforwardly. It is liberating to be able to share feelings openly, bare oneself and deal with the aftermath as it comes. No one appreciates subtle manipulation and in the end serves no one, not even the perpetrator. It is a work in progress, but I strive to make it my new standard—open dialogue, honest, and real.

I can understand how any HSP might be considered passive-aggressive. However, there is no research to suggest this is the case. I can imagine some HSPs taking this strategy. If they do, like me, I think they would feel incredibly guilty for using it as a strategy, even if it's a defensive one.

I am an emotional junkie. I love the highs and sometimes find I relish the lows as well. To feel, to me, is to be alive. I am an unadulterated sports fan, a fanatic about certain teams, follow them religiously, experiencing the highs of their victories and the lows of their defeats. It is a microcosm of the emotional junkie's experience. Mood swings follow the defeats, wallowing in self-pity, which invariably leads to the highs of victory and ebullient joy. It is a steep swinging pendulum that leads to overstimulation in my HSP nature. Yet I get back in the saddle and do it every sports season, making no sense over the addiction to the emotion attached to the sport.

Love follows the same line. It's deeper, more personal, and has a greater effect on me. Love is emotional candy, with the same effects that sugar has on a toddler. These rushes of emotion and hormones usually accentuate most new relationships. The swings can be monumental, yet I find the sensation addictive. The moods can range from inspired and hopeful to depressed and forlorn. Because of the HSP emotional reactivity trait and my exercising the emotional hormonal system, I find that the enhanced feelings are quite a sensation. Even unpleasant emotions have purpose and meaning. I experience them all, riding the roller coaster, ups and downs, knowing full well that they will tax and exhaust me. Yet I continue to experience them over and over again. I'm an emotional gypsy with an addiction to feelings, wide and disparate.

For years, I ignored the call to embrace the Anima in me. As an HSM, it is easier to follow in the footprint of high sensitivity with higher emotions, more empathy, and the propensity to nurture and counsel. I tend to express my emotions more outwardly, which may seem to some more effeminate. As I have matured, I now understand more about my true nature; I realize this expression is more human, not more female, not less male, just more human.

I consider myself to be more of a Highly Sensitive Extrovert (HSE) if given the definition Jacqueline Strickland, noted HSP counselor, applies. I seek novel sensations and new situations, sometimes unconsciously steering myself to these new opportunities to grow and stimulate my brain. Then after the experience of a new situation, I need to retreat into my inner sanctum for contemplation and processing and recovery.

I am creative and like to think that I have visionary tendencies. That may be because I like to see the big picture, the ten thousand foot view, leaving the details for those who prefer the confinement of narrow vision.

I value the spiritual in myself and the Universe. I consider my spirituality to be an inward journey that is a progression built upon my experiences. The more I experience, the greater the leaps I make in my journey. The older I get, the more I realize that the experiences I allow for myself are the things that teach me how to expand my comfort zone. Being an HSP is an interesting and challenging way to experience life. It has limitations, but also the potential for enormous growth and insight. We sensitive folk tend to dance on the edge of a pin, never knowing if we are going to plunge off the edge or delight in daring a complicated dance within a confined workspace. I am learning to relish the experiences regardless of the seeming danger, pushing up against my cautious nature, to allow the world to flow through me.

CHAPTER 8:

Struggles of Being an HSM

Walking the Path of Fear

What does it mean to walk the path of fear? As Carlos Castaneda once said, and I paraphrase, walking a path of fear is walking as if death is stalking us, always worried that one wrong move and death will overtake us. It's a subconscious thing. Fear is our warning system, planted deep within our minds, smothered by our amygdala, and embellished by our conscious minds.

Fear is a warning of impending, imagined death. Surviving is avoiding death. But how does this affect our ability to live genuine, authentic lives? Is living a life wasted, ravaged by fearfulness really a life? Our mission in life is simple: learn, grow, and for the spiritually minded, love. Everything else is gravy. It doesn't matter how each of us filters the world, filters wide open or mostly shut; we all have to bend to the mission.

Fear is a driver of our behavior. Fear is a healthy impulse. Fear can be learned and it can be imagined. Our reactions to fear are often comprised of four actions: freeze, to ponder the circumstance; fight, to resist the threat; flight, to escape the threat; or fright, to internalize the threat, which can become overwhelming.[51] For many HSPs, the last action is too often the case. We are driven back to the comfort zone, that place where the threat is controllable or no longer there.

But what are we really afraid of? To die, to be hurt, to be misunderstood, to be shamed or made fun of, to be afraid to learn something new or grow? Perhaps we fear the growth we may experience will be the death of who we are, a kind of existential death. A death of self and the dismantling of our ego, our essence. Or maybe this is just an overwhelm thing. Do we fear the onslaught of too much threatening information, too much to process with a rush of adrenaline? Is overwhelm like drowning in a tidal wave, out of control, and rushing into the unknown?

HSPs often find themselves walking in this pathway of fear. Is fear-avoidance a personality characteristic of HSPs? This is not to say that HSPs can't be brave or courageous or don't do things that require overcoming fear. But we live so much in our heads that before the threat is even real, we have imagined endless possibilities, some not so positive. It's no wonder that many HSPs are threatened when their comfort zone is questioned. The comfort zone is not an expansive mechanism; restorative, yes, but not the ideal mechanism for growth.

For humans, habituation to fear is hardwired. This ability to habituate to the thing we fear is what allows us to try novel and new experiences. It increases our capacity for survival. This is not just for the HSP world to ponder, but for all humans. Avoiding the thing(s) we fear prevents this habituation; this getting used to the fear and repeated retreat into the comfort zone, does not relieve the fear. It avoids it, allowing the fear to anchor within. The only way out is through the fear, says psychologist Noam Shpancer.[52] This requires expanding the comfort zone enough to face the fear and overcome it repeatedly. Experience brings confidence. Confidence is expansive and grows your comfort zone.

So, where is this root of fear? Is it in the amygdala, the brain's warning system? This connection—a limbic to cerebellum circuit—takes the subconscious warning signal and embellishes it with conscious emotions, creating fear and sometimes anxiety.[53] Since HSPs' sensory sensitivity is much greater than the population at large, we seem more prone to excessive fears and overwhelm because of our circuitry. According to Dr. Elaine Aron, we need to pay attention to where we feel the fear generally in our bodies.[54] We will register sooner than most. In that moment of freeze, it is our opportunity to consider the odds of our perceived threat happening and then act accordingly. We often confuse the arousal of the stimulation with the fear or emotion of the situation. But when it is time to act, we need to consider a thoughtful strategy and go with it.

Consider the attributes of courage. No one who is courageous is fearless. Realize your vulnerability, acknowledge the fear, and allow yourself to be exposed to the fear. The exposure will give you experience, valuable experience. Stay positive; sometimes just saying the right things at the right time can help associate positive actions with a negative stimulus, helping you overcome the fearful thoughts. Practice bravely going beyond your comfort zone, and you will grow as a result.

So often, we HSPs think our comfort zone is the place where we can handle the fear, our fortress, our mailed armor, our protection. Yet staying solidly in the comfort zone for a lifetime without altering it will keep us walking the path of fear. We need to consider going beyond, risking the imagined type of "death" we fear so much and expand and rebirth that comfort zone.

So, here are my tips for overcoming that fear of which I speak:

1. Recognize that death is not a probable outcome of walking a much bolder path. I know that sounds silly, but we will face embarrassment, we will face failure, we will face pain and suffering, but those things will not annihilate us. I believe the root of all fear is the fear of death. Access the probability of your death in that fearful moment, and you will realize to some extent the reaction you are having is not the fear of your death, but something much more trivial. It's a starting point.

2. I believe what keeps us looking out the windows of our glasshouses is the need to escape boredom and sameness. There may be comfort in routine, but there is a deficit of stimulation. Just because we get overstimulated quickly doesn't mean we don't need or crave that same stimulation seemingly braver folk do. Walking a path of courage means being willing to be overwhelmed at times to assimilate that stimulation. The comfort zone is a place of rest, an inn, or tavern on a long journey. But it is not the journey. The journey is out *there*, not inside.

3. You don't have to walk alone. HSPs are not the crowd magnet that non-HSPs might be. We are sometimes solitary, like monks in a monastery. Tending to our daily chores, focused inward, not minding the solitude, comfortable within the walls. Then there are vespers, the chance to mingle with others, walk the gardens with other souls. Find your special friend or friends to walk with you, maybe empathetic non-HSPs, to encourage you to continue challenging yourself.

4. Remember, too, that you are greater than your fear. Your fear is based on unchallenged assumptions about yourself and the environment. Overcoming fear requires a degree of faith that you can rise above this very primal emotion. Allow yourself to meet fear head-on, allow yourself to experience the wonder of how your thoughts shape and change your beliefs. Rewiring the brain sometimes requires non-adrenaline fueled courage. It can be as pragmatic as thinking in a new way, testing it out in the real world, adjusting then repeating until you are no longer fearful. When we understand the root of fear, we understand that it's malleable, and because of our (HSPs) heightened sensitivity, we exaggerate the fear' feeling of emotion, giving it more power than it deserves. Stop walking the path of fear by stop thinking the same thoughts

that gave the neural pathway its energy in the beginning. You can change your life, your circumstances, and still be the highly sensitive man you were born to be: cautious and thoughtful, yet quietly brave.

Being a Loner or Being Alone

When I was little, I loved to play in my room for hours with toy soldiers, miniature cars, and Lincoln Logs. Sometimes it was like I was directing a movie, filled with dramatic scenes, terse dialogue, and the careful movement of characters upon my little stage. I had great fun with this.

Sometimes the neighbor kids rang the doorbell and asked me to come out and play. I would fake a headache or stomach ache or anything else; I could only think of returning to my solitude. I wasn't like this all the time; about half the time, I went outside and to play, build forts in the woods, or play a game of catch or kickball in the street. But when I needed downtime, I retreated to my room and reveled in being alone.

I was fortunate, as I was the only boy in the family and the oldest, so I got my own room. It was truly my castle, my fortress, and I used it well. Sometimes, my friends thought I was weird about this, remarking wryly that I should probably see a doctor about all those headaches and stomach aches. It became a bit of a joke in the neighborhood. But I always knew instinctively when I needed to shelter in my room; regardless of my peers' commentary, I carried on.

I sometimes wondered if it was because I was a lone wolf, a solitary boy who needed solitude that made me different. Back then, I had not yet registered that I was wired from the beginning for this type of solitude, the need for alone time. Now as an HSM adult, I recognize the importance to my system of parking myself away for a while, processing, recharging and quieting down my brain.

When describing to others what it's like to be an HSP, I will cup my hands together, like praying hands, where the tips of my fingers barely touch, with the palms bent like open sails. I then open the fingertips just a bit wider, perhaps a few inches and say that this is like the non-HSP brain, where the gap between fingers is the aperture of their sensory reception, the flow of data being what a non-HSP receives at any given time, not limited but not overflowing.

I then open the fingers wider, much wider, so that the aperture is much larger and say that this demonstrates the comparative difference of how an HSP receives sensory data. The gap is substantial. These gaps stay pretty constant for each group, with, I suppose, some variation for stressful times. The constant bombardment of information takes its toll on HSPs, usually followed by some sense of overwhelm and then the need to withdraw to quiet quarters. This is the necessary downtime all HSPs need. This is the importance of solitude to HSPs, that period of silent regrouping, of catch up processing time, of freeing and purging the queue, and mostly of resting alone time.

How often this occurs varies from one HSP to another. Some need more time than others; some need complete alone time, while others may require a tamping down of stimulation and social contact. But be assured, all HSPs need this time. We don't function well without it.

Just like my boyhood friends, there is likely much confusion about the need for this sanctuary for HSPs among friends, family, partners, co-workers, and social acquaintances. This need for "aloneness," may make us seem like recluses to others, maybe even dangerously shy or socially anxious.

Although those attributes may apply to some, for the most part, this has nothing to do with our need for temporary seclusion. Like introverts (which many of us are), we tend to draw significant amounts of energy from within. The outside world tends to drain us of that energy, and to refill our tanks, we need the space and time to do that. Most of the world sees that as odd and can't quite grasp why we shun 24/7 connection. By nature, we are not always on, favoring the need to be off at times.

In this area, I think HSMs have a slight advantage over HSP females. Culturally, men who are lone wolves carry a cachet or mystique about them; you know, the dark, quiet types. Independent and brooding, the stuff of solitary heroes. Think of the lone woodsman in Alaska, independent and aloof. Women, on the other hand, are expected to be more social, which can present some perceptual problems for HSP women who also need to isolate to recoup their energy. This can add some stigma to them that is not merited but gets delivered anyway. Think the bookish librarian, alone among the stacks, who prefers a quiet tea over shots of Tequila with her girlfriends.

There's a thin line between being alone and being lonely. For some people, being alone at all for short periods conjures up thoughts of abandonment and/or loneliness. To an HSP, though, that sweet solitude, that break from humanity is the elixir of life, something to return to often and in proportion to the stress of life. But it can be too much.

Isolation to an HSP can be addictive. In a healthy manner, it has purpose and place but taken too far, it can be a prelude to social avoidance, fear, and anxiety. If HSMs are naturally shy, then stepping out of the comfort zone can be challenging. Rushing back to the sanctitude of aloneness, although a refuge, can also become a prison. Knowing the upper threshold of solitude, as it borders on the cold plains of loneliness, is important for all of us HSPs. I wonder if we are limited by our hardware, our wiring, to constantly live on the edge of that isolated border with loneliness with occasional forays into the warmth and shelter of companionship.

In many ways, we HSPs go against the grain of social interaction. We tug back and forth between the non-HSP world and our own shelters. The cost of this sometimes may mean the loss of friends, real and potential, misunderstanding among our family and peers and the unnecessary labeling of us as social isolates and troubled souls.

I sometimes think for me it's a selfish indulgence that keeps me disconnected, especially from my family. Not intentional, I pull myself back to the comfort of my own solitude, alone with my thoughts and sometimes without a reference that society can provide me. I wonder, what have I missed? What learning, what interaction, and what emotion did I not experience? And, yes, I feel that now, more than ever as I age.

As with all things in life, it's about balance. As HSPs, we need the downtime, that's obvious, but we also need the opportunity for social growth. For getting out there in the world, pushing our comfort zones from time to time, growing, and experiencing the world outside of our heads. As much as I love being alone, I need social interaction and contact. Sometimes boldly and sometimes quietly, but getting out there and mixing it up with others is just the intoxication I need to feel alive again.

I think it helps for us HSPs to be involved with socially active partners or friends. They serve as brokers and intermediaries into the greater world. Find one and attach yourself to him or her. But choose one who is mindful of your HSP needs and respects your requirement for downtime. Do things that will energize you, charge your batteries, and channel some of that energy to social affairs and interactions with others.

Getting prime facetime is experientially beneficial for you and for those you interact with. Be sure to understand your limits and communicate them to those who care. They can have your back in social outings. Reach out to others; don't wait on others to reach out to you. There is growth inherent in doing this, and it keeps you attached to the planet on which you live. Above all, seek out kindred spirits, people who will respect you and will desire your company.

And when you step out into the world, make sure you are mostly in environments that you can thrive in: positive, optimistic, healing places. It's easy to get mired in the negativity surrounding our world since we absorb so much of that deeply. It's not always simple to shrug off as many non-HSPs can. Make your base camp a place that nurtures your tender and creative spirit. Then go hiking bravely on the trails of social interaction.

So, tell me. What metaphor describes us best: lone wolf or pack dog that sometimes needs the quiet sanctuary of the den?

Decision-Making in an Instant Gratification World

Expectations for how long it takes to make a decision has shrunk in the past thirty years. This is largely because our reliance on instant technology that can either produce near-instant results or the illusion of instantaneous gratification. This quick decision-making has in many ways rewired our brains to expect hasty decisions, often based on little information inputs or with wide information gaps.

With text messaging and social media, we get faster response times, and now our society looks for leaders, particularly to make instant decisions. Technology is beginning to rewire our brains to expect more instant response decision-making, teaching us to make battlefield quick decisions without the benefit of key inputs or training. It can leave everyone feeling battle fatigued.

This type of decision seems to lack reflection and appeals to our more primitive limbic emotional processing systems. We can see more and more bad decisions being made across society, from teenagers to seniors, from politics to religion, from corporate to private worlds; it's happening all over.[55]

I'm not saying it's all bad. There have and always will be times when quick decisions are imperative; think of an emergency room, in NORAD's control center, or flying a plane in bad weather. But more often now, decisions are expected quickly when more reflective thinking is needed. This carries over into business, and in the field I once worked—information technology—it is rampant. We have created a great and ponderous beast called the internet, which requires 24/7 attention and feeding. All our technology is tied to that one way or another, a giant communication network with billions of nodes, requiring perhaps as many or more decisions every day.

HSPs don't work this way. We are deep processing thinkers, and we are observational, receiving a large quantity of inputs from multiple sensory paths. Instead of bypass processing, we are absorbed by all the inputs and have to sort, categorize, and process the data. This takes time and runs contrary to modern cultural expectations. "I'll get back to you," doesn't cut it today. Leaders expect workers and workers expect leaders to instant process to decisions; no rumination, no mulling and culling; just get the answer ... NOW.

Part of the stress HSPs face working in industries that require this type of quick thinking has to do with the expectation of making decisions on unprocessed information, hastily sifting through the inputs, and creating a less than perfect output. HSPs are highly conscientious individuals, and doing this kind of half-baked thinking goes directly against our wiring. The stress comes from the pressure of having to decide without being given ample time to process deeply.

Now, we can do this like everyone else, but it's not comfortable. To be asked to do this all the time can be almost debilitating. Going against our nature is what we are expected to do all the time, and indeed, not doing that can have real-world consequences for many HSPs in the workplace. The increased pressure and stress can short circuit our processing, delaying further decision-making or in some cases, shutting us down.

But the world is not changing for our needs, at least not anytime soon. If you want to work today, you'll need to find a way to cope, adapt, or join in the fray to deal with the pressure to move more quickly. Adaptation is the key, but with all things for HSPs, self-preservation is the lock. You'll need that to stay secure.

Let's look at some things that may help:

- There are three main types of decision strategies.[56] Deductive, which is a rigid set of rules applied to proven facts; inductive, which is more about suggestive logic, you infer from a set of data that appears to be true; and finally, abductive, which relies less on absolutes but uses creative and intuitive logic to arrive at a decision. Much of decision-making depends on inference. Not every decision you make can be deduced from known information. Learn to practice inferring a decision by doing some intense upfront processing, then stopping and making inferences from what you have. A good example might be deciding on a new restaurant to try. Do some cursory research with an online app like Yelp, gather up info on a few good candidates, and then make a decision based on your primary criteria. You can infer things from pictures of the food, previous reviews, menu items, etc. You can generalize this to other things, like buying clothes, choosing a movie to watch, picking a book to read. Put a timeline on your decision-making process, and when it's time to decide, pull the trigger.

- Give up the perfectionism strategy. This is sometimes called maladaptive perfectionism.[57] Perfectionism implies that there is such a thing as a perfect decision. Nada, not gonna happen. In an imperfect world, nothing is perfect, not even you. The irony about perfectionism is that it doesn't originate in extreme self-confidence, but rather it's a veiled mask for insecurity. HSPs are notoriously tied to perfectionism, and when used for review/ edit mode, it has some benefits, but to strive for it in everything will not aid you, but will slow you down. Perfect decisions don't exist. Let go of that.

- The hardest thing for HSPs under pressure is to battle overwhelm, which kills decision-making in its tracks. The brain scrambles start to shut down, and often, we are left like deer in the headlights. Stop and focus on the results. What is the objective? Sometimes you can buy some time by asking for clarity on the request. We are very adept at picking up the vibe of the requestors (often panicked themselves) that we mirror them. Calm them down by getting as much detailed information as possible about the decision they are looking for; this can calm us down, too. Questions like: 1) what is the expected outcome, how does that look (sound or feel) like? This gets down to the subconscious drivers on a decision. 2) What are they most concerned about (bosses, customers, peers)? As you gather the data, start processing, and as more clarity comes from refocusing, you can start to accelerate your decision time. Reining in your brain should be the number one priority so that you can put it to full use.

- At some point, let go and make the decision. Frame your decision around solutions that meet the necessary criteria with a focus on risk, consequences, and feasibility. If you work in an environment that encourages hacking, then take a swag at the decision sooner. Successive approximation is a great learning strategy but works with decisions, too. Hack it till you make it. If your workplace favors good, but quick decisions, then process and stall, but at some point infer or intuit a decision, and give it your best shot. You won't always be right, but you made an effort without balking—then you can recalibrate. Process, learn and reload.

- Be prepared for the fallout. This may be the hardest part. As HSPs, we all, to some extent, know that feedback can hurt. If we are wrong too often, it can have dire consequences. And we process that emotionally and deeply. If you work in an environment where fire drills are the norm, and you are too stressed out to carry on, then, perhaps a job search is in order. Remember, self-preservation first. Of course, this applies to everyone, not just HSPs. It is imperative that you develop a quick mind relaxation hack that will calm you down during and after stressful situations. Meditation, a power nap, relaxation audio, a massage, exercise, breathing properly when under fire techniques, or brain training can help. To some extent, all jobs have elements of the stress-induced decision. Know this: you can do this, and the more you do it, the better it gets. So, as we say in hypnosis—relax and let go.

Taking and Giving Criticism

When I was a young boy, I often felt the sting of my father's criticism. As a highly sensitive male, I always took to heart his feedback and would retreat to my room. No matter how hard I tried to please him, I always found there was something else I could have done to improve or performed better in his eyes. It was a painful lesson I learned young ... that sometimes you just can't please everyone.

Like many men of his generation, I finally understood he tried to bury the fact that he was an HSM by not acknowledging those characteristics in himself that he saw in me. His answer was to force me to take the same route he had, which was a denial of his sensitivity.

It was fashionable and trendy at that time to rebel against your parents, and I fell in line. We often had tense moments, I began to loathe being around him, and then abruptly, he died. I never got that opportunity to explore with him our HSP characteristics—an opportunity that would, I believe, have bridged the gap between us. His criticism still stings to this day.

Highly sensitive people are often criticized for their perceived hyper-sensitivity to criticism and are often accused of this primarily from people who are not very sensitive or empathetic. This is often compounded by HSPs self-admitting to being overly sensitive to harsh or brash criticism.[58] The truth is we HSPs internalize criticism and become our own worst critics.

When we are criticized, especially unexpectedly, we tend to overcorrect because we have overthought the criticism. In other words, we don't look for the criticism as feedback, but rather and sometimes harshly, internalize the delivery of the criticism and overlook the message. With that in mind, many HSPs tend to people-please to avoid criticism. We quickly learn the expectations of the critics and modify our behavior to avoid the causes of their criticism. When we don't take this tact, we often find that external criticism, coupled with our internal criticism, overwhelms us with emotion. This leads to defensiveness, withdrawal, or shutting down.

When defensiveness becomes the regular coping strategy, an almost narcissistic attitude develops that we are not at fault, but rather the critic is faulty in his or her analysis.[59] The walls go up, and productive communication shuts down. When ego gets involved, we, like most people, do not want to feel that we should be submissive to other's critiques or if the criticism is harsh or unfounded to the devaluation of our ego. As Dr. Steven Stosny says, "the valued self cooperates, the devalued self resists."[60]

Criticism takes many forms, and the deliveries reflect that. The criticism that goes wrong and fails to connect often focuses on character and not behavior, and is filled with blame. When criticism is not focused on improvement and is presented in an unconstructive manner, it is not likely to be received well. This is especially true for highly sensitive people.

The reaction of oversensitivity to criticism may be learned from childhood.[61] The childhood environment, whether over critical or even non-critical, can influence the child's ability to receive criticism later in life. Oversensitivity to criticism may have roots in narcissism, perfectionism, or obsessiveness. All these traits may have been learned at the direction of the parents. If you compound the sensitive nature of HSPs with the childhood environment that may create a hypersensitivity to criticism, it's easy to see how constructive feedback or harsh attacks can be lumped together and then avoided.

HSPs tend to ruminate over conflict, which can lock us into not releasing the criticism. Releasing the criticism is like unwrapping a gift, discarding it, and keeping the wrapping. We tend to focus too much on the packaging and forget that the gift is the prize, not the wrapping. We tend to avoid conflict, which includes criticism, because of some inherent feelings of vulnerability over differing opinions or just the risk and fears of disagreement.

When receiving criticism, we need clarification of the criticism to help us remain authentic and in preserving our sense of validation. We sometimes tend to overlook the facts and focus on the emotions involved, which attaches us too much to the suggested outcome instead of regarding it as a possibility for consideration. Research suggests there is a correlation between our hypersensitivity to criticism and our perception of negative bias toward criticism[62].

Many HSMs compartmentalize feelings to avoid overwhelm. Our handling of criticism falls into this category. Sometimes delayed reactions occur as a result of bottling up the emotion, leading to withdrawal, anger, or retaliation. The key to handling criticism is to remain calm, that is to say, keep the emotion objective with self-regulation of a peaceful internal state. This takes practice. Meditation, exercise, being out in nature, following a spiritual practice, Yoga, Tai-Chi or brain training will help aid in being able to conjure this state when needed. Your reaction to criticism is by now automatic, and through mindful awareness, you can begin to control the reaction.

As males, do we need to find better ways to handle criticism? Yes. Part of the problem is that many people who are in positions to critique others are miserable at offering feedback. To the larger, non-HSP population, criticism may only be a mere annoyance, but to many HSMs, it's a personal affront. I believe HSPs are capable of handling criticism. Yes, we tend to over sensationalize some of it, but truthfully, if given in the spirit of helping us improve, I certainly think we can handle it even if we don't agree with it. Part of what we need to do is help educate those around us with suggestions on how to best offer us feedback. If the idea behind the criticism is to affect change, then certainly those in positions to offer us criticism should be open to criticism of their feedback.

Humans are self-correcting organisms. As a species, we have the ability to offer correction advice to each other for the overall preservation of the group. In today's online environment, with social media being what it is, we are experiencing emboldened criticism of each other, some merited, some unmerited. Some of this criticism will sting, yet avoidance of it is impossible. The only thing we can do is to control our reaction to this criticism and realize that in every criticism there is an opportunity and sometimes a kernel of truth.

All feedback is good feedback. Even the harshest and most insensitive means that at some level, you have affected someone else in such a way that has caused them to react to you. You are not a shadow; you live life in the open. That is a good thing.

Here are some tips for handling criticism:

1. Understand that you are going to be more sensitive to criticism than most folks. Part of it is wiring (nature) part of it is related to how you learned to receive criticism as a child (nurture).

2. Anticipating and avoiding criticism is part of the HSP way. But that may inhibit our learning and experience. Try walking *into* criticism

as an experiment. Test your tolerance. See how you handle it. This means walking outside the comfort zone again.

3. You cannot avoid criticism from insensitive people, but you *can* handle the way you react to it. Insensitive people are everywhere; many are strangers, and many are family members. Learn to handle this by using a concentric circle approach. Focus your attention on those who are in the closer, inner circles. They are the ones who know you best and are in the best position to give you constructive feedback. The farther the critic is away from the center, the less emotion is attached to their criticism. Still, look for opportunities to grow even from those on the outer circles, but don't let them sink your boat.

4. Might as well let folks know they are hurting your feelings, but stay calm and without excessive emotion. Just call it out and let them know the best way to affect you is in a constructive, positive way. Give them feedback on their feedback. Their response will be telling.

5. Balance your reaction by evaluating the criticism and bypassing the tone or delivery. Look for the nugget of opportunity to learn about you and the person evaluating you.

6. Remember, everything is not a threat. Calm down a little or a lot depending on circumstances. All feedback can be good.

HSPs and Arguments

Now we focus on those times when criticism leads to arguments and how HSPs often struggle with conflict. How is that generally bright, intelligent, deep-thinking people seem to wilt in the heat of a contentious argument? It's as if a bit gets flipped in our brains, and we shut down, unable to keep up with the fast pace of heated argumentative situations. I have often wondered about that in myself. It's as if I lose processing power to fight back or at least contend with the high emotion of the situation. The minute the temperature heats up, my force fields go up, and my brain scrambles. Yet my ego won't let me stay quiet, even if my arguments are a scrabble board of mixed thoughts and my parries fall into almost nonsensical logic.

I have never quite understood what happens to deflate my ability to counterpoint, especially against clever people who seem to thrive in these types of situations. What am I afraid of? Loss of face? Shaming? Losing favor with the person I'm arguing with? It seems the overwhelm causes unbridled defensiveness, a welling up of emotion, and my perfectionism kick in together to create a stew of mush, which then causes me to lose control of my thoughts and move from single threading to a kaleidoscope of mixed emotion and thought too incoherent to vocalize. Perhaps my thoughtful manner, and in this case I mean pensive, leads to a type of "I'm right no matter what," because I thought a lot about this, therefore I must be right.

It is imperative to externally test our ideas and thoughts, not so much to gain consensus but to test our theories in the real world. Part of that is to hear and debate counterpoints in our line of thinking. But if testing leads to pushback on our ideas, ideas that are a representation of who we are, then this can ultimately lead to avoidance behavior, i.e., for arguing our point, because we are not willing to accept that maybe we are wrong in our thinking. And this shatters an internal myth about ourselves. If so, I cannot see this avoidance behavior as being a realistic strategy for HSPs in testing our ideas, much less for anyone else.

The overwhelm, nevertheless, is very real. Overwhelm comes from within, especially for HSPs. In the heat of an argument, stressors arise that lead our minds to recognize that in arguing with someone else, we have a situation with an unpredictable outcome.[63] A very contentious argument is also full of raw emotion. This kindling lit with the emotion of the moment sets off a brush fire in our neural circuitry that can quickly short-circuit our minds.

Moving quickly into defensive mode, we are caught in a battle between our flee or fight instincts, mostly focused on self-preservation, and therefore we shut down our brain's effectiveness in following rational intellectual capacity. The sting of defeat in an argument is deeply felt. The human brain processes emotional pain in the same way it processes physical pain. The same areas light up in the *anterior insula* and the *anterior cingulate cortex* with physical and emotional pain, in an apparent evolutionary efficiency.[64]

I often wonder if the amygdala in HSPs is overactive. The Deep Layer Superior Colliculus (DLSC) area of the brain works in conjunction with the amygdala to regulate emotional response in threatening situations.[65] HSPs' response to stress situations seems to predispose us to always be on high alert, based on our unique genetics and our life experiences. This constant flashing of alerts for sometimes exaggerated situations, like arguing, may affect our hippocampus and other key areas of the brain in negative ways. This is prominent in situations where HSPs, or for that matter, anyone who has lived through traumatic life experiences. Much of this is harbored in the port of our subconscious mind.

The intensity of feeling is no doubt greater in HSPs, compounding this problem. Greater feelings of anxiety in response to stress may lead to malfunction of the brain, especially in stressful argumentative situations. The repressed anger ensuing from a stinging defeat may lead to increased muscular tension and side effects in the body, as we "hold within" our feelings of not being able to make ourselves heard in an argument.

More importantly, I think this can lead HSPs toward a lifetime of argument avoidance, especially those that are conflictual and highly charged emotionally. This may lead to less expression of opinion in public forums, standing up for oneself in political or philosophical debates, or in work environment discussions. Some friends and family may even feel that we are hiding something from them and can construe negative imaginings about who we really are. Not a good situation.

The Thomas-Kilman Conflict Mode Instrument defines several types of modes or styles of dealing with conflict.[66] They range from the most aggressive to more avoidant styles, each style with a marker for assertiveness and cooperativeness. The most assertive style, *competing*, is assertive and non-collaborative. *The collaborating* style is assertive, but as the name implies collaborative. *Avoiding* style is both non-assertive and non-collaborative. The *accommodating* style is non-assertive but collaborating, and finally, the *compromising* style is right in the middle on both assertive and collaborating. It would seem that most HSPs would fall in the avoiding, accommodating, or compromising style of handling conflict, with the worst case being the avoidant strategy and perhaps the most successful being the compromising strategy, or with some practice and skill, the collaborating style.

In another angle on the effects of personality and arguing skills, the Myers-Briggs personality inventory, which is based on Carl Jung's personality types, can be extrapolated on key personality functions to indicate tendencies during arguments.[67] For example, Thinkers (T) no doubt focus on the facts and tangible evidence, whereas, Feelers (F) focus on the interpersonal dynamics of the people involved in the argument. People who are Judgers (J) might focus on temporal issues, how the now impacts the future, where conversely, Perceivers (P) focus on inputs and if the conflict is being addressed. Most HSPs tend to be NFs (intuitive feelers), so according to this, sensitive folks are more concerned with the emotional dynamics of the argument and the impacts caused to relationships, perhaps empathizing with our opponent and deferring to keep the peace.

This, in turn, may lead to internal conflict between defending self and our position versus feeling empathy toward the person we are arguing with. The internalized stress and conflict may be a leading reason our brains shut down, scrambled by conflicting directives. How then do we slow down our brains, single thread our thoughts, and think lucidly during an argument?

Interestingly, as is noted later in the book, the effects of alcohol and some drugs may seem to achieve this objective. These external agents affect the inhibition systems within the brain, which, of course, affects behavior. Some of the main attributes of usage are: 1) anxiety suppression, 2) disinhibition, 3) ego inflation, 4) thought deceleration, and 5) emotional suppression.[68]

In my own experience, I have noticed this to be true. However, there is a tipping point, where the effects are counterproductive and lead to many more issues that are not productive. In no way am I advocating the use of substances to enhance the ability to handle conflict. It simply illustrates that the capacity to regulate emotional throughput can be done, even if we are using an external agent.

Far better approaches are handled without introducing external chemistry. This gets back to emotional regulation, which can and should be done internally. Here are some strategies for dealing with arguments:

1. First, remember conflict avoidance is not an effective strategy for life. Life is drama; drama is life. Remaining calm in an argument is key. Learning to slow down your brain and single thread thoughts will allow you to access that great arsenal of information within you. Calm under stress should be your mantra. In the heat of an argument remember to: a) step back and take a moment, a mental timeout—"give me a minute"; b) do some dopamine pumping—make a salient point, pause, let the dopamine reward kick in, then move to another point; c) lastly, do some stress throttling (perceive what the stress is and calm it down with calming thoughts).

2. Drugs and alcohol are not good prescriptions for this problem. Let's face it, they may seem to work in the short term, or in occasional situations, but they are, in the long term, an unhealthy and

counterproductive strategy. The power to change is within you. I believe being an HSP is a wonderful gift. The energy within us is sometimes overwhelmingly powerful, yet harnessed and channeled, it can be wondrous.

3. Read *The Gentle Art of Verbal Self Defense*, by Suzette Haden Elgin. It is a great and handy guide to dealing with argumentative and aggressive people. This can give you some training on taking back the argument. It will help you understand the importance of language, both verbal and body, avoiding taking the bait in arguments, use of sensory preferences in language and how to use that to your advantage, and understanding some of the presuppositions in arguments. With this information, you can help build cogent and unemotional argument counterpoints or points to help you stay calm in the argument. It is very much like verbal Aikido.

4. Again, learn to build confidence in yourself by learning calming techniques: meditation, brain training, yoga, tai chi, or aikido. Confidence breeds calm. Many of these things do not require group settings. Once learned, some can be practiced at home in private.

5. Learn the art of letting go. At some point, you, like all of us, are going to lose an argument. The HSP way of ruminating the thing to death, then beating yourself up for a faulty effort, or worse still, coming up with talking points a day after the argument is pointless. You must learn to let go and let go quickly before the self-flagellation starts. Once set in, you will feel worse and reinforce an incorrect message about yourself.

6. Finally, I must say that all HSPs are not defective here, but I suspect that many can identify. If you grew up in an HSP family, then you need to spend more time learning the art of persuasion. If you grew up in a competitive or contentious or debating family, you are probably in a better position to deal with argumentative situations.

You can still learn how to argue more effectively and still preserve your sensitivity. And don't forget, it is not necessary to hang out with willfully argumentative and contentious people. Everyone has their moments, but if you recognize the pattern and you will—boot them from your life. Life is truly too short to deal with that.

Violence in the Media and the Effects on HSPs

Somewhere along the way, as I was growing up, violence took a wrong turn in the media. Movies, TV, print; all began to show more graphic violence. I don't know what the starting point was, or when; I just know it started getting more detailed, more bloody. Of course, there were always horror movies, slasher types full of gaudy special effects and makeup, but somewhere along the way, the technology got really good, and bloodletting began in full swing.

For a highly sensing boy, I saw this as a turnoff. What happened to the days when a gunshot went off, there was a quick cut, and a dead body lay on the ground? Sometimes with blood, sometimes without. I got the message; the character was dead. I didn't need to see him bleed out to make that point. The excessive reliance on violence for dramatic conflict seems like lazy writing to me. The subtlety of death and dying disappeared, and so did a certain naiveté upon the viewing public.

Modeling of violence in the media can desensitize us all into the acceptance of violence or at least aggression as an acceptable method for resolving egregious problems or for seeking justice, whether it is a war against perceived enemies, capital punishment, or personally arming oneself to the teeth to protect against "bad guys."

Nowadays, watching almost any historical drama on television or in films is rife with realistic, and I could argue hyper-real blood and guts, as villains are slain to exact justice. One can simply no longer turn away from the violence, and even as adults, the visceral and subtle unconscious effects alter all of us.

There have been many studies over the years vilifying the effects of passively watching violence in the media. The National Institute of Mental Health found that children watching violent media may become desensitized to others' pain, and they may be more likely to behave in aggressive and harmful ways to others.[69] It has even been suggested that this learned behavior may follow into adulthood. Violent video games have a similar effect. Ninety-eight percent of video games contain violence and since 97% of adolescents play video games, the reach of violent modeling goes way beyond Saturday morning cartoons.

Violence is found in music, YouTube, radio, on cell phones, the internet, and now especially in social media. This constant exposure to aggression creates aggressive thoughts and can produce less empathy toward others. The focus of aggression is the intent to harm another, where the other is looking to avoid this harm. It takes many forms: relational aggression, i.e., spreading harmful rumors; cyber-aggression via electronic messages; and verbal aggression. With over 42.5 aggressive acts per hour on television and with a clear increase in violence in movies over the last forty years, it is no wonder that the effect culturally on children is growing. These children, of course, grow up to be adults. When these acts of aggression take a more severe form, we are looking at violent actions.[70]

Many of you may say, well, these studies have not been able to prove long-term effects or many of the studies are flawed or invalid. Some even argue that viewing violence has a cathartic effect on aggression. No studies show this to be true. It is very difficult, if not ethically impossible, to construct a study in which a cause and effect relationship can be established by watching violent media with behavior in which murder or violence is the result of the study.

Yet it is clear we can measure arousal rates when watching violent media: heart rate, respiration, and higher blood pressure. There have been MRI (magnetic resonance imagery) studies where noticeable differences in brain activity have been shown after just one week of watching violent video games.[71] Other studies have noted short- and long-term effects associated with video violence. Primary among the short-term effects have been the arousal via emotional stimulation, which causes a visceral response. And of course, mimicry, which causes the viewer to imitate behavior, watched in a less violent but aggressive way—generally creates more aggressive thoughts.

The long-term effects may affect observational learning skills and alter emotional states, thought schemas, normative beliefs about violence, and executable behavior scripts. It may cause desensitization with increased exposure, aggressive behavior, bullying, increased fears, depression, nightmares, and other sleep disturbances. The key to all of this is repetition. Repeating the viewing, especially with video gaming, where repetition increases skill level, increases the retention and acceptance of violence as a means to an end. [72]

This affects children and adults with the continuous bombardment of violence or aggressive behavior, especially with the actions of hero characters, models that the world is a dangerous place and that justice is only served by righteous indignation, often in violent form. Because this is constantly presented as reality via the media, the unconscious mind, not the greatest at distinguishing reality from fiction learns that violence, if not honorable, is at least tolerable to settle injustices.

How does violence in the media affect HSPs and in particular, HSMs? Why do we watch it if it is offensive and abhorrent to our sensibilities? I find excessive violence in film and television to be distracting to the story. It creates a strong visceral reaction, a shock if you will, that I feel in my body. I never get sick to the stomach, but feel a slight, steady revulsion to excessive violence, even knowing it's not real. If it's severe enough, I will turn my head, but as of late, I force myself to bear through it. It's over soon enough, but the story is altered for me. Even with plot justification for the violence, I tend to be more tense, watching the remainder as if waiting for someone to jump out from behind to startle me. Gratuitous violence is just that—plugged into storylines at regular intervals to give the mind and body a shock. It sells tickets.

My larger concern is, what is all of this violence doing to us as a culture? Is it altering the way our brains perceive violence? One could argue that we have always been violent, aggressive creatures. But at what point do we rise above our baser instincts and evolve, moving past violence. If it is affecting us all, does it mean we HSPs are being altered along with the rest of humanity?

As HSMs, we need to aid in tamping down the violence in our sphere of influence. Perhaps taking more care with our children in monitoring or sanctioning violent media viewing. If you are teachers, counselors, therapists, ministers, or others in the helping professions, use your opportunities wisely to offer suggestions to caregivers and parents about the effects of violent media watching on children and adults.

We can lead efforts to offer guidelines, based in part on our sensibilities to the media themselves for acceptable levels of dramatic aggression that serves a dramatic purpose without sensationalizing extreme blood, mutilation, or gore. This should be gentle guidance, not out and out restrictive suggestions.

We react differently to violence than non-HSPs; we do more feeling, thinking, recounting, and I would say more reviewing with emotion and arousal. Others may enjoy or thrill to the exploitative violence in the media, much like a teenager thrills at a joy ride in a stolen car. But repeated exposure, with the consequences sinking unconscious and manifesting in unsavory ways, is something we as a society must guard against.

Watch the news, read a paper, listen to the radio. It's already happening.

Being too Sensitive in a Macho World

"Son, are you a man or a mouse?" My dad delivered these few words to me every time I got a bit too weepy as a little boy. Growing up in the '50s and '60s, it was not wise for little boys to show too many traits of emotional sensitivity. Might look like a sissy, if you know what I mean. So, my father would chide me with this little question, and I would abruptly stop my sensitive ways and buck up and act like the little man I was supposed to be.

As the years went by, I began to shield myself from this type of criticism by trying to live the manly life I was taught to live. But it always felt a bit disingenuous and inauthentic. The older I got, the more I began to realize that I was no less a man because I could feel deep emotion, get in touch with my inner core, and freely express the emotion within. When I began to read about the highly sensitive personality type, I felt vindicated and liberated. Dr. Elaine Aron gets a lifetime achievement award from me. And I'm sure a lot of HSMs feel the same way.

When I first started researching this topic, I was looking for male sensitivity and found that the first page or two of the search was focused on penile sensitivity. Interesting, but not what I had in mind. But I suppose there is some metaphorical tie-in too obtuse for me to elaborate on.

Is there a sensitivity spectrum within HSMs? Are some HSMs more sensitive than others, more prone to emotional display or sensory overload, than say, other HSMs? I, for one, believe there is some truth to this. I mean, after all, we are all individuals, and science accounts for individual differences. We may have the same predisposition for an active amygdala, but perhaps the signals get muffled more so in some than others. Maybe there is some broad gradation starting with a threshold HSM, who is lowest on the scale of HSM sensitivity, a moderate HSM that straddles the wide middle, and a high HSM, one bordering on hypersensitivity. This could explain some of the diversity in HSM capacity and expression of that sensitivity. I know all HSMs are not what the general population would peg high sensitivity to be.

Of course, no one is better or worse than the other, just a way to stratify further the traits of HSPs. This might explain why some HSMs weep at sad movies, while others just get the obligatory lump in the throat and wet eyes. In any case, regardless of where you fall on the spectrum, if you are an HSM, you are a man with fully functioning tear ducts. Be proud of that.

This still remains about sensing capability, our high capacity to sense our world. It's the inputs that affect us so. Sensitivity is the reaction to that sensing, and perhaps this sets us apart from our non-HSP fellows. So whether it is sights, sounds, smell, taste, or touch, or even the unconscious sense of intuition, we are always sensing deeply. And it will always affect us deeply. And, yes, we react sensitively and passionately. Yet we HSMs are still men; we are simply broadening the masculine definition.

Fitting into a world that values machismo, the hyper-male, and toughness is always going to be a struggle for HSMs. The ridiculous focus on aggressive and dominant behavior, which is often seen as the epitome of masculinity in our culture, naturally divorces the American male from the emotions that are native to all humans. In other words, you are no longer a male unless you reflect a set of traits that are better suited for 10,000 B.C. than the twenty-first century.

You can see this in our militaristic, warrior archetype that is reflected throughout our society in board rooms, bedrooms, and now bathrooms. We are still fighting imaginary wars every day at work, at home, and play. Even some women have adapted to this model to succeed in this dysfunctional paradigm.

Our world is very troubled. The political discourse these last few years, the racial divides, the wars, the poverty, and all the detritus that swirls around this world, makes me think there has never been a better time for HSPs and HSMs to find our place in this world. It's a time that is ripe for a shift away from the machismo politics of the Reagan Republican brand and back to a more compassionate, empathetic form of government.

If this shift fails to take hold, I fear we are heading for a dark place as a culture and as a people. The HSP is often the canary in the mineshaft. Pay attention, world. We are uncomfortable in this manufactured male macho world that generally insecure and paranoid males have created. We HSMs need to assert ourselves in a distinct HSM way and penetrate the corporate ranks, the world of politics, religion, art, and journalism and serve as new role models for men everywhere. It is our sensing nature that will help change this world, and as men, we can help reshape the balance of things. We need to do something challenging for us—stand out.

Since most of us will not be in politics or will be religious leaders, we can start somewhere closer to home and at work.

HSMs are not always in leadership roles, especially at work. We tend to work in the background, quietly and diligently, getting along, being good soldiers. But I think it's time to start talking about a change in the workplace. HSPs are generally the first to detect toxic work environments and need to speak out about conditions that we sense are not conducive to productivity. That is our prime objective as the alert mechanism to the larger group. We need to start talking about being HSPs and explaining to our managers and co-workers and Human Resources that we may have some different requirements to be at our best. The research shows that a lot of what we find necessary for a good productive work environment is similar to what our non-HSP coworkers also find important.

And when given the opportunity, we need to accept leadership roles and promote a more cooperative and empathetic workplace. HSM males can model this new paradigm for a more compassionate, caring male that may shift all that yang energy to balance with the feminine yin energy. That can easily filter within the entire organization. Sounds new-agey; well, maybe so, but science says that we are energy and the polarity has been imbalanced for a long time now.

I believe in balance. HSMs can't always be about feeling our pain, expressing emotional outpourings, and living in flight or fight all the time. Sometimes we need to "suck it up," which means being willing to adapt, staying fluid and flowing with the energy around us. We often retract at negativity and recoil or retreat, but sometimes staying authentic means letting the storm blow around you, putting away the protective umbrella, and letting the rain fall in your face. Sure, you get wet, but you don't drown, regardless of how you feel. Sometimes you're the man; sometimes you're the mouse. But remember, the man doesn't have to be unemotional and stoic. Courage and bravery come from a deep place within us all. Ride the wave, do one brave thing, and never trust a man who doesn't cry.

My Experiences

I could write volumes about my fear-based living model. It started very young as avoidance of behaviors or situations that caused fear in me. It could have developed as a result of fearing criticism. I was a master of procrastination and as such, would often put off to the last minute doing things like schoolwork, yard work, chores around the house, and would later face the consequences. I began to learn that I could avoid the punishment or criticism of not doing what I was told by creating some conversational diversion. In other words, I learned to lie about the reason I failed to complete the task and became very good at excuse-making.

As you can see, the root of this is fear. Fear-based living gives way to excuse-making and ultimately to avoidance behaviors. As an HSP, avoiding criticism was a primary goal. I either worked very hard to be a model student, son, and friend or if I was afraid of failure, or not measuring up, found convenient excuses not to face my fear head-on. Having parents who were both HSP doesn't always help. Straightening me out and perhaps forcing me to at least attempt to do the thing I fear would have given me valuable experiences in learning to cope with failure and disappointment. But more often than not, my father was an absent influence in my life. My mother, not one to take on unpleasant tasks, often gave in to what I wanted to keep the peace. Regardless, I learned a strategy that was to be repeated often in my adult life to my regret.

Working for years in a corporate information technology environment, I learned early on that the machine never sleeps, so neither did I. When you are in a 24/7 on-call environment you are at bat all the time. One CIO even created our division logo based on a burning light bulb. He matter-of-factly proclaimed that we would be "Always on."

This means that decisions are being made all the time, day or night. Some decisions could affect millions of dollars in account activity; a bad decision could cost customers, reputation, and needless to say, money. I learned quickly to make decisions fast, not always my comfort zone. Some people love the excitement of early morning conference calls, like some battlefield situation. Not me.

For me, as an HSP, deliberation and contemplation are where I make my best decisions. This is not to say I can't make snap decisions; it's just that I overthink and look at all the options. This takes time. Time is something corporations value and don't seem to have. It was a difficult work situation for me, but I dealt with it. In life, my decisions are often slow to come, pondering, and waiting for inspiration, then out of the blue an answer appears and generally shocks those around me. Watch the quiet ones, they may seem to be doing nothing, but in reality a lot is going on in their heads. I know.

I have found that I would never make it on a debate team. My brain is just not wired for rapid-fire arguments, which is why I avoid them as much as possible. Couple this with the wild-card emotions in a heated discussion, and mostly, I'm toast when anger kicks in, and temperature goes up. The problem with this strategy is that it is impossible to avoid confrontation forever. At some point, you will be drawn into an argument, and the unpleasantness of emotional debate begins.

Avoiding arguments means avoiding conflict—another mistake. I have said this before: conflict is drama, and drama is life, and there is no way to avoid life, especially if you are living it. I never learned to calm my mind in an argument. I so easily get sucked into the emotion of the moment, add elements of ego, makes a perfect recipe for getting my ass kicked in an argument. I'm not sure there is a cure for this, but see the earlier reference to verbal self-defense.

If you are hiking a trail deep in the forest on a trail you'd never hiked before, wouldn't you want a guide who picked up the subtle signs of nature: an animal track, a storm coming, a bad place in the trail, the best place to camp? I bet you might pay for that information because, in some ways, it could be lifesaving. The expert guides use their sensory information and previous experience to add value to your experience. Their ability to sense the subtle makes them valuable, not a pain in the ass. Highly sensitive people are like that. I am like that, so, yes, I'm sensitive, but too sensitive? Not if you see my value.

CHAPTER 9:

Piling On – High Sensation Seeking, INFP/J, Introversion

High Sensation Seeking

The idea of thrill-seeking highly sensitive people may seem a bit out of character. The notion of nice, quiet, pensive, peace-loving individuals taking off on wild adventures as novelty seeking daredevils doesn't match up with the stereotype of HSPs. Believe it or not, a subset of HSPs fit that profile and are high sensation seeking (HSS) folks or to spell it out: High Sensation Seeking Highly Sensitive People HSS/HSP.

Dr. Tracy Cooper reports that about 30 percent of the HSP population fit this label. Most of them are male.[73] There are four primary traits that high sensation seeking people display. One, they are *thrill and adventure seekers*, i.e., drawn to adrenaline-pumping risky sports and activities like mountain climbing, bungee jumping, motocross, etc. These are the kind of activities you would most expect from a daredevil. Two, they are *experience seekers*, looking for novel mind-bending mental sensations; think of psychoactive substances or sensory bending experiences. Three, they display moments of *disinhibition*, mostly in the realm of social or sexual activities (wild parties, inebriation, or multiple sexual partners), hence, a relaxation of social boundaries and the willingness to cross them. Finally, they are prone to *boredom susceptibility*, the tendency toward aversion of repetitious activity, and seek novelty as stimulation. HSS/HSPs tend to fall mainly in the last three traits, granted, with some caveats.

This can be seen as reckless behavior, uncharacteristic of traditional HSP traits. However, the dual nature of HSS/HSP individuals presents many internal conflicts—working both sides of the caution versus novelty endpoints. This conflict is a classic one foot on the gas, one on the brake, which I suppose creates some novel forward motion, but doesn't test the boundaries of thrill-seeking to its limits.

For most HSS/HSPs, high sensation seeking is about the novelty of the experience.[74] Changing the landscape for a new view seems a bit more modest and a controlled method of allowing for a taste of what might seem dangerous without risking life or limb. We HSPs tend to have a more pronounced Behavioral Inhibition System;[75] thus, brakes get applied when the ride gets too dangerous. Although some of this behavior borders on impulsivity (taken from my own experience), it is still guided by a more cautious retracting or overriding behavior reining in when the drift is too uncomfortable.

What is the balance between walking the high wire and resting safely on the net? How much and what type of sensation is necessary to overtake the underlying boredom of being quiet and reflective? Since most HSPs are introverted, it seems a far cry from living in the cocoon of the internal world, which is already being bombarded by a greater amount of sensory data. Why fetch more sensation, even when bored, if the idea is to avoid overstimulation?

It seems almost a cruel hoax to possess these two opposing characteristics. One pushing inward, one pulling outward, one processing experience, one seeking experience, teasing the limits of an already sensitive system. Can this sensation seeking be a controlled, throttled pleasure, with none of the irresponsibility of reckless and dangerous impulse? It seems at times to be an unconscious draw to seek overstimulation, an addiction to adrenaline, however modest, only to offset quickly with reflection and solitude.

And what of this cycle, to what extreme can it go? Are some HSPs sensation seekers, walking as it were, without a net, making bad decisions, knowing the consequences, yet yielding to some inner drive for increased sensation? Like diving headlong into a freezing pool, only to jump out and run back inside by the crackling fire. An odd balance of fire and ice, flipping between the two, just enough to keep the fire hot and the ice cold.

Can any of this be self-destructive? Is the impulsivity of taking risks for the novel sensation balanced by a keen sense of risk perception? Are HSS/HSPs more likely to access the reward/gamble ratio and to step out of a typical HSP cautionary personality to seek novel experiences just to keep from being bored? The answer is yes and no. Perhaps there is a deeper drive to create that motivates seeking out novel experience to be able to fashion something new and useful. The motivator is boredom; the outcome is creativity with reward and stimulation.

With a third of the HSP population showing this trait of novelty seeking, it certainly explains the high level of creativity that emerges from the HSP community. To be creative, one must be willing to seek new ways of looking at things, to put parts together in unusual ways, and to be willing to risk criticism for your creations. The reward of success is a big rush of dopamine for having braved and crafted one's indulgences.[76] The added splash of adrenaline doesn't hurt either.

How do you tell if you are an HSS/HSP? Dr. Elaine Aron has constructed a test that was designed for HSPs to determine if you are a high sensation-seeking individual. Here's the link: https://hsperson.com/test/high-sensation-seeking-test/.

I scored high enough on the test to be considered an HSS/HSP.

My experiences as an HSS/HSP follow a familiar pattern. Always seeking some secure situation—a job, a marriage, a relationship, a life—then abruptly leaving, almost at a whim, when boredom kicks in. Then being lost for a period, seeking, looking sometimes recklessly, finding a new novel situation to anchor me, only to leave again, a drifter on the run. Sometimes doing stupid things or taking risky gambles, zigging and zagging off the path added in the mix, then getting comfortable for stretches. Then boredom sets in again, creating changes that have consequences and require remediation.

But the boredom is not what you might think of as boredom. It's unsettling, restless, not like a little kid, or a too-bright child unable to find the creative ability to stay active. It's like an internal clock that says, "enough, time to move on." A prompting, a calling to change venues. I hardly understand it; others never understand it. A neutral, unemotional epiphany that says it's time to seek other sensations.

I want to think that this process is all trending upward, a giant learning process, like climbing the tread of a larger than life wheel. But who knows? In the end, it is always looking for that balance between boredom and overstimulation, a good and sensitive man who sometimes makes perplexing decisions.

INFP/INFJ Personality Types

The complications of being an HSP are already pretty demanding, but adding the rare personality type of INFJ to your identity is another layer of complexity. Well, actually, INFJ type is probably more common in HSPs than they are in the general population. Many of the INFJ attributes overlap with common HSM characteristics, so it's possible that it really doesn't add too much more complexity, but if you factor in the rarity of this personality—approximately one to three percent of the world population, it is likely that INFJs are even a smaller subset of HSPs. In males, it's even rarer with only one percent of all males presenting as INFJ, and I would guess that all are HSMs[77]. So what exactly is an INFJ?

Carl Jung defined certain personality types as part of his body of work, largely based on cognitive function and style. From that seminal work, psychologists Isabel Myers and Katherine Briggs further developed an instrument for testing personality typology called the Myers-Briggs Type Indicator (MBTI).[78]

The focus is on sixteen different personality types composed of four major indicators: Extroversion/Introversion, Sensing/Intuition, Thinking/Feeling, and Judgment/Perception.[79] Each of the four elements reflects a particular style of dealing with the world, for example, **Extroversion** is outwardly energetic, while **Introversion** is inwardly energetic; the same is true for Sensing (fact-based) versus Intuition (insight-N). Another dichotomy is **Thinking** (cognitive logic) or **Feeling** (values and emotion), and finally the plan of attack, **Judgment** (structure, plan), and **Perception** (flow guided). The combination of the four elements produces sixteen basic personality types, each with its own style and process for interacting with the world. If you think about this, our personality develops as we age and serves as an outward mask we present to the world. It's hardly static and highly interactive.

By now, you should be getting a pretty good handle on the HSP personality type and in particular, the HSM, or male version of HSP. What is interesting as of late is there has been a lot of attention on the Introvert personality type, such as in Susan Cain's book, *Quiet: The Power of Introverts in a World That Can't Stop Talking*. What is not being talked about as much but will be, I believe, is the overlap in the HSP personality type and the Introvert personality. In fact, about 70 percent of HSPs are introverts. What percent HSPs make of introverts as a whole is still unclear.

Let's delve a little deeper into the INFJ personality type.

INFJs are indeed rare individuals. They exhibit many of the characteristics of HSPs[80]. They are intuition dominant, relying a great deal on
this subconscious process for assessing the world. They tend to see things
in patterns, big pictures, and symbolic meaning. They live largely in the
abstract, are quite independent, enjoy working behind the scenes, and are
very private individuals. Ironically, they can seem to be extraverted and
animated when engaged in passionate dialogue about something they care
about and can even sport a personal charisma that is arresting, if not a bit
off type. They love to work in environments that are harmonious and, if
put in chaotic and hectic situations, can withdraw because of overwhelm.
They have keen insight into problem-solving, even though they are less
rational in their thinking and rely heavily on their feelings and intuition.

Emotion, gut feel, and internal sensing play a big role in how they
interact with the world. There is often a strict perfectionism about INFJs
that can seem almost snobbish as they survey their footprint in the world,
conscientiousness on steroids. They are easily hurt by what they may seem
is an indifferent world, which may not have time for their grandiose visions
and emotionally intuitive problem-solving methodology. You can easily see
why artists, creative types, activists, healers, and spiritually inclined folk
are represented in this group; in part, the same types you see in HSPs. HSPs
tend to be represented well in the MBTI areas that feature Introversion,
Feeling, and Intuition (INFJ, INFP, INTJ, INTP).[81]

INFJs are caring, imaginative people. Some examples of INFJs are
Gandhi, Eleanor Roosevelt, Florence Nightingale, Shirley MacLaine, Jimmy
Carter, and even Carl Jung. A great crowd to be running with, but INFJs
have some negative baggage, too. INFJs have the highest marital dissatis-
faction ratings of any of the personality types—go figure.[82]

Under stress, they can act very impulsively, even destructively, make
decisions without thinking or evaluating consequences. They can be hypercritical of others, find fault everywhere, and display an OCD-like obsession

with meaningless details. At times, INFJs can go against their moral code and break the rules, become very selfish, and display a shadow self that is not their core values. Again, like most HSPs, the INFJ needs downtime to reevaluate, reenergize, and decompress.

Now, does being an HSM magnify the INFJ traits if you are both? If being an HSM is as much a physiological based (Sensory Processing Sensitivity) personality type as INFJ is a cognitive personality type, then it would seem logical that being an HSM would amplify, through heightened sensitivity, the traits inherent in being an INFJ.

Of course, if all INFJs are, in fact, HSPs, then there would be no other option. I wonder if that is not a valid assumption. Perhaps I'm wildly speculating here about the mix, since both personality types are small populations, but not all HSPs are INFJs. Certainly, too, not all HSMs are INFJs, so at the end of the day, I think when you see this combination, you have a rare cross-breeding of personality types that can make life challenging, interesting, and unique.

That so few men are HSM/INFJ means interacting in an often unsympathetic world that reacts to rare personality types in sometimes callous or harsh ways; you can see where the problems might arise for HSM/INFJs. My conclusion is not that the personality combo is bad or maladaptive; I think it might be more problematic because of its uniqueness. In the end, being understood is a key to happiness, and for HSM/INFJs that is often a hard commodity to find.

Here are a few tips if you believe you may be an HSM who is also an INFJ:

1. If you haven't done so, take the MBTI test to determine your personality type. I have found the test to be reliable. I took it the first time when I was nineteen and have taken it multiple times over my life. The test has been consistent and reliable in calling out my INFJ nature. It's an interesting insight into who you are;

realize that it is not a complete mapping of you. https://www.
mbtionline.com/?utm_source=MBF&utm_medium=link&utm_
campaign=online

2. Recognize the rarity of your personality type in just the sheer numbers. It's sometimes going to be hard to find people you relate to and interact well with you. Being an outlier doesn't mean you have to be an outcast. You are unique, even within your uniqueness.

3. Read the book, _Please Understand Me_, by David Keirsey and Marilyn Bates. A great book on the personality typology we have discussed. Seeing some of your unique personality traits on paper may help to put it in perspective.

4. Realize you are here for a reason, you have a purpose. This is spoken like a true INFJ. You will have to live outside of your comfort zone as an HSM and an INFJ, and at times, as is now the new buzz word, show grit.

5. It is more important for you to find your place in life, your unique place, more so than it is for most folks. Meaningful work, meaningful relationships, and a meaningful life are important to you. Understand _you_ and how you function and understand the above principles of meaningfulness, and you will thrive.

Introversion versus Extraversion - Are we Innies or Outies?

When one thinks about the highly sensitive personality type, it is easy to classify all HSPs as introverted. You know, the quiet, introspective, shy, socially inept, or averse individual who would rather spend a quiet night alone reading a good book rather than socializing with a crowd or group of friends. The reality is that although true, most HSPs are introverted, not all are. It is estimated that about 30 percent of HSPs are extraverted or externally oriented, yet still maintain the basic profile of sensitivity. That is, they are easily overstimulated, have the same great sense of the subtle, show great empathy toward others, and process information deeply.

The basic personality trait of introversion/extraversion, like most personality traits, runs along a continuum. Like the trait of sensitivity, it can fluctuate over time and can change with life experiences, generally slightly, being either enhanced or moderated.

Extraverts, by and large, seek gratification from the external world. They readily engage in social, political, and community[83] activities that provide them with external goals to achieve and then internalize the reward. Introverts, conversely, seek solitary reflection and introspection, looking for internal rewards. Introverts prefer small groups or individual interaction, limited close friendships and mostly quiet activities. Extraverts tend to be happier and find it easier to garner rewards in our outwardly focused culture. Introverts self-report less happiness, although it seems that their reports are more inwardly biased, with less external confirmation. Introverts generally are not rewarded as much as extraverts because they tend to be more inwardly focused. Introverts, however, tend to be more intellectual and are considered gifted.

There appears to be some brain function variability between extraverts and introverts. Extraverts tend to have a greater sensitivity to the dopamine system, which provides some of the reward benefits noted above. Introverts tend to be more frontal lobe functioning and exhibit greater internal processing, which is exhibited on the intellectual side.

Within the sensitivity group, extraverts exist. They are known as Highly Sensitive Extraverts or HSEs.[84] HSEs are introspective, kind, creative, empathetic, and perceptive like their HSP Introvert (HSI) cohort, and unlike most non-HSP extraverts tend to go inward like the HSP introvert does for deep processing. HSEs differ from HSIs in that they need to venture out more into the external world for stimulation and seek to experience novel situations. Positive environments, the kind sensitive people thrive in, bring out more extraversion and externality for the HSE, according to Jacqueline Strickland, HSP advisor, therapist, and a noted HSE.[85]

HSEs often find that they are high sensation seekers, looking for new experiences, pushing their boundaries without overloading their capacities. These new sensations are often emotional or experiential but are not to be confused with what most consider being adrenaline junkies. They are, in many ways, outliers in the HSP community, perhaps even leaders for sensitives to model about expanding boundaries of learning. HSEs also need their downtime, just as HSIs do. The key difference is that HSEs use their downtime mainly for rest and recovery and not as a point of refuge or place to do their main deep contemplation.

Highly sensitive people, although largely introverted can be extraverted and can display characteristics of non-HSP extraverts. As Strickland notes, regardless of this distinction, at the heart and core, HSEs are sensitives following the DOES model. Because of this, I believe the continuum of introversion/extraversion is very fluid. It is useful in life to be flexible; it is useful in life to be adaptable, and to become more extraverted has its advantages. I'm not sure there is a set point in which we as individuals fall along the spectrum of introversion/extraversion, but I think we can hop along the line as circumstances warrant, perhaps even adopting new characteristics that are most comfortable and provide us with the most gain. Introverts have to adapt more than extraverts.

Our culture rewards extraversion, so to succeed, introverts must be able to "come out" to meet the world's expectations. Just like a left-handed person often needs to adapt to a right-handed world, introverts must do the same. In doing so, just as the lefty becomes more ambidextrous, introverts become more ambivert, which has advantages.

My Experiences

I often wondered what led me to seek out novelty experiences, when typically, I shy away from new situations. I did a lot of starting over during my early youth, having moved around four or five times before we settled into life in South Carolina. Perhaps that set me up for seeking out different sensations, different friends, and different locales later in life. Sometimes I feel I need a shock to my system—to jump start it if you will—to propel it in a new direction, even if the whole experience can be uncomfortable.

At some level of consciousness, I know when and what to pursue, by creating the circumstances that will create the situation for growth. At times I seem to be rather stupid and create haphazard plans that lead me to these new situations. I consider myself to be relatively intelligent, aware, and prudent and cautious, but these experiences surface, and they take me on a journey into new territory.

This is a unique characteristic of a subset of HSPs, known as High Sensation Seeking individuals. The term belies the sometimes subtle nature of this quality; it's not about jumping off high buildings or engaging in extremely dangerous and risky behavior, but more about deviating from a personal norm to gather novel experiences and experience emotional and physical sensations.

I tend to experience this in relationships. I can go for years in a steady relationship, and then one day, unexpectedly, I start seeking different companionship. The idea of breaking away from someone I've been with for a while is exciting and maybe even forbidden. It's as if one day I wake up and a shift takes place in my brain, and I notice that I'm looking elsewhere. I am not an unempathetic companion or lover, I know there are consequences for doing what I do, and I always regret hurting someone I love, but the urge to move is quite strong. Ironically, I have always told myself that I wanted to be in a lifelong relationship with a single individual. Yet I continue to exhibit this behavior over and over.

As of late, I have been on the move quite a bit, changing locales depending on circumstances. This starting all over again manifests in making new friends, taking in new environments, and learning new things. I wonder if I am a novelty seeker and if there is some invisible threshold that I must cross to begin anew, one that lays just below conscious awareness, one that seeks new experience regardless of the pain or uncertainty the decision to experience newness brings. As an HSM, this creates conflict within me, and I labor over every move, yet know I must do it. There is always an adrenaline rush, like the beginning of a new romantic relationship. I seem to get the biggest sensation experiences from new relationships. As I get older, this novelty is wearing thin, and I believe I'd like to stick with someone from here on out.

I am a part of one of the smallest personality populations on the planet. In Myers-Brigg lingo, I am an INFJ/P. I straddle the line between the two groups, mostly falling in INFJ. Add to that, I am a man, and you create an even smaller subset.

Part of our finding our place in life is developing a sense of self in relationship to others. When your tribe of personality types is hard to find and people you can relate to are often few and far between, this makes it difficult to make close friends who really understand you. In some ways, I feel like I am trapped in this personality type; it can be confining. The quirkiness of the personality combined with the sensing/feeling of being an HSM makes it all seem too much at times.

There are rewards for being a part of this personality combo platter; you see things differently, uniquely, and creatively. People don't often understand what you see, but it makes viewing life through this unique prism very interesting. This feels like piling on in the personality department. It's not a disorder, but rather a unique combining of rare personality traits, making it seem that nature culls you out for some type of special mission. I don't regret the traits, I relish the uniqueness, but sometimes I wish there could be more moderation of the extremes of the personality type.

The first letter of the INFJ/P personality type indicates introversion. I feel as I have aged, I have evolved into something of an extraverted-introvert or even an ambivert, although that doesn't feel like it fits.

As a child, I was extremely shy and introverted. I relished playing alone and was uncomfortable in situations in which I had to be outgoing. I was a fussy child and preferred to be involved in solitary activities.

In my early school years, I began, rather painfully, in learning to be more social, making friends at school and in the neighborhoods. Around sixth grade, I got involved in Boy Scouts and continued my growth toward full socialization. By high school, I was comfortable in and out of class, made quite a few friends, some extraverts as well, and developed a decent social network.

I believe that introversion/extraversion is a continuum. As we age, we grow, we expand our horizons on the continuum. We may roost closest to the area on the line that we were born into, but we can travel up and down the line as needed. This is especially true for introverts, where socialization is imperative and most difficult. There is a higher need for introverts to adapt and so we do.

In adulthood, I continue to straddle the line. I still have a strong introvert nature, but I have adopted an extravert social strategy that suits me. The conflicts are obvious, the push-pull, and sometimes no one landing spot to settle. I consider myself to be an aspiring extravert, with introvert roots and sensibilities. It is at best a tenuous equilibrium.

CHAPTER 10:

HSM Traps

Junk Food and HSMs

I am both health maven and junk food junkie. It depends upon the mood. It seems I gyrate between a cycle of diet and health focus, studiously avoiding avoid junk food, only to return to the clutches of fast foods and a maddening desire to satisfy a genetically inherited sweet tooth. I wonder if my sensitivity or heightened sensory awareness makes me more prone to indulge in the pleasures of junk food. Is it just about the sensation of taste, smell, and mouthfeel or is there brain chemistry involved as well? This section is about the HSM and being junk food junkies.

Ever since I was a kid, I have been a bit of a junkie for the foods that today we know contribute to multiple health issues. I could soothe a disappointment or overcome a hurt feeling with a sugary soda (Pepsi) or a sweet and crunchy candy (Chick-o-stick). It seemed a reliable way to soothe raw emotions. I grew up as a tall and skinny kid, active and always in motion, so eating junk food never dealt me the same misfortunes of those who gained extra weight with over-consumption of sugar.

Back then, high fructose corn syrup was not as prolific as it is today, so I had the good fortune, like most of my generation, of consuming good ol' straight sugar made from beets or cane. This only lessened the blow by a degree or two, but I think it kept us from becoming a generation of obese sugar junkies.

Today things are different. Junk food is designed with the intent to addict you or as the manufacturers would prefer saying—crave more of their product. Their foods, and I use that term loosely, are specifically designed to appeal to the brain and the senses. The appeal is more than a quick treat; it is made to keep us coming back for more—continually.

Working with food engineers, manufacturers carefully design junk food to elicit neurological, psychological, and physiological responses in the consumer. Things like *dynamical contrast*, where a hard shell of a candy contrasts with its soft, gooey inner layer; *salivary response*, where just the thought of the food brings forth a physiological response; *vanishing caloric response*—a fancy way of saying, because of the "lightness" of the food it fools the brain into thinking you are consuming fewer calories and you eat more; *sensory-specific response*—satisfying a brain need for food variety. The food is designed again to fool the brain by not providing too much satiation and prevent a dulling of your senses and future avoidance of that food. *Engineered caloric density* is a way of mixing ingredients to pass the brain's food test, but not enough to pass the "full" test; and finally, *past memory association*—this is the psychological part, where your brain associates this food with some pleasant past experience.[86]

I added the above verbiage to illustrate a point about how junk food is designed to be addictive. If you have a personality prone to addiction, it is easy to fall prey to this game played with your body and mind by food conglomerates. This falls easily into the category of food addiction. As a hypnotist, I have worked with many people over the years, looking for help in losing weight. One of the main components of the weight issue is the ease with which we become addicted to certain foods. This is no accident. The emotional ties we have to food, especially foods we consider to be comfort foods, are very strong and difficult to break.

Many of the triggers for food addiction are physiological, the interaction from the brain to the body, brought about by the ingredients in the food we are consuming. This is a complex interaction and can involve the brain and the gut, both centers of neurological control. When food is engineered to affect a response in the consumer, you can see the danger. Food addiction also has a psychological component, largely emotional. Food as self-medication has, at its root, the use of food for coping with difficult life situations. Throw in social pressures—family, friends, media, social occasions— and you can see how pressures within and without can push us over the line.

The pull of sugar on behavior is very powerful, as are starchy carbs, which ultimately turn to glucose in the body, creating this cycle of repetitive behavior. Indulging in the junk food of choice creates a body response, a kick of dopamine as a reinforcer, a rush of sugar into our bodies, creating a sugar high, and within a short period, a drop off of energy and crash.

What happens internally is even more devastating. The continued pumping of sugar-producing foods into the body leads to more insulin production, which is used to absorb the energy into the cells, and at some point, a saturation of the cells occurs, leaving the body to store the excess as fat. This condition can lead to insulin resistance, which is a precursor to a whole host of diseases.[87] Not good for your long term health outlook.

Can this affect HSMs or HSPs more so than the general population? I think it can. Because the research supports that HSPs are processing more sensory data and are prone to overwhelm more often, it seems to reason that HSPs are operating under more stress than the general population. Not necessarily under the greatest stress, but as a group, stressed more often, which could be a motivator in turning to junk foods for a calming effect.

Recent studies have shown that a select group of high stressed females ate more "comfort foods" to alleviate stress than individuals with less stress in their lives.[88] The high levels of the stress hormone cortisol creates an increase in cravings for sugar, carb, fat types of foods and the consumption of these foods lowered stress rates, albeit only temporarily. Could HSPs also be more prone to doing the same thing? Certainly, some of us do.

Since HSPs tend to present more intense moods as a result of our sensory processing sensitivity traits, food also can heighten mood expression from a biological standpoint. Should HSPs avoid sugar and processed carb foods to help calm down some of our emotional responses? The consumption of sugar, in particular, can suppress the activity of a key growth hormone in the brain, brain-derived neurotrophic factor (BDNF), which, when levels are low corresponds with depression and schizophrenia.[89] And increased sugar consumption can affect blood sugar levels in the body, affecting mood. There is enough enhanced brain chemistry naturally with HSPs that there is no need to flood our systems with junk food highs and crashes.

To top this off, Jennifer Cohen has studied a correlation between personality types and preferred junk food.[90] Although HSPs were not called out as a personality type, I can surmise from the personality descriptions where HSPs might fall. The criteria for snack foods, aka junk foods, were largely in the processed carb category, but traits like loyalty, integrity, perfectionism, and thoughtfulness kind of fit into the HSP wheelhouse. The foods corresponding to those categories were: meat snacks, cheese curls, tortilla chips, and crackers. No chick-o-sticks ... bummer.

Here are a few thought for HSPs on junk food consumption:

1. Junk food cycles are an endless cycle. We live in a junk food world where we are constantly bombarded with ads to entice us at our weakest moments. The sugar highs and sugar lows don't seem to stop us from consuming. It's not just the sweet stuff; it's the wheat stuff, too. It's a losing battle until you consciously break the cycle. Even being aware of your moods (easy for HSPs to do) after junk food consumption should bring some motivation to jumping off

the bandwagon. Focus your attention on health. We of all people should be leading the way here; I think it affects us more.

2. Look for positive mood foods, foods that will enhance your brain functions and control the ebb and flow of mood factors. Dark chocolate, protein, coffee, bananas, and berries; even though they may contain some sugar, they contain other nutrients that can positively affect your brain's functioning.

3. Learn to taste, not engorge. I have always wanted to see a manufacturer step up with a product that was called "Just Enough." This line of products would have just enough sugar or fat or both to taste, enough to recognize and with minimal product size—just enough to give you the experience without bombarding you with excess. It's a slight corruption of the Okinawan philosophy of *Hara Hachi Bu* or "eat to 80% of fullness." We need to learn to retake our senses back from a corrupt food industry, who see food as nothing more than product for profit and not for nutrition or health.

4. Disengage in automatic behaviors by being mindful of your eating habits. By feeding brain chemistry via seductive but harmful foods, in turn, creates and powers automation—automatic behaviors that often occur outside of your awareness. The cycle can be broken with your attention.

5. For HSMs, here's one for the ages: strive to be that slender, mindful soul that is as much in touch with his body as his mind—knowing that physical health is directly connected to mental and spiritual health.

Fantasy World

It occurs to me that Highly Sensitive People tend to live a mostly trusting life. I think we generally look for the good in others, are optimistic about outcomes, maybe to a fault, and generally foster a rich internal life that supports this belief. The general characteristics of HSPs as outlined by Dr. Elaine Aron's are 1) a depth of processing input data, 2) tendency toward over-stimulation, 3) emotional responsiveness and empathetic response, and 4) a certain sensitivity to subtleties. So, how do these characteristics foster a trusting and maybe borderline naïve outlook on life?

Jacquelyn Strickland has noted (see previous chapter) that most HSPs fall into the NF (intuitive feeling) category on the Myers Briggs personality inventory.[91] NFs tend to be highly idealistic visionaries who focus on big-picture ideation and do not typically get down in the weeds with detail and minutiae. Ironic that our depth of processing is typically emotionally based versus a more objective analytical processing of information that many more analytical personalities take. We like the feeling of ideas as opposed to the critical analysis of ideas. This is by no means saying that HSPs are not analytical or have the capacity for critical thinking. However, I believe we prefer the feel of ideas and I would add the playing with these ideas in our minds.

Now, if you combine the general characteristics of HSPs with the personality tendencies of HSP NFs, what I think you get is a rich inner world in which we tend to play with ideas and judge their worthiness based upon our feelings or emotional reactions. Processing deeply for us means a deep rumination of thought and emotion toward an external stimulus. We deep dive with our feelings carrying thoughts and ideas with us on our rich inner journeys.

Part of the problem with this strategy is that it often leads to overstimulation, both from external and internal sources, as we turn the idea over and over in our heads. Because we live so much in our emotions, based on what I think is our need to experience emotional flow, our response is typically emotional, impulsive, and not always rooted in rational thought or grounded in critical analysis.

It has been noted in studies that HSPs tend to respond mostly in emotional centers in the brain when presented with positive or negative images.[92] It's almost as if we filter our world through our emotions; i.e., how does it feel? This could explain why the same study suggested that HSPs exhibit differential susceptibility, which means we do better in positive (read emotions) versus negative environments. This, of course, impacts our internal world processing.

HSPs may also show a stronger optimism bias, which is a somewhat naïve view that bad things won't happen to us.[93] Without external confirmation of our theories about life, we may find that we stoke up our psychological immune systems with those beliefs that cushion the blow of negativity in our lives and give emotional respite toward negative events. This sometimes prevents us from learning our life lessons through objective analysis, albeit temporarily protecting us from the blow. In addition, this emotional optimism may give us a sense of control when events in our lives seem uncontrollable.

Does this make us overestimate the reality of our lives or get overly optimistic about our careers, plans, relationships, projects, and ideas when faced with pushback in the real world? Should we suppress our intuition or feelings when dealing with the outside world in making key decisions? Is our rich inner world composed of emotional fantasies untamed and wild and driving us to poor decision-making?

Perhaps we should consider how we might become more critical in our thinking. Critical thinking was essential to my success in the information technology field; I had to learn to become more analytical, not only as a technical resource but as a manager as well. Problem-solving requires a certain calm state in the brain, laying the facts all around you and dissecting and discerning the objective pieces before you. I learned I was quite good at it. Yet, throughout, I knew my strength was in the big picture overview and not in the details. It was, I thought, a good compromise, considering how my brain works naturally. Somehow, I was able to make it work.

But do all HSPs need to be more critical in our decisions and interactions, or more skeptical or even cynical? At the extreme end of the spectrum, cynical thinking is rooted in fear. It seems more in more in our world, critical or skeptical thinking has been overrun with cynicism. In business and science, I sense a more cynical view from these areas on outlier or new ideas as if to keep the herd in check. Cynicism is hard and vindictive; it is not open-minded and displays a lack of the characteristics that HSPs own. It is the damaged outer portal of someone who has been burned and has full shields up for protection. Not something HSPs should aspire to replicate.

The premise of this chapter was to look at the way HSPs process internally and the effects of our rich inner life—sometimes fantastic, sometimes fanciful. Are we more susceptible to others taking advantage of us, for our trusting, nurturing nature? Do we live too much in our inner worlds? This is especially targeted at the Introvert HSPs, which make up 70 percent of our base, and to narrow the field a bit more, adding the introverted HSPs who are NF on the Myers Briggs.

Because NFs focus on abstractions in speech including using rich metaphors, promote diplomacy and harmony, foster altruism, believe in optimism fueled by positivity, trust intuition, are romantic in thought and deed, and focus on what could be, rather than what is, we tend to be easy targets for those who prey on many of these characteristics.[94] Yes, it seems we are a lot of Don Quixotes chasing windmills. The idea that we are prone to mysticism continues to put us in the realm of outliers. Our rich inner life provides us with a wealth of new ideas, mostly untested, still soft, not hardened by the real world, but still new ways to think.

Our enthusiasm for these new ideas can be easily crushed by cynical observers who intend on keeping a mythological status quo, press us back into the herd. These are folks we need to be wary of and avoid. In a previous chapter, I spoke of receiving criticism and fostering a more accepting nature toward constructive criticism when given by those who indeed wish to help us and to realize the ideas that emerge from this font of creativity within us are like newly released magma, fluid and still malleable. With the help of those we cultivate around us to give us that external testing and feedback, we can then shape the ideas into practical and useful and insightful ideas that have real value. Yes, we can develop our critical faculties, as many of us have, but releasing some of our internal world to the external world for evaluation, confirmation, and agreement, to me, is a good thing.

I realize not all HSPs are lumped into the same bucket. We are all unique; we can navigate the world in our own ways. Many people write that HSPs are too broad of a group to lump into categories, and perhaps some truth is there. However, I still feel that too many people have identified and are continuing to identify with like characteristics attributed to the highly sensitive person. The discovery continues; the more we share with each other our thoughts, our feelings, and our ideas the more we all grow.

Personality Hypochondria

Highly sensitive people are often seen as being overly dramatic. This might include imagining all types and manner of disease, both physical and psychological. Being extra sensitive to physical stimulus also makes HSPs prone to sensing issues and problems with their bodies or generally with their psychological wellbeing. It doesn't mean that all of this is psychosomatic or exploding little issues and making them into larger ones, but it can happen. I've seen it with HSPs, myself included.

Hypochondria is a disorder where an individual worries excessively about having a perceived illness. We lay people often refer to this when speaking of those we know who seem to contract every illness imaginable and exploit the malady for sympathy or attention. It is, however, a real issue often tied to those with Obsessive-Compulsive Disorder (OCD).[95] Hypochondria is often brought about by stress, family deaths, anxiety, phobias, and even obsessive internet searches about disease.

There is a strong relationship between neurosis and hypochondria. The strong comparisons to OCD are suggested by the intrusive thinking and repetitive behaviors of someone acting on unrealistic impulses. Hypochondriacs tend to be paranoid, obsessive-compulsive, exhibit avoidant behavior, can be self-defeating and passive-aggressive.[96]

The point here is not to suggest or tie SPS with hypochondria, but to examine if the characteristic behaviors of someone with hypochondria can be correlated with those who have heightened sensory and somatic awareness and that whether those symptoms associated with hypochondria, perhaps in a mild form, are sometimes expressed in the SPS personality.

HSPs tend to feel pain more than the general population and have been socialized to report that pain less, because often they are more often criticized for expressing their sensitivity to pain, whether psychological or physical.[97] My observational experience around HSPs has led me to believe they are often more aware of differences in themselves than most non-HSPs, especially differences that might be considered disorders. That awareness makes them more cognitive of their pain, even if they don't express it openly. In several online groups I belong to, I have noticed a more openness about expressing these issues when the audience is perceived as more understanding and sympathetic than when that expression makes them more vulnerable, such as in non-HSPs groups.

The trap for HSPs is because of increased awareness to adopt an illness or personality trait, whether real or imagined, that instead of following up with medical or mental health providers, they adopt the trait as if it were real and incorporate that into their overall personality. Sometimes it aids their personality scripts, sometimes it inhibits. The question is whether this occurs more often in HSPs than in non-HSPs.

A study that set out to find if there were strong correlations between those with SPS characteristics and hypochondria produced an interesting finding.[98] The presumption was that because those with SPS often display behaviors of social anxiety, avoidant personality, anxiety and depression, stress and ill health, and agoraphobic avoidances, they may be more likely with their higher self-focus to display more hypochondriacal fear and an elevated focus on physical sensation. Although not definitive, the study did show that there was a high correlation between high SPS traits and hypochondria. It makes sense that individuals with high sensory awareness and sensitivity to the environment coupled with deep thinking processes likely perceive illness when the sensory data suggested it, regardless of whether it is corroborated medically.

When this assumption is not tested externally, such as under a doctor's care, then it is easy to see how HSPs might find themselves believing they have more issues than they actually do. This thinking can be very limiting, and I believe can trap HSPs into using this line of thinking into limiting experiences and using the disease as an excuse not to participate more fully in life. This creates a type of personality hypochondria in which the individual uses the perceived disease as a shield for protection and seclusion.

Being the Victim and Self-Pity

Another trap for HSPs is playing the victim or falling into indulgent self-pity. HSPs, with their heightened sensory awareness, emotional reactivity, and empathy, can often find themselves in situations where they are easily victimized. There seems to be a natural attraction between narcissists and HSPs. This is a classic prey-predator relationship, and HSPs tend to easily fall into it because of idealistic expectations, issues with being too empathetic, and their natural internalization of feelings.

Being a victim and playing the victim are generally two different things. Sometimes, however, they are together. Victims tend to see events happening to them instead of being responsible for events and consequences. Victims feel ineffective and overwhelmed by events and assume there is some overall fairness in life. Because life seldom is fair, this drives victim behavior toward internal brooding, in some cases driving righteous indignation and a sense of entitlement.[99] HSPs tend towards this type of thinking. It's not a stretch to see the internal brooding as being part of recursive repetitive rumination that HSPs display. The sense of right and wrong, the moral compass that many HSPs follow could, in cynical cases, lead to that sense of entitlement and resentment when life becomes unjust.

I believe as a whole HSPs want to do the right thing. Their clarion empathy wants to see justice in life and a sense of fairness. This idealism, although admirable, can be a downfall when clung to beyond the randomness of life. Perhaps this is where HSPs can fall into a sense of victimization and hopelessness.

This can lead to adopting a trait of victim sensitivity, which is a stable trait in which a victim senses a mistrust, jealousy, suspicion, and tendency toward uncooperativeness.[100] At the core of this is trust. Most people who display this trait have a critical life event that perpetuates this sensitivity and damages trust externally. The central event has the following characteristics: self-relevant, life-goal obstructing, comes upon them unpredictably, and is completely out of their control. Childhood sexual abuse comes to mind. All this leads to avoidant behaviors, things that many of us HSPs are aware of.

Having the personality trait of SPS is a two-edged sword. On the one hand, it heightens our sense of experience and with a proper sense of self-worth, can lead to insights, creativity, and emotional depth and maturity. But so often, HSPs do not get the necessary support to maintain high self-esteem and find themselves at odds with parents, family, friends, and colleagues.

With all of that deep processing we do, it is easy to get locked into a continuous loop of self-pity and victimization. Over time it can become an entrenched way of thinking. Not getting enough external confirmation to test our internal theories about ourselves is a way to self-delusion and doubt. The discovery of the trait of SPS is so new, and so much research is needed to determine effective strategies for raising SPS kids and developing coping skills for SPS adults that as a group, we almost have to ferret these out for ourselves. But beware of the traps, and there are many for HSPs. As a group, we are often misunderstood, and many of those perpetrators are misinformed and uneducated about the traits we possess, both good and not so good.

My Experiences

Coping is the number one preoccupation I have with my HSP traits; finding ways to deal with anxiety, stress, or the creeping up of depression. I love my junk food. I don't partake of it all the time, but especially when I feel frustrated or overly stressed, sitting down with some carbohydrate rich food or sugar-laced concoction takes my mind off the strain of life. Both types of food are converted quickly into sugar in the body, and the brain and body chemistry kicks in. I get that quick lift, a sugar high, and then the subsequent crash just after. I sometimes wonder, too, if I am addicted to the whole cycle, both the trough and the crest.

Lately, I have purposely stripped myself of carbohydrates and sugar to lose weight and break this addiction. It works, but requires me to find other ways to cope with stress and frustration. I sense that HSPs should just avoid sugar-laced foods altogether; they are like cocaine, good for the moment, but treacherous for the long run. Nevertheless, I feel like a junk food junkie and will have to be vigilant for the remainder of my life, recognizing that food is not a comfort if it makes me uncomfortable getting into my pants.

I am a hopeless romantic, but also a hopeless optimist. I don't know whether it is the idea I have adopted that states that your thoughts dictate your outcomes, and staying positive ensures good results, or just an insane naiveté that believes good things are my reward for trying to be a good person. The problem with either strategy is that positive outcomes result from work, trial and error, mistakes, issues, and persistence. It requires some critical analysis, some problem-solving, and sometimes good or bad luck to reach a goal. Hopeful wishing, although a nice distraction, and perhaps there is some credence to putting positive thoughts out in the universe, does not alone provide success in life.

I have always been drawn to the "new agey" ideas of controlling one's destiny through mind power, I think because as an introverted HSP, I live a lot in my head, swimming and sometimes drowning in my thoughts. It also conforms to this notion about not having to confirm your beliefs externally. If you never have to leave your head, you never have to confirm or reject your most comforting beliefs. And what of confirmation? How long do you test your ideas externally before you must let them go?

The balance between relinquishing an idea that's not working and holding on persistently testing to validate is also difficult to determine. I have often held to beliefs long past their useful life, because a part of me didn't want to test the idea outside my head. My beliefs can be like flowers in a garden, beautiful to look at, but reluctant to pick them, knowing that will destroy them, and just letting them be.

For a long time, I saw being an HSP as a weakness. Even before sensory processing sensitivity was widely known, and certainly before I knew about it, I saw my traits as a weakness. My sensitivity was something to hide from the world. Being a man and being sensitive were two things I could not reconcile. When I first learned of high sensitivity, I related strongly to the characteristics, but still was reluctant to embrace them. I saw myself as a victim of genetics and the environment. I was always the odd man out and certainly felt that life wasn't fair. Life had cast me with an ill-fitting costume and was making me march onto the stage, absorbing the guffaws of the audience, who laughed and mocked me as I spoke my lines.

I did not appreciate my uniqueness but only thought about fitting in. Years went by before I realized that the sensitivity was a gift from nature, and an opportunity to be very special and important. Playing the victim is an easy role to fall into. It doesn't require much effort to acquire the trappings of victimhood and use that as a flimsy shield. I used my sensitivity in all the wrong ways, making excuses for opting out of my unique life opportunity and making myself miserable trying to fit into a life and lifestyle that was not comfortable for me. It wasn't until I was in my late fifties that I realized not being my authentic self was literally killing me.

It has been hard giving up the victim role, acknowledging that life is difficult and that there is more to learn in error than in success. I have now embraced my sensitivity and feel a unique charter to defend it at all costs. My courage has risen as I discover my mission in life. Being HSP in a non-HSP leaning world is not easy, but it can be fulfilling. The more exposure I have to other HSPs and HSMs makes this a worthwhile journey.

In the end, the trap for me was that it was easier to retreat than to advance. And to advance, one needs to move out of comfort zones, move forward into uncharted territory, test internal theories in a cruel and unforgiving outside world—learn from them, discard flawed thinking, and grow. There is no other alternative except to be reclusive and slowly die. This is the lot of all life on this planet. We HSPs are unique, we interpret, we observe, we process, and digest, but it can't stop there. It must be externalized for our uniqueness to be realized. An idea floating around in a brain is just a potential. An idea shared is a realization. That is the trap to beware of—that is the solution to act upon.

CHAPTER 11:

False Courage

Early Rite of Passage or Coping Tool

S everal years ago, my son and his girlfriend came up from Los Angeles to visit. We spent a week hanging out at night, visiting the local breweries and restaurants, and I must confess, I drank a wee bit more that week than I normally do. This is a perfect segue to this chapter's topic of HSMs and strong drink.

I have had my fair share of spirits during the course of my life, often to celebrate, sometimes to fill a void, frequently as a social lubricant, but very seldom to improve my mood. Growing up in the southeastern United States, where drinking is sport and young men are often required to prove manliness by the quantity of alcohol consumption, I was baptized in this rite of passage during the early days of high school. Alcohol is the great social leveler and for brief moments made me equal to the socially adept.

It was so wretched to me that I began a second vice, cigarette smoking, to combat the bitter and often burning taste of alcohol. It seemed a fair trade to help a tall and skinny, pimply-faced young man gain social confidence among peers. I drank, I got confidence, and an inner personality emerged that was affable and full of social grace. At least until I, as all young men do, overconsumed and promptly deposited my day's food intake into the back seat of my best friend's parents' car. Not cool, but repeated again and again until the lesson of moderation was learned.

But all this really said about me was that I was prone to overwhelm, to shyness, and to social awkwardness, and that I believed I needed to consume some external substance to make me more of what I thought the world wanted from me; it was the nerve to be cool.

I am sure that many young men and young women face similar challenges, but as an HSM, these seem so much more exaggerated internally, and alcohol seemed to offer comfort and relief.

When Overwhelm Seems too Much, Does Alcohol Really Help?

As HSPs and particularly HSMs, we often pretend not to be overwhelmed by our environment so as to fit in and to project being in control. However, since our nervous systems are keenly and tightly wound, we feel and experience sensory information much more intensely than some of our peers. It's hard to process what we feel and what we sense without some coping mechanism.

For many HSMs, alcohol serves that purpose. Just look around at the world of art, music, and creativity. How many great artists mire themselves in addictive habits of substance abuse to quell the waves of emotions, expectations, and demands of their creative endeavors? Many of these creative creatures are HSPs and in particular HSMs.

The burden of being misunderstood and feeling too much becomes too much, and at some point there is a crossing of a threshold that drives the need for quick, albeit temporary, relief. The price paid is often devastating, and the damage greater than bearing the burden unassisted or alone.

Turning an HSM Introvert into a Raving Extravert

As stated earlier, one of the primary reasons I started drinking alcohol was to disinhibit myself in social interactions. It made me more comfortable and talkative. It was easy for me to make small talk, to be a bit more casual, and speak my mind. I was more like an extravert. And for those times at parties, celebrations, gatherings, it was a convenient persona to take on. I could mingle; I could be loud and yes, a bit cocky.

Since HSPs are typically not risk-takers, fully engaging in drinking behavior makes us feel a bit edgy and pushes us to poke at our own boundaries. Yet we tend to be more sensitive to the effects of alcohol and more easily pay the price of over-imbibing. Alas, plow ahead we do, at least some of us. We feel the social pressures to drink more intensely and conform to please. That, with an altered state of our personality, helps with the anxiety of social overload. Forgive me for generalizing, but visualize the bespectacled, quiet admin, or the nerdy computer tech at the annual Christmas party cutting loose on the dance floor and propositioning half the room. Yes, it can get dangerous. But it doesn't have to be.

Tamping Down Versus Numbing

I wonder what is really going on here. Are we trying to change our personalities to fit in? Or is there some effort to tamp down or numb down some internal pain, anxiety, or fear that we feel we can't overcome otherwise? Is overwhelm so poorly misunderstood among HSPs that we follow a path that is neither natural nor safe for us to follow? Since many HSPs are introverts (not all, but most) and introverts tend toward some degree of self-loathing at some point in their lives—which can lead to depression—what are the dangers that substance abuse can become problematic for introverted HSMs? It appears there is a correlation between alcohol abuse and depressed introverts.[101] Sadly, it's strong enough to raise eyebrows and flag as a warning. I think this is especially true for HSMs who easily panic, get anxious, or are otherwise uncomfortable in social situations; again, yet another thing to be cautious about as HSMs.

Dealing with Our Stuff

All in all, I think we need to continue down the path of owning our stuff. This notion that we are so fragile and prone to overwhelm, although not overstated, needs to be ameliorated in ways that allow us to function in the world more comfortably. The idea that we can control everything in our environment tends to box us in, retards spontaneity, and limits us in so many ways. Having that drink at the office party or loosening up at the company picnic or family gathering with a beer or a glass of wine is a way of coping with heightened sensitivity.

Granted, it shouldn't be our go-to solution for every life challenge, but occasionally bellying up to the bar can actually teach us about our inner selves. Alcohol can introduce us to an alternate reality, as it were. It can teach us how to overcome fear, to let loose and celebrate with others, especially our non-HSP family and peers. In the end, our nature is different. I think we have a gift, but one that is very high maintenance. The people around us feel it; we feel it and can easily set us apart, which creates isolation.

Celebrations with alcohol can bring us together. It can open us up to the world. But it has to be used with respect and caution. Granted, it's not for everyone. It can be used as way to ease into social situations that might otherwise challenge us. It's not so much the alcohol, but the context in which it is used. I see no problem using a drink or two to alleviate and relax what many see as a difficult, but not life-threatening situation. Conversely, I don't advocate its use as a way to numb pain, depression, or deep-seated anxiety. There are better ways to tend to those problem areas. I think we all know that.

As for myself, I will continue to be a social drinker. I'm older now, know my limits and boundaries, and stay within them. I like the little buzz of a slightly altered state, the relaxed calming feeling of a few drinks. My HSP characteristics and cautious, risk-averse nature keeps me from overindulging. It's a good balance. I think many of you out there will agree.

Prescription Drugs for Overwhelm

Self-medication use in America is utilized by about 17 percent of the population.[102] That means many individuals self-treat their undiagnosed medical issues with prescription and non-prescription medication. Some of this is for recreational use, some are for mood or mind-altering purposes, and some are for self-soothing.[103] The primary drivers for the use of self-soothing medications are to eliminate stress, anxiety, mental illness, and psychological trauma. The user purposely selects the drug that produces the desired effect, many times discovering the magic elixir through trial and error.

Many times an individual will use a drug as a disinhibitor to express feelings of affection and closeness or conversely, to release feelings of anger or aggression. People suffering from a social anxiety disorder may use these substances to fit in or feel more relaxed in context of social settings that would otherwise make them uncomfortable. The use of depressants to disinhibit, stimulants to excite the nervous system, opiates for analgesic effects, or cannabis for its psychoactive properties, allows individuals to take matters into their own hands, often with unconstrained use, giving them the ability to ameliorate emotional pain or social dysfunction.

The use of psychoactive substances such as cannabis, LSD, mescaline, and psilocybin, which have the ability to alter conscious perception, often bringing valuable insights into the user's awareness, has a long history with mankind.[104] Often used for religious and spiritual purposes, they have been used for recreational use, most notably in the sixties and seventies, sometimes in a reckless fashion and without due respect for the power of the drug. Naïve users can create more problems than they bargained for without proper training or understanding of dosage and the proper setting for meaningful and useful experiences (Set and Setting).[105]

HSPs would seem likely candidates for the use of various substances to help control feelings of anxiety, stress, and social discomfort. Use of some types of medication to tamp down those feelings of anxiety and stress makes sense for some HSPs. The use of depressants and cannabis might aid HSPs in dealing with uncomfortable social situations. I know I have used them before in my own social interactions and found them to help me relax and become more outgoing and social.

Although these milder sedatives might have some benefit for HSPs, I am not advocating non-prescription use of drugs for anyone. In some states, cannabis is legal and can be used by adults without concern for breaking the law. Harder narcotics should be avoided, and I believe that HSPs will find their use to be harsh on mind and body. The same may be true for some psychedelic drugs, although they have long held promise for personal psychological work, and most are illegal. Without guidance, HSPs may find the experience to be too much to handle and should likely be avoided. It has been suggested that because of their nervous system makeup, HSPs are more susceptible to addiction and would be wise to select their use of substances judiciously.

The problem with all of these substances—alcohol and drugs—is the elimination of facing the experience with nothing more than your own awareness. Most HSPs, when life gets overwhelming, retreat to their sanctuary to reprocess and rest, thus sometimes eliminating life experiences that could allow them to grow both socially and personally. Many of us HSPs look for some external device or gimmick to allow us to pass through the social membrane and defy our personality's own constraints. The idea of changing our body chemistry in order to interact more effectively has many downsides, least of which is that we are not learning to adapt to the environment. There is a dependence on something external, which is temporal, that we ingest to get us into the desired state in which we can function; it is not an adaptation of our personality, but rather an alteration.

I've known many HSPs, myself included, who have taken that route in order to fit in or overcome our innate cautiousness and apprehension about walking into circumstances we are not comfortable with.

My Experiences
Alcohol

I started drinking about fifteen years of age. My dad drank, generally bourbon cocktails, but I figured if he drank, it must have been okay for me to imbibe. My first experiences were not uncommon. The first taste of beer was disgusting, bitter and rather tasteless. I would watch other friends guzzle cheap lager, and I could barely choke down one. The mark of manhood was "submarining" a beer, which essentially forces the beer down your gullet in one gulp.

The first time I got drunk was initially a fun experience, followed by the inevitable throwing up and waking up with a beer hangover, the worst hangover of all. At that time, just like a baby rattler, I hadn't learned to throttle the poison, so I violated all rules of sensible drinking.

It taught me that I was more than what I presented, even surprising me at times and how charming, witty, and outgoing I could be. It was my primary social lubricant. It loosened me up, made me comfortable around strangers and I felt like I fitted in socially. It helped me boost my confidence.

The negative side was that it made me do some really stupid teenage things. Some were reckless (driving under the influence, saying too much at times, taking some ridiculous risks), and others were just unfathomable. I look back and think now, what was going through my mind?

I was young and foolish. It brought me out in ways that I could not have done with the knowledge I had at the time. But alcohol is like that. It's a strange mistress; she can seem to love you and then in a flash betray and make you miserable.

For years alcohol was my ticket to confident social intercourse. College parties, clubs, social organizations, corporate events – all had access to alcohol. I lined up, got a few drinks in me, and I become Mr. Personality. I quit drinking like a teenager but still found that drinking at social functions was my best strategy for circulating.

I have learned to be more confident in all social circumstances without drinking. I am more outgoing, speak louder, engage people more, and trust that I can navigate a party like a pro, but that doesn't mean I still don't get my butterflies. I have a complicated relationship with alcohol, like most people who drink do. I believe that had I not been an HSP, my inclination would have been to avoid it. I used it as a tool, much like using a sledgehammer to crack a walnut. It will work, but it's overkill.

Marijuana

I started smoking pot about the time I started smoking cigarettes. It was becoming fashionable during that time, and many of my friends had already started smoking. It was readily available, and with a few connections, would easily get a nickel or dime bag or a full ounce of pot.

I really liked the way it made me feel. Getting high was so different than drinking. It was more cerebral and contemplative than getting hammered with Country Club Malt Liquor. I never got sick or threw up, no matter how much I smoked. I kind of liked the whole ritual of smoking, the papers, grinding the buds up to a powder, the rolling machines, the incense to mask the smell, and passing around the joint. It was communal and real hippie-like, perfect for the times.

Getting stoned alone, I liked to listen to music. It allowed me to pick out things in the songs, things I wouldn't ordinarily notice. It gave me insights into the meaning of the lyrics and let me hear things in the music, subtle things, things that in my normal awareness I would have missed.

I never saw cannabis as a way to break social territory. To me, it was a solitary retreat into my mind. It was good to get high with a select group of friends I trusted. We had philosophical and religious conversations, digging deep within trying to find meaning in our lives. Eventually, the conversations would devolve into just laughter and comedy. I smoked with good friends who made me laugh until I cried; it was that good. We'd do skits and act out characters, but mostly laugh at how silly and ridiculous we could be.

Marijuana opened up doors of creativity for me. It was a revelation. I never got down while smoking. I just ended up starving and looking for odd foods at the 7-11 store at odd hours of the night.

I continued to smoke pot until my late twenties when I got married. With kids in the house, I felt a little weird about modeling smoking an illegal substance, so I quit. That lasted until the State of Oregon legalized marijuana use, and I began to experiment with the occasional high. In a lot of ways, it was not the same, although the selection was much greater, and it was now legal and easier to get. I mostly smoked in order to enjoy music more. Going out high was taboo for me, so I kept it mostly secret.

As the trend continues to progress on legalizing marijuana, it makes sense to me for HSPs to try it. There is already a myriad of studies that show enormous medical potential for cannabis, and I can readily see this translating into psychotherapy at some point in the future.

Again, using an external substance to affect an internal change may not be for everyone. I think for me, it was an instrumental part of my growing up and learning about me. It allowed me to access parts of my personality, my being, if you will, that helped me to grow. I think there is merit here. Each individual should make their own decision.

Cocaine, LSD

Around 1979 I had just moved out to Hollywood to live with a friend. Cocaine was everywhere. It was the designer drug of the period and was easily available if you had the money. I did not, but I hung out with a few people who did. I'm glad my funds did not allow me to be exposed to it any more than I did.

The times I tried it, I really liked it. I liked it enough that I would have been snorting lines all the time if I could have afforded it. I would have been addicted. It was too good to be true, and fortunately for me, it was not to be a part of my life. A few years later, I was out of Hollywood, married and a parent. I left that lifestyle behind. Cocaine gave me confidence and energy I didn't know I had. It's not a good mix for an HSP, or for that matter, anyone. Cocaine offers a false sense of courage; it's a delusion and an illusion.

Growing up, I was a bit too timid to drop acid. A lot of folks at my high school did, but I just couldn't see losing control of one's consciousness for that experience. I was likely a product of the anti-LSD campaign that the government was peddling at the time. I remember doing a research paper on it in high school, partly to learn more about it, and what I read scared my poor HSP nature off.

I finally tried it in Hollywood. A friend of a friend gave me a tab of something he claimed was acid. It was over the Christmas holidays, and my roommate was gone. I took the tab and waited. I was alone and locked into the apartment, an old twenties style Spanish building on the second floor. Off in the distance, I could see the Hollywood sign. Not much happened that night. I remember believing a UFO was circling the apartment and was looking for me. I called a woman I was dating and talked to her for several hours. I was pretty paranoid; things seemed a little distorted, but no dancing elephants, no plasticine colors, and no magic revelations. I'm not sure what I took, but it probably wasn't what I was told. I was up most of the night and fell asleep disappointed. I never tried it again.

Curiously, now as I'm getting older, I am interested in trying a psychedelic for therapeutic reasons. Many people are now finding "shamans" and doing ayahuasca for experiences with interesting results. It's starting to gain credibility again as a possible treatment solution for depression and alcoholism. I hope this momentum continues. Under controlled circumstances, with experienced guides, I can see the benefit, especially for HSPs. Accessing parts of the unconscious may seem daunting for HSPs, but I believe the insights can be growth opportunities. I am advocating this only because there are therapists who do this and are experienced at handling the emotional abreactions and other outcomes.

I think what happened in the sixties was mostly stupid, gullible people trying a very powerful substance, looking for instant insight. Some got it; some didn't. I think it's time to reevaluate this in a controlled manner that allows for the best experience for the sojourner. Perhaps only the bravest of the HSPs will consider it, but I for one am looking forward to it.

Prescription Meds Opioids, Sleeping Aids, Anti-Depressants

Just like most people, I have had some access to prescription meds, those in particular that are mind/state altering and have been rife with abuse. There are times when I just want to feel numb, and those are the times that if I have them, I will take a pain pill or a sleep aid or a muscle relaxer to get rest. I don't advocate this, not even with myself. It's a slippery slope, and I truly want to avoid it.

I tried a short stint with anti-depressants. I was going through a diffi-cult time in my life a few years ago and asked my doctor for help. He gave me a quick questionnaire on my mental state and determined (amazingly) that I could use an anti-depressant. I was given a generic equivalent of Lexapro and took it for several months. What I found was that it "flat-lined" my emotions. I didn't feel down, but I didn't feel up, either. During this period of time, I broke up with my girlfriend and instead of feeling depressed, I felt nothing. I thought it would be good not to feel anything about the breakup, but for me, it was a loss—a loss of feeling of anything that seems to matter the most.

As an HSP, feelings are everything to me. Yes, I can go on a rollercoaster at times, up and down, but that is my normal experience. I expect that. It's not always pleasant, but it is what I do. I couldn't find within myself enough to write anything down about the relationship that I lost. No feelings, and without the feelings, the words would not come. It was an awful experience, one I would not recommend for dealing with normal emotional upheaval. I talked to my doctor, and with his clearance, I quit taking the meds.

Within a week or so, I started getting my expected feelings back, and of course, I felt like shit. But then I realized that was a normal range of emotions coming through. And I realized that I needed to experience that full range to appreciate my ability to feel so deeply. It is part of me, it is part of all HSPs, and it is part of all humanity to experience the wide-ranging wheel of feelings. The real nuggets of truth in life are in the extremes of emotion—great joy and great pain bear great fruits of learning. The barren middle is where we exist most of the time, but without the opportunity to feel the extremes we miss out on our humanity.

I am afraid we HSPs tend to *live* more in the extremes. We need to be careful not to dwell there too long. There are ways to swing the pendu-lum back to the middle, to make life bearable, to make it work—it's all about balance.

Wherever we find our courage, make sure it is true to you. The false courage that can be gained externally from substances that don't gently move the pendulum can be very dangerous. Tread cautiously in those areas. Do your HSP research, think deeply about your choices, look for ways to moderate and modulate your emotions. The learning is in the doing, and we all have our own paths to follow. Press on, keep looking; it will be there.

Chapter 12:

The Negative Side of Being an HSP

The Dark Trap of Insecurity

Does high sensitivity produce high insecurity in HSP males? With all that extra processing power, the more intense the emoting, the greater likelihood of high-level meltdowns, and when faced with the outside world's response or pressures, doesn't it make sense that with such feedback, insecurity will flourish?

Are highly sensitive males more likely to be insecure than the larger non-HSP male population? The elements of being an HSP—high sensitivity, deep mental processing, overwhelm, and emotional reactivity—might seem on the surface to contribute to insecurity, especially in HSP boys. With overstimulation, overthinking, and presenting emotionally as less than the ideal masculine in dealing with emotions, does this inherently lead to feelings of insecurity and lack of self-esteem? It seems other factors are more important than simply how we process emotions.

The environment plays a greater role in providing the feedback necessary from parents and friends that reinforce feelings of insecurity and low self-esteem.[106] In other words, there is no genetic predisposition for insecurity. Insecurity is learned. If there is a tendency toward insecurity in HSP males, that is a product of nurture and not nature. Studies suggest that when HSPs are raised in nurturing homes with understanding and supportive parents, they thrive. Conversely, as you might expect, in opposite conditions, they respond more negatively than less sensitive kids.

Where, then, does insecurity come from? There are a multitude of sources from which the seeds of insecurity are sown. As stated earlier, parental figures play an enormous shaping role in developing a child's self-concept. Disapproving authority figures, uninvolved and disinterested caregivers, bullying parents all send the wrong types of messages to sensitive young minds.[107]

Without the benefit of adult size mental filters, kids naturally process this feedback as is and take the negative message to heart. Later in life, when academic, athletic, or more serious traumatic events present themselves as challenges, rigid beliefs from childhood, which have never been challenged, become set. The insecure child becomes an insecure adult. Social media serves to confirm these beliefs: "I am not worthy."

Does this become a lifelong affliction? Like cement, once set, does it become immutable? The impacts are quite clear. Low self-esteem, insecurity, and low confidence affect every aspect of life. From career choices to mate selection, academics, sports, sex performance, income potential, you name it, they all are impacted, and for men, the question of how you are viewed as a man.

The self-comparison game starts early and so begins the insecurity. [108] Current examples have to include social media, where comparisons run rampant, and the unreality of reality weighs in for review. Everyone is doing better than what the insecure eye sees. Filter this through the HSP lens, and you see amplification through greater self-talk, constant comparison processing, overreaching emotionally, and stoking the fires that will one day consume the fragile ego.

What can we surmise that the arc of this behavior will lead to? Do insecure people self-sabotage to minimalize overstimulating experiences?

Does this ultimately lead to withdrawal, overcompensation, and self-loathing? At what point do insecure men believe there is a point of no return?

People who lack self-confidence learn early to seek approval externally.[109] They moderate and lower positive expectations and naturally deflect compliments. Yet somehow, the lack of self-confidence is not all-pervasive in an individual's personality, although it may seem that way. It's not dependent on actual abilities, but the focus is rather on unrealistic expectations set by parents and authority figures transferred as beliefs in the individual.

Many assumptions the insecure individual possesses are: 1) they must be loved and approved by every important person in their lives, 2) they must be thoroughly competent and high achieving in all aspects of their lives, and 3) their focus is always on past performance, not present or future potentials.[110] Their thoughts are permeated with 'all or nothing' thinking, often seeing the dark side of situations, magnifying the negative. Further, with their uncritical acceptance of runaway emotions as truth, overemphasizing "shoulds," self-labeling, and seeing challenges through the prevailing belief of inadequacy and incompetence, they perpetuate their own self-myth.

Is it any wonder that emotional insecurity ensues? This becomes a feeling of general unease or nervousness that may be triggered by external factors, resulting in feelings of not being worthy of love, alas, an inadequate and worthless human being.[111]

It's a slippery slope from childhood to manhood or an upward climb with unsteady footing for those unsure of themselves. When you're not getting the feedback you deserve, you need, you crave—the impacts are real. It's all learned and the process, I dare say, intensifies when you are an HSP. Everything gets amplified; the internal voices are louder, the uncorrected logic, fueled by emotion, cuts a broader, wider path in your self-esteem. Who knows how prevalent it is in HSMs. We don't all have parents who get us. How many fathers likely see beyond their own expectations, and instead, see their sons as the budding man, still malleable, like fresh, soft clay ready to be molded into its strongest, best form.

How do we prevent this from developing in our HSP boys? How do we gently bring them along, not making them dependent, yet lighting that flame of courage, independence, and self-love that will empower them throughout their lives? We, as parents, need to give the positive spin on HSP characteristics and yet instill confidence in them as people, as men, even being different men who are sometimes swimming against the cultural tide.

We need to show what a healthy, masculine role model is like. Help them to be confident in their inherent qualities. Help them become emotionally strong men, teaching them to express the full range of human emotion. Teach them to avoid the dark trap of insecurity. Teach them confidence and self-assurance, *sans* the arrogance, overconfidence, and bravado of small-minded men. That confidence will allow HSP traits to grow and flourish without heavy internal conflicts. Healthier boys make healthier men.

Here are six things that will help our HSP boys:

1. Help them understand their nature. Educate them about the Sensory Processing Sensitivity trait they possess. Show them how unique and special they are.

2. Stop comparing them to non-HSP boys and men. Eliminate that game early on. The idea is not to isolate them, but rather to integrate them without losing themselves in the process.

3. Give them tasks where they can gain confidence in their abilities. Challenge and encourage. Growth comes from pushing beyond the comfort zone.

4. Help them learn to push the envelope a bit, gently getting them to expand their horizons. Nothing builds confidence more than experience. Nothing adds experience like challenges.

5. Show them support when they falter; don't let them wallow in self-pity or loathing.

6. Teach them to respect themselves and others.

The Call of the Void

The French have a term, *L'Appel Du Vide*,[112] the call of the void, to describe that intrusive call to oblivion, of self-destruction or of jumping impulsively into the abyss, that we all experience from time to time. The moment happens to most of us in a split second, standing near a ledge, or driving in a car, wherein we contemplate cutting across the line into oncoming traffic. It is like Carlos Castaneda's ideology of death stalking us, tempting us with a moment where we are dared to chase the reaper. A snap inner voice that says "Jump!" and for a split second, our minds drift over into the call to nothingness. A single moment of distraction, an alternate reality, and then just as suddenly back to normalcy with a deep sigh.

Living a lot of our lives inside our heads, many HSP self-concepts come from the conclusions we have drawn from our own deep analysis and deep processing. Many times we don't validate those conclusions externally because of our sensitivity to criticism and our fragile egos. We make ourselves subject to deep hurt when our carefully considered assumptions are proven wrong by expressing them to others. Deep processing does not always mean correct conclusions. In fact, I would argue that many of our conclusions are off the mark, like computer code stuck in an endless loop.

At times this can create a bit of an existential crisis with us, causing doubt about who we are, what we are, and thoughts on the possible need to construct a new model within our egos. A very conscientious individual can be severely rattled when confronted with logical holes in their reasoning or in their emotional position.

Are HSPs subject to the *un petite l'appel du vide* thoughts? Or are we more practical, suffer the insults, process heavily, then pop our little heads out of the hole again, no worse for wear? Suicidal ideation, fleeting thoughts, role-playing, or incompletion of actually ending it all is not so uncommon.[113] But it is a serious matter. Nearly four percent of adult Americans report having these moments. The underlying causes often come from mood disorders, depression, or simply by feeling alone, abandoned or the stress of life. But what I am speaking of here is not that.

These moments of existential crisis, a moment when the individual questions if his or her life has meaning, purpose, or value, may lead to conjuring a *l'appel du vide* moment.[114] More often, it may pop up as a spontaneous subconscious thought. Could heavy, deep processing of a bad decision or wrong conclusion lead one to doubt oneself or provide too many options to choose from, leading to this same internal crisis?

Maybe this is just a miscalculation. Can over-processing of highly energized emotional input cause us HSPs to over calculate, causing an internal crisis? Dr. Elaine Aron acknowledges to our deep processing cycles with the acronym, D.O.E.S.[115] The D represents the HSP depth of processing, that deep contemplation of what others might see as minutiae. The O stands for overstimulation, a common characteristic of HSPs, our world of overwhelm. The E is for emotional reactivity and empathy, our energizing qualities, and finally, the S is for seeing the subtle or our high marking sensitivity. Granted, all these qualities have and can be seen as positive in many ways, bringing us the ability to be intuitive, empathetic, cautious, and careful planners.

Sometimes the pain is the lesson. Suffering through deep processing should eventually lead to some type of action, but with HSPs there is not always follow through. A constant churn of revisiting, rethinking, and reevaluating conclusions may not be a great strategy for solutions. Even with our need for solitude, alone time, silent reflection—in the end, a decision or action is needed. Too much solitude can lead to a distortion of perception, increased anxiety, and perhaps sensory illusions.[116]

When a computer program is flawed, it follows the code, regardless of the flaw, and loops back endlessly to the beginning, only to start again. It wastes computer time and resources, perhaps generating needless output, yet never concluding. When confronted with a painful reality, are HSPs subject to endless loop processing?

Our inaction can lead us to those moments of *l'appel du vide*, even while our deep processing leads us to wish we could let go of the processing cycle. We fall into a bottomless pit, not deciding, not concluding, caught, lost in too much information, and in our imaginations stare blithely through a rain-soaked windshield at the oncoming traffic ahead, flashing a moment of nonexistence for a respite.

So, what do we do? Follow up the deep processing with some type of action. Don't get caught in the whirlpool, getting sucked down into the vortex of overthinking. Don't let frustration get you down; head up, keep looking to break the trend of over-processing. And if that moment of *l'appel du vide* comes into conscious awareness—consider it rather as a leap of faith. Yes, process as we do, but at some point face the uncomfortableness and take action to resolve. Take the leap into the void of uncertainty but leave the leap from the cliff alone.

Note: *Suicide is a serious matter. If you are having recurring suicidal thoughts, please seek immediate help from a medical or mental health professional. The gist of this section is to take the French concept of "the call of the void" and use it in a metaphorical way, describing a brief mental escape. L'appel du vide in this context is also used to mean responding to the call as a mental leap of faith or better yet, taking a calculated risk toward positive action, expressed as leaping into the unknown. Breaking the habit of over-thinking is probably a good thing, but don't abandon careful, considerate deep evaluation. Consider it carefully, as I know you will.*

When Dark Gets Desperate, Suicide, Men and High Sensitivity

Throughout the book I've been talking about the intense feelings HSPs can have. Part of the discussion is developing healthy coping skills in dealing with these strong feelings. Men, especially in this country, have been socialized to suppress their feelings in order to appear more "manly."

Yet contrary to evidence, suppressing feelings is not healthy at all. In fact, it may be contributing to the leading cause of suicide among middle-aged and older men. It had me thinking there could be an intersection between some HSP men who are also older and have been socialized to keep feelings under wrap may contribute to an unhealthy sense of hopelessness or helplessness. Helplessness is a learned behavior to act or behave helplessly even when there is the power to change the harmful or unpleasant circumstance.[117] This behavior contributes to depression, and depression, in turn, contributes to suicide.

Depression is the leading cause of suicide. With ten percent of the population reporting feelings of sadness, six percent reporting feelings of hopelessness, and five percent reporting a sense of worthlessness, it can easily seem like these factors are contributing to our nation's depression epidemic.[118] Women are more likely to be sad than men and singles more so than those who are partnered. Although women have a two-to-one ratio for depression in most developing countries, research shows that while men and women have comparable levels of depression, they express it differently.

Nevertheless, men's suicide rates are higher than women's. In spite of the fact that 70 percent of suicides are caused by the wide umbrella of depression and that women report higher incidences of depression, actual suicides are a staggering 4:1 in favor of men. This rate of suicide in men increases with age.[119]

It's worth noting, yet not surprising, that men seldom seek help for depression. Women are more likely to seek help. Women tend to ruminate on depression, holding it inward, whereas men tend to act (externalize) depression with drink and risky behavior. Suicide rates are higher, with men over 50.[120] Interestingly, low population states have higher suicide rates as do military personnel, LGBTQ communities, and those suffering with chronic pain.

There is some genetic tendency toward suicidal behavior, i.e., the Hemingways. Whether there is genetics at play or this is learned behavior seems debatable. Edwin Schneidman, a noted psychologist, proposed a suicide model in which the victims tend toward unbearable psychological pain, isolation, and a persistent perception that death is the only solution.[121] Of course, there are other contributing factors—loneliness, bullying, discrimination, and separation from family—especially men as non-custodial parents. The upshot is that depression, helplessness, hopelessness, and worthlessness contribute to feelings that might lead to suicide.

And men who are desperate are often the ones who act on this.

What about us highly sensitive people? Would it seem HSPs, and in particular, highly sensitive men, are any more likely to reach that tipping point born out of desperation? Is there any evidence to suggest that because of intense emotional processing and/or with the added factor of additional mental health issues, HSMs are at a higher risk for suicide?

According to Dr. Tracy Cooper, HSPs are prone to depressive and anxious thinking because of a more elaborate depth of processing in their thinking.[122] This thinking can lead to bouts of depression and sadness. But does that put HSMs at more risk of suicidal behavior? In Dr. Cooper's blog, he references Dr. Thomas Joiner, who has reformulated the major causes of suicide for predictive purposes. These causes are framed to highlight the weighted burden men often experience when helplessness and hopelessness set in. It is many ways a reflection of the unrealistic expectations men often shoulder in silence.

Dr. Joiner's list of criteria consists of the following: 1) a sense of not belonging or being alone, possibly because men often fear ridicule or shame for sharing feelings considered unmanly, 2) a sense of not contributing or of being a burden, and with our current economic climate, men can feel as though they do not contribute as much financially as in previous eras, creating a sense of guilt, and 3) finally, Dr. Joiner suggests that one must have the capability for suicide, the will to die, to override the evolutionary urge to survive, and the willingness to act.[123] Even as research shows that suicidal intention is transient and fleeting, there may be that moment in time, as Dr. Elaine Aron says, that the thought, played with, becomes an accidental action, and one breaches the portal of death.[124]

Speaking specifically to HSPs, Dr. Aron shows some optimism for the HSP population in regard to suicide. She suggests because of the HSP depth of processing feelings, our sometimes rampant perfectionism, the fact that HSPs are often bullied because of our uniqueness, and at some level can build a fed-up attitude we harbor toward our sensitivity, causes that otherwise turn others toward dark depression, can be thwarted in HSPs because of our natural empathy, caution, and willingness to think things through before acting. This may keep HSPs from following through on such a permanent and drastic measure.

Yet I wonder, if Sensory Processing Sensitivity (SPS), the prominent trait of HSPs, creates opportunities for HSPs to experience difficulties in processing deep-seated or highly emotional trauma, i.e., PTSD. Conversely, are HSPs any better suited to handle the emotional overwhelm, something that we routinely experience, and are we more likely to share the deep, dark feelings with others? Do HSPs, including highly sensitive men, perhaps more so than the general population, seek out help when needed to avert something catastrophic like suicide? I have not been able to find specific research supporting this, but feel comfortable assuming there is some degree of truth to that.

What could be a soft crack in the above resilience hypothesis of sensitive men might be with HSP men over sixty suffering traits suggested by

Dr. Joiner, who may not be aware of their SPS traits and may labor under archaic male role models. Regardless of their awareness of their sensitivity, and by that I mean acceptance of it, they may hold their feelings in private to seem more masculine and yet suffer deeply within and not connect with others. As research has shown, if they had been raised in negative environments as children, the overall effect can be compounded. With negative copings skills and low self-esteem, this can dovetail quickly into a serious situation.

While acknowledging the seriousness of talking about suicide, which may seem like attention-seeking behavior, you cannot assume the individual is not capable of the act. If you know of someone showing these behaviors listed below, or if you are displaying these, get help immediately:[125]

1. Unrelenting low moods
2. Pessimism
3. Demonstrable hopelessness
4. Desperation
5. Deep anxiety
6. Withdrawal
7. Sleep issues
8. Drug or alcohol abuse
9. Impulsiveness or risk-taking behavior
10. Verbal threat of suicide

Suicide is always a failed strategy in lieu of better coping skills. A fatalistic approach to life is a failure to comprehend the value of every life. It is failed thinking, spurred by deep and often unconscious programming, the result of unfortunate learning or experiences. These can be remedied with professional help. Seek out help if you are even contemplating suicide. The National Suicide Hotline is 1-800-273-8255.

Footnote:

In this last decade two high-profile males over sixty-years-old committed suicide. Robin Williams suffered from Lewy Body Dementia, a disease that causes multiple perplexing physical and psychological problems.[126] The net result of confusion, helplessness, and depression led to his actions. I suspect Mr. Williams was an HSP, but I have no way of verifying that. His thoughtful, sensitive, and gentle nature could easily be observed. Like many, I miss his brilliance and his talent.

According to accounts, Anthony Bourdain suffered from depression[127] with a reported desire to die. Yet he shouldered a "strong man" mentality, never asking for help. He suffered in many ways, alone, as many men do. Successful suicide is largely a male problem. His support of the #MeToo movement suggests great empathy. I will also miss his lusty appreciation of great food and great culture and his dry wit.

CHAPTER 13:

The Positive Side of Being an HSM

In the sixties and seventies being different—or more importantly—being yourself was encouraged. A time when being unique was a good thing. Non-conformance was seen as a positive. Self-image for me was evolving, yet somehow I was still concerned about how I measured up as a man. My sensitivity in most things tended to seem awkward to friends, girlfriends, and others. I was taller than most boys, beanpole skinny, but athletic and likable. That probably saved me from a few butt whippings or being the target of bullies.

Somewhere in the mid-90s, I found out about Highly Sensitive People. I can't remember the exact route I took, but somehow I discovered Elaine Aron's book on sensitivity and sensitive people. When I read the book, my eyes opened and realized it was about me and for me. It was life-changing. It was like being found, after years of lonely wondering in the "what am I?" wilderness.

Even later when high sensitivity was given a measure of credence, being an HSP male among HSPs seemed fine, but being an HSP among non-HSP men was different. I seemed to have more female friends than male friends, although I did have male friends. A few close male friends.

Nevertheless, I still struggled with my sensitivity and my masculinity as it was defined for me by society. I began to question how this template for being a man fit in with my internal model and feelings. The fact was it didn't. I knew something had to give. Now that I'm older, I have learned about the importance of being authentic and true to oneself. I have learned to embrace my sensitivity, and I am now an advocate for the characteristics in myself and in men who have the same qualities. I'm proud to be a sensitive man, son of a sensitive man, and father and grandfather to sensitive children.

A good friend of mine, an intuitive life coach, gave me a reading once to help me understand myself. In it, she described that my life purpose was to be an observer of life and to put these observations to paper. Later I recognized that calling had led me to write. It fits me well. A chance to think, to ponder deeply, to verbalize my thoughts and opinions and do it in an environment I choose.

In this chapter I focus on what I consider positive HSP characteristics. Here's a short list of things that readily come to mind—positive HSP originated traits.

It's All Good to Me

Looking over the unique and often peculiar traits of HSPs, one can conclude that being sensitive is a hornet's nest of problems, both physically and psychologically. So many non-HSPs pass judgment on the often restless and turbulent HSP personality that it can be like shooting fish in a barrel. Many HSPs internalize this criticism and make that a mantel of their persona. This is unfortunate and focuses only on the negative side of the HSP coin.

I am tired of focusing on HSP/HSM negativity. I have been confronted with this my whole life and am just now beginning to challenge these assumptions. To stay locked in this negativity keeps HSMs locked in their shells, never free to explore the great and mystical gifts they have been given. It blocks and hinders growth and possibilities that lie deep within us. Rather, I would like to focus on the positive traits that each HSM carries inherently. Let's look at some of the key traits I think make sensitivity a positive characteristic. Of course, I'm looking at this from my own unique lens, but nevertheless, I see this in other HSPs.

Adaptability

Because of their keen observation skills and desire to be inconspicuous, HSPs have created great skills on being adaptive. This chameleon-like quality allows them to almost stealthily blend into environments and become the observer in which they can learn the best survival methods.

I know for myself, this ability to mirror my environment allows me to penetrate the world of others and to listen, learn and adapt. It allows me to gain trust and connection to others that I might not be able to do if I failed to blend. The nice part about this is that I don't compromise my identity in order to fit in, almost like a magic cloak that I can hide behind in order to gain access.

Perhaps this adaptation is an extension of fitting in. It allows me to blend with a variety of people. The camouflage allows me to learn and observe. This is part of rapport building with people—it builds trust and empathy. It expands my comfort zone and raises my learning levels. That is a good thing.

This adaptation allows me to observe and learn in many situations—at school, at work in social settings, in public venues, etc. I can "float" around inconspicuously, not drawing attention to myself, yet scout and mingle. This adaptability is in part driven by empathy in wanting to connect deeply with others and to be understood through observation and interaction.

My cautious nature can actually be seen as a form of adaptability. It allows me to leverage a slow, steady reveal of a situation, giving me time to internalize the needed adaptation, allowing time for absorbing and expanding my comfort zone at my own pace. I see this as an adaptation: to be different superficially, inherently unique, and still maintain my HSP identity.

Communication Skills

The skill to articulate ideas and then externalize the communication is due to the HSP quality of deep processing and is another key positive characteristic. If you couple this with my deep desire to be understood, the ability to communicate with anyone becomes imperative. It allows me to frame my wording to fit what I know about others, giving them a touchpoint to understand my point of view. The key to good communication is in the listening and in particular listening for nuance from the speaker. Because we HSPs are empathetic, we often listen to better understand how to communicate with our audience, whether one or many.

It is sad we are often not confident speakers. Because many of us are naturally quiet individuals, we tend not to get the reinforcement we need to become confident communicators. This does not mean we can't be excellent communicators. We have the inherent tools to do so. Because we grasp intuitively what our audience needs to hear and how it must be communicated, we strike deep into the heart of what good communication should be.

Communicating by paying attention, learning to observe who I'm communicating with, and being able to give feedback, I am mindful of the words I choose and the effects they have on my audience.

One of my greatest challenges as an HSM is to communicate in a starkly authentic way. Often I prioritize the listener over my own needs, anticipating what the listener is expecting and deviate from my own truth. It has been a life lesson for me to get the priority straight. I have the skills to speak, but I sometimes deviate on the message to please the listener.

Yet the more I lay straight the message, adhering to what is authentic for me, the more comfortable I feel, and ironically the better I am received. All HSPs should work to be/express more authentically their truth.

Empathy/Compassion

My ability to relate to others, feeling their joy and their pain, has made me an empathetic person. I have used this quality to be an empathetic leader at work and in my relationships with others. It is a very useful quality for building rapport with others and staying connected at a deep level. HSPs are naturally more empathetic; it is an end result of all the HSP characteristics.

I have been conscientious, a distinct HSP trait, my entire life—from my first school reports cards to work reviews and life in general. It expands beyond myself outward to others. As a thoughtful participant in my relationships, I am conscientious toward my partner's needs, mindful that this is more than just a quality; it is how you project into the world.

The cycle begins with us seeing "others," perceiving them through our sensory input and making a physical connection to them. We then begin the process of feeling the "others," the emotional carriers that provide more depth of information. This process involves internalizing, bringing their emotional content within our own framework, absorbing, observing and aiding us to understand "others." We can become bombarded with sensory data that may place us in a condition of overwhelm as we assume the verbal and nonverbal cues from this other person.

Next, we begin to become the "others," able in many ways to see the world from their point of view. This strong empathy allows us to become one with them, increasing our understanding of their needs and desires. This isn't some magical experience; it is something we all share. It's more work for most, but HSM/Ps, seem to do this naturally. The fact that so many HSPs are in the helping professions is no coincidence, and this trait is attributed to this ability. Empathy drives compassion, which drives a desire to help.

It makes us more vulnerable to the unscrupulous who prey on our giving nature in order to manipulate us. Nevertheless, the trait is overall a positive and humanitarian one, if not sometimes misunderstood.

Awareness

With a keen natural sense of observation of the world, our environment, both externally and internally, HSPs lay the groundwork for our uncanny awareness of life and self. Our ability to absorb the sensory input we receive draws into the lair of our deep processing and creates an increased awareness of the external world. This awareness grows the older we get, each new layer, like sediment on exposed rock. It builds our knowledge, creating a base for wisdom that others might miss.

I have always been emotionally aware of the environment. Being so makes me feel a bit more alive than most. I feel more keenly aware of myself, and the feelings of those around me making me a better observer and hopefully a better writer as a result. This characteristic maps to the HSP characteristic of processing more sensory data.

I am also a lover of all things sensual: music, art, theater, film, food, drink, intimacy, touch, taste, sight, and sound. I love quality over quantity. There is just something authentic about a quality sensual experience. Some people call it good taste. I call it fully embracing life. As an HSP there always was the concern about too much of a good thing, so, I add, I try to do this in moderation.

I like to think that I'm more creative in how I take all these observations and make conclusions based on how I process the information. This is especially useful in writing. Over the years it has made my observations unique. This relates to the deep processing HSPs do.

Somehow we HSPs find that we are often ahead of our time. Not necessarily because of genius or a rare special intelligence, but by the sheer power of observation and deep processing. The odd thing is that many HSPs are shy, cautious creatures who fail to test some of their best and boldest hypotheses. The external testing brings confirmation and confidence, two things we often sorely lack. There is a certain spiritual side to this sensitivity that allows HSPs to move more toward natural wisdom.

This natural wisdom is the foundation of true enlightenment, or now more fashionably called, awareness. We often hide our awareness because of our lack of confidence or maybe the brash boldness that seems to elude us. Consensus kills this type of growth, especially in HSPs, typically sheathed in self-deprecating resignation that there is nothing special about their thoughts or ideas.

The deeper thinking and empathy contribute to the inherent need to have spiritual awareness; to see beyond the physical and understand the purpose, meaning and the deep, deep emotions of love and joy. It is the drive for harmony in my life, helping me to rise above my baser self and see myself in an existential and spiritual way in the world around me.

Finally, the greatest of all these HSP traits is the gift of intuitive insights. Intuition is a really deep observation of subtle sensory inputs and works on anything from business trends, football predictions, to understanding the subtle nuances of life, deciphering politics and getting to the root motive of others. It's not always correct and the more specific the insight, the harder to get it right. Often it's just a feeling, a sense, an understanding. The hardest part is learning to trust that intuition. There's more than appears on the surface—like most HSPs.

I, for one, see this as our special gift, our great contribution to human society and survival of the species. The threats to humanity are not so much physical as they are spiritual or existential. The world needs gentle, thoughtful, and innovative HSPs.

All these qualities have served me well. Some are valued by others, some are less valued; I value them all. Above all, being an HSM has made me unique and at times, a pariah. Some people don't know what to do with me, others embrace the differences and accept me for who I am. I have learned to be careful about whom I choose as friends and keep my inner circle small.

I am grateful for the qualities that I now see as powerful gifts given to me via a combination of genetics and environment. I discover more qualities every year and embrace them.

CHAPTER 14:

HSMs in Everyday Life

Do Sports and the HSP Males Mix Well?

As I have gotten older, I have mellowed on my love of all things related to the University of North Carolina athletics. I never attended the school but was born in the state: alumni via propinquity. My children truly feared a Carolina loss and often hid when they could see things going south. We laugh about it now, but I'm sure it was terrifying seeing the old man rant at amplitude for a missed free throw or a squandered scoring opportunity.

That was about as freewheeling with my emotions as I got. And I would let loose. Today, not so much; I am more tempered by age and realize, wisely, the goings-on of twenty-something athletes is nothing to get bent up about. And in my reflection, I wonder, as an older HSP male, why I allowed this to happen in the first place.

As sports fans, HSP or non-HSP, we are tragically tied to the fates of our teams. A fan is a fanatic and typically emotionally vested in the outcome of their favorite team's performance. We all become emotional; we all channel the inner HSP, full of rich, deep, and strong emotion viewing our sporting event of choice. Of course, fueled by alcohol or some other such social lubricant, we can intensify that emotion, making the small fan into a large and emboldened *fan*.

As HSMs, we can overcome our reluctance for emotional public display by joining in with other like-minded fans, shout and scream, rant and rave, and feel like part of something bigger. Perhaps for some HSMs, the roar of the crowd, the rowdiness of seatmates, the blaring bands, the PA blasting is a bit much in person, but safer to follow on the big screen at home, with a touch of a remote control.

Even still, I have often found that moments of heart-pounding sports action can find me slipping into another room, waiting on the outcome, signaled by the crowd's roar or silence to clue me in on what happened. Not being able to watch is strangling my support, I suppose, but makes it easier. Nevertheless, being a fan can be linked to feelings of well-being, happiness, less loneliness and isolation. Giving you community gives you a common communication language, an inter-generational connection, and the freedom to express emotion in public with reckless abandon, especially for men.[128] Maybe even more so for HSMs.

It really is like being in love. The range of emotions is almost identical—up and down with a team's fortunes, heartbreak, and ecstasy, winning and losing, sometimes all in a neat two-hour drama or a months-long season. And at the end of the season, if your team makes the final round of action, you either soar into the following year with a victory or sink with disappointment in a loss that lingers and is re-triggered with every SportsCenter highlight or YouTube video clip. It can be agonizing.

So why would HSM males put themselves through this? Typically, we are not the best athletes. We are not often drawn to competitive sports, as players or as viewers (alright, maybe more of the latter). Why do some of us do this? A place to vent, be aggressive, and walk out with all of your teeth.

Like most young males, HSM males are socialized into sport. It is the manly thing to do, to engage in competition, to test our strength against other males, to foster the warrior within and to progress toward a masculine archetype, defined by our culture. It is the staging area to grow the ambiguous boy and transform him into the man society expects him to be. Right.

As HSMs we generally refrain from violence as a first resort, but watching particularly violent sports, such as hockey, football, and even baseball seems to be the antithesis of what HSMs find entertaining. But you can't take the HSM out of the context of the culture we reside in. In America, football is religion, and no one can say this sport is not about snot knocking violence. We hoot and holler about a great hit, a bone-jarring tackle, or a bruising run by a halfback.

Many studies have shown that violence modeled, even for adults watching away from the action, can lead to violence away from the game.[129] Where does that lead HSM sports fans? Is this some vestige of our early childhood training? Are we proving our manhood by watching or participating in such games or are we simply getting along to save face with our male cohorts? It doesn't seem to make sense, but I know there are many among us, myself included, who pass through this ritual every Fall.

As George Orwell describes it, "Serious sport has nothing to do with fair play. It is bound up with hatred, jealousy, boastfulness, disregard of all rules, and sadistic pleasure in violence. In other words, it is a war without shooting."[130] How can we not be affected by it? Where is the balance?

As for the athletes involved, how many of them are HSMs? If HSMs are 20 percent of the population, it stands to reason there have to be some college and pro athletes represented. If so, how does that affect their sports performance? Does criticism mess with their heads, hence, impact performance? Do they get *too* emotional during losses or during stages of defeat that impact the team? Or are they more passionate, more driven, and more conscientious about their game and tend to excel?

I can't imagine there being any mutual exclusivity to being sensitive or highly sensing and athletic ability. In fact, many top athletes are not above showing that sensitivity in reflection of a completed game/match/meet.

I point to athletes who show a great deal of passion and compassion, as possible HSM model athletes: Michael Jordan, Tim Tebow, LeBron James, and Tiger Woods.

I still love sports.

Regardless of where you stand on this topic, since HSM males are a wide spectrum, and yes, I believe HSP attributes range from moderate sensitivity to extreme sensitivity, we males can fall anywhere on that strata. I can't speak for the whole, but I can say for me, I still love sports. I play less of the team variety these days, but I love to participate when I can. I watch my teams and vicariously enjoy their success and failures. It puts me in touch with something greater, a sense of belonging (even remotely), and I relish that.

But I wonder sometimes how I can be so variegated with HSM interests—art, music, writing, spirituality, and enjoying the natural wonders around me—and still be drawn to combative, competitive, and yes, sometimes a violent world of sports. Perhaps it's my type O blood. A friend told me that type O is an ancient hunter-gatherer blood type. Maybe that predisposes me toward some instinctive bloodletting activities.

HSMs and the Workplace

After taking an early retirement from a good job in corporate America, starting and failing at my own business, relocating to help out my mother, I am thinking about getting back in a corporate job.

Now, to be honest, I never liked working in corporate America and never thought I'd ever have to go back there to find employment. But life has its interesting way of steering you in different directions, sometimes in a circular fashion. Now that I am back pursuing a regular job again, I have given a lot of thought to what kind of job or job environment best suits me as a highly sensitive man. And more broadly, what kind of environment is best for HSPs, regardless of the industry?

Lately, I've seen more and more articles published about the trend toward looking for more empathetic and emotionally intelligent workers. There seems to be some movement in favor of the soft skills that HSPs tend to naturally have and are most comfortable using at work and home. This makes for interesting TED talks, but where exactly are these types of jobs? It seems almost impossible to find an IT firm—a competitive, high stress and almost soulless job—that would even consider these newly valued traits, the qualities which HSPs bring to the table.

As an IT manager, I know I brought a penchant for clear communication, empathy for staff, emphasis on esprit de corps, a genuine interest in staff as people, and a recognition that we all rise or fall together. I was well liked by my teams and respected by other managers within the organization. Like most HSPs, I valued deeper meaning in the job, more harmony, and cohesiveness within the team and a desire to get the job done right, even if it meant doing it more deliberately.

I enjoyed coaching my teams and enjoyed watching them grow and develop as the years went by. These are traits HSPs bring to management. I was most comfortable when my style was not constantly challenged or undue pressure was not placed on my teams and myself that I thought was unreasonable. I was fortunate for many years to report to a manager who valued my contributions and the management style I employed.

As deep thinkers and emotionally connected individuals, do HSPs make better managers or even better workers? I think the answer is clearly yes. Because we are more reflective, we naturally process more data and information more carefully, making us—if given the time—more accurate thinkers. We absorb more information, and although this may cause overwhelm if not given space and time to process, we can analyze more data points than most and formulate a clearer big picture perspective. Because of our enormous potential for empathy, we also tend to be more nuanced in our handling and dealing with people. Not only does this make us better team members, but especially better leaders.

Our characteristics such as high perception, empathy, focus on justice and fairness, loyalty, our passion, creativity, and generosity collectively make us almost the perfect employee. Yet where is the box on the application form where you can check off for HSP? Nowhere. Largely because we are often seen by non-HSPs as individuals with singular HSP characteristics in the negative, such as high sensitivity, or overly emotional, or prone to overwhelm, we get a bad rap. However, the perspective is entirely different when the collective of our HSP characteristics is seen as a whole. The prejudice against HSPs is based on ignorance, pure and simple. In fact, I think companies should be seeking out HSPs for three main reasons: creativity, loyalty, and empathy.

How we perform as employees in the workplace is a function of the environment itself. Given encouragement, space, and time, we are among the most gifted, most talented staff any company can have. Yet if the environment is toxic, at least to HSPs, we can wilt like flowers in a waterless vase. Seems simple enough.

The notion of HSPs as a personality type is gaining traction among those in the world of psychology and the world of the arts, but doesn't seem to be making a whole lot of headway in corporate HR or in management suites. Much still needs to be done to promote the benefits or hiring and nurturing of HSPs and training managers on how to get the most from the highly sensing worker. There is no question we are represented in numbers (20 percent of the population), and straddle across racial, gender, and ethnic lines. If 20 percent of your employees are underperforming because your environment sucks, whose fault is that? And what is that telling you about you?

For HSMs and HSPs, because of all things discussed in this chapter, we tend toward working in areas where competitiveness, aggressiveness, and high energy are at a minimum, which of course relegates many of us to low demand, low paying jobs. Sad but true. Is it possible to have high meaningfulness at work and high pay? Do these two things ever meet in the work vortex?

Yes, I think it can be found, but needs a more considerate approach to job seeking. It requires more flexibility and more willingness to do an exhaustive search, but I believe it can happen.

Here are some tips on finding the best fit jobs for HSMs.

- First, be very clear about the qualities and characteristics of the job best suited for your personality. You may not get them all in a job, but rank the ones that are deal breakers. This is an important preliminary step. Remember, you will not be able to control everything in environments in which you are not either the owner or the site manager.

- Recognize your unique personality characteristics. Not all HSPs are great artists or brilliant intuitive thinkers, but as a general rule, we have patterned characteristics that are native to HSP personalities. Value them as currency. This will be a part of your resume and calling card.

- Next, look hard and define your strengths, regardless of how often you may not see them listed on job descriptions. You may have a strength that is needed, but is not listed; nevertheless, it may give you a decided edge. Access your weaknesses as well. Determine a strategy to handle them in the workplace either with training, developing new skills, or sometimes just writing them off. Don't fret about not being ideal. The latter strategy may be useful for HSPs because we tend toward perfectionism.

- Look for employers who value employee health, wellness, and diversity. Award-winning companies in those areas tend to have happier employees. Avoid companies with reputations for toxic environments for HSPs—dynamic, ambiguous, stressful environments that value high energy over thoughtful, methodical, and nuanced modes of operation. You will not succeed there even if everyone you know has gone through that gauntlet and lived to tell about it. Nada.

- Think six degrees of separation; this is code for networking. You don't need to know the endpoint person (i.e., the hiring manager), just the one who knows the one who knows the one, etc. Finally, make it fun, like a scavenger hunt. Make a game of finding the hiring manager. A resume will never, ever, ever present you has a human being. A brief talk will.

- Finally, boldly go forward. Value yourself and know that you will thrive in the right environment. Most worker bees don't know this. You do because you are a highly sensing person.

Politics

The Highly Sensitive Male and Politics: Where Do We Gravitate?

Lately, we have been cast into an incredulous political battle. Particularly interesting has been the run for the presidency over the last several cycles. I have never seen such a time of political backstabbing, muckraking, outright lying with no consequences, and general political nastiness.

No one wants to discuss real issues; no one seems to care. It's all about showboating the TV ratings with outrageous claims and stunts. HSPs hate this crap. Because of our empathic nature, we hate seeing people, regardless of their political views, get their asses handed to them on a platter during a debate. It's unpleasant, unsettling, and unsavory. Most of us just tune it out. It offers no value, no redemption, and no reason to focus our attention. In fact, it's very embarrassing. Yes, we are embarrassed for the country.

So where do HSMs tend to gravitate politically? I don't have any study, survey, or empirical evidence for this, but I surmise we lean mostly toward the party that shows the most heart. We are a liberal-leaning, progressive thinking lot and likely hang out with folks who share our joint, collective empathy toward our fellow man and the planet. That's doesn't sound Republican or Libertarian to me these days.

The Highly Mythical Empathic Party or What is Red and Blue with a Little Bit of Green?

If a political party existed that HSPs found most appealing it would be, perhaps, a lot blue, maybe some red, and a little green. This would be the Empathic Party, a fictitious collection of people who actually give a damn about the population of this country, and I mean the entire population of this country. This used to mean the Democratic Party, the party of the people, the party of equality, the party of the middle class.

The State of Our Country Since Reaganomics: The Rule of the Reptilian class

So what happened? In a word, Reaganomics. The election of Ronald Reagan in 1980 completely changed the dynamic of political discourse in this country. The civility and bipartisanship of days before were promptly washed away, and a new political agenda was foisted on the American populace. Ronald Reagan, a make-believe cowboy, rode into town and with him, a gang of elitist, reptilian-brained operatives began to use the politics of survival, making politics no longer a profession of discourse and debate, but rather guerrilla warfare. Do you remember Lee Atwater? How about the manipulation of media with Roger Ailes?

This strategy shut down an era of sensible politics and occasional collaboration from both sides of the aisle. From then on it was war. Character assassination was the new norm. Political intrigue devolved into the swampy depths as opponents were branded as un-American for disagreeing with the new jingoism of the Reagan era.

The destruction of the middle class had begun, as with the diminished role of government as a moderating force against greed and self-aggrandizement; the big wheels ran amok.

This move toward what I term *reptilian politics* is really about where the focus of political thought originates. It is clear to me that most of this "thought" emanates from the reptilian part of the human brain, the part that focuses on raw emotion, on the survival of the individual, and the destruction of anything that gets in the way of that motive.

You can cap that with intellectual neo-cortex rationalization and make it look like its deep and important, but in the end, it's the same driver that has kept us in a regressed mode for millennia, the consequences of which are damage to ourselves, our climate, and our future. Think war, poverty, famine, and concentration of wealth in the hands of the most powerful and greedy individuals.

This has led us to our most current crisis: an Empathy Deficit Disorder.[131] We are growing less and less empathetic, and it shows in our politics. I mean really, Donald Trump has been polling the support of about 40 percent of the population, and probably many more who can't or won't admit that he represents their beliefs. We are in a serious crisis.

Where HSMs and HSPs Can Make a Difference

In a 2014 Pew poll about empathy in politics, liberals and conservatives were asked about how important certain values were to teach to children.[132] Conservatives focused on religion, obedience, and hard work. Liberals cared more about tolerance, empathy, curiosity, and creativity. These are traits mostly shared by HSPs and are characteristic of individuals with a high degree and capacity for empathy. This would include, of course, highly sensitive males.

Although we make up only 20 percent of the population, HSPs need to make our voices heard. That's hard for us, especially in this combative political climate. But we are that ocean wave powerfully and relentlessly smashing against the rocky shore gently shaping and altering the landscape of the shoreline with persistence and consistency. It does not require that we change the world immediately and drastically, but our influence can be gentle, yet powerful through our art, our words, our wise counsel, and the emotion that empathy brings. Sometimes a whisper is as effective as a shout when heard by the right ears.

This is where the mammalian brain kicks in. The emphasis is on the collective as opposed to the often selfish motivations of an individual focused society. The collective society focus is greater in terms of survival of the species than the almost desperate reptilian need for individual survival.

Fulfilling the Evolutionary Mission

Our purpose (HSPs) is to warn the species, to calm the impulsive and reckless warrior heart, and offer good counsel to our leaders, and be good stewards and leaders ourselves when placed in those positions. We are the balance and the early warning system for the species. It is not a trivial responsibility. Future generations may depend on our reining the havoc wreaked on our society by a one-dimensional policy that disregards the future for the ever-present quarterly result. This is a madness that can be tamed with the aid of the collective wisdom of our HSP males and females. It's time to gently kick some shit and make ourselves noticed.

Film and Art and HSMs

What makes film especially meaningful to Highly Sensitive Men? I think it starts with the idea that film is the most complete art form. It combines sound and sight, light and motion, emotion and feeling all into a neat package. It allows the viewer to become the omniscient observer with a dynamic viewpoint, giving us the opportunity to take both passive and active roles in the unfolding of a story. It can inspire and uplift and allow us to vicariously experience living a fantasy through the characters, plot, and action. What's not to like about that?

Films cover a panorama of emotion from sadness to anger, love to loss, joy and fulfillment, horror and surprise. We respond as if the events are real, with engagement that hangs on the precipice of mutual experience with the characters. This is a great opportunity for naturally empathetic people to explore emotions within a safe and controlled environment. We respond to the sequence of images flashed upon the screen in story format and get lost, I dare say, hypnotized, by what our eyes and ears behold. It may be the greatest thing to happen to storytelling since the campfire.

Watching movies does have a direct psychological effect on the viewer. Studies show that there are distinct physiological responses to plot points within the story.[133] Whether it's increased blood pressure or heart rate, tears or heavy breathing, we have all felt the visceral effects of being at the movies. Movies can have positive effects on the viewer from a cognitive standpoint. You may see something inspiring or moving, and this reaction can contribute to positive feelings you may have toward yourself or others.

This phenomenon can be triggered by what scientists refer to as *mirror neurons* in the brain.[134] These neurons help us mirror the activities of others and can contribute largely to social cooperation and encouraging empathy. This sounds exactly like something that highly sensitive people are drawn to, which is why I think HSPs in general, like myself, enjoy the movie experience. HSPs are thought to draw heavily on mirror neurons to create our great empathetic nature.

Now wrap this all around with an emotionally charged movie soundtrack, and you have an experience unlike anything else in entertainment or education. Studies show the emotional effects of music in movies on the audience, which those of us enthusiastic movie fans have known for years.[135] A sound score carefully and artfully done can elevate a story and film to heights of emotional vibration that cements the experience for all viewers. What's really interesting about the score is that it often rides just below conscious awareness. We know it's there, just like we know there's someone sitting two rows down from us, but we don't consciously care. A good score, I believe, affects and guides our subconscious more than we think. It charges and cues the emotion centers within, which ultimately can make a movie memorable or not.

What kind of movies do men prefer? Well, in a word: action. Most men are looking for action, sex, and nudity.[136] It appears too much like the primal objective takes over for men in the movie house. Men like "real men" in the movies, doing real men stuff, which often involves blowing stuff up, driving fast cars, or bedding beautiful women. Although a couple of those sound interesting to me, they can't hold my attention for two hours. I hope as young men mature they will expand their horizons a bit, and start taking plot and characterization into account, but perhaps, that's asking too much.

As an HSP male, I find myself a little bit out on an island. I like a good plot, a good story, good directing, writing, and acting and in the end, something that moves the emotional meter. Relatability is key to me. I will add, I want to walk out of the theater thinking about the movie over coffee, or dinner. I don't care about seeing a single car sacrificed or a super-hero demolish a city single-handedly. I want the movie to, well, move me emotionally, viscerally, and create a lasting memory. I suspect most HSMs feel the same.

I don't like trashing whole genres of film. Art is art, whatever form it takes, and I begrudgingly admit some great action movies have been made and yes, I enjoyed them. But the corporate cookie cutter approach to film making that basically takes the Pavlovian approach, if a dog salivates at a bell, we are going to make movies about bells and bells only, doesn't work for me. Many others agree, including producer, Stephen Simon, who has been an advocate for bringing back character and plot-driven movies. See his book, *Bringing Back the Old Hollywood.*

Another question is if there are HSMs in the movie industry. Of course, it's an art form. As we've already discussed, HSMs are and can be sensitive artist types. I dare say that a majority of male actors in Hollywood, perhaps worldwide, are HSMs. I have no scientific proof of that but map the profile of being an HSM to being an actor, and well, they overlap pretty nicely. At least that applies to the really good actors, directors, etc. (pardon my smugness here).

Are HSMs portrayed often in movies? Yes, but not nearly enough. Some of the best movies, the male protagonists have been to some extent, sensitive men. I'm thinking of movies like *Forrest Gump, Dead Poets Society, Dances with Wolves, Field of Dreams, It's a Wonderful Life, Good Will Hunting*, and the list extends back into the history vaults at TCM. What you often see in movies is the male character showing some sensitivity as a means for character growth, but often not explored deeply enough (as we HSMs want). Hell, even John Wayne played a sensitive guy in *The Quiet Man*, but couldn't get out of the movie without a half hour fistfight with his nemesis.

I'm sure back then the male audience would have abandoned the theater if he didn't start slugging away at some point.

* HSMs and Money – The Law of Distraction

As HSPs, we inherently understand the fundamentals of money acquisition and possess many of the characteristics needed to acquire money, but more often than not, refuse to play the game or participate because of the taxing nature on our personalities. Let's look at this.

By nature, HSPs are cautious creatures, which makes us less likely to be willing to engage in behavior that risks assaulting our sensibilities. We are in many ways risk averse. However, according to Dr. Tracy Cooper, about 30 percent of HSPs are high sensation seeking individuals (see previous chapter). So, we are not entirely a tribe of non-risk takers. Those high sensation seeking HSPs are like other risk takers, looking for novel experiences, able to disinhibit long enough to engage in risky behavior and get bored easily with the same old, same old.

Why don't more HSPs become prominent in business or startups or in the art of making money? Why aren't we front and center on getting promotions at work, implementing our ideas in the marketplace, making sales, pitching our ideas to investors, sticking our necks out there, and risking everything for an idea that has money-making potential? Oddly, I don't think it's the risk that factors in here.

One has to consider the nature of business or the nature of making money. One is either in the business of labor creation or in the business of labor offering. The motive of all business is to make a profit for the enterprise. Economic purists argue that this is a noble and time-honored task. To profit in a business is to be efficient and innovative—two things HSPs are fairly good at. To profit in business is to be able to provide rewards to shareholders and owners and to perpetuate the business as an entity.

Much like evolutionary survival, a strong, profitable business thrives and continues. And much like a true reflection of Darwin's evolution of species, modern, capitalistic business must compete to survive. Survival becomes the prime objective. Think of crushing competition, dominating the marketplace, and hoarding resources; this is what we prize in our culture. It's what we deem as winning (watching the scoreboard).

This applies equally to individuals at a microeconomic level, too. It comes back to how we earn, acquire, and accumulate money. It's how things get done, and it's rampant in our culture. There is a little lechery in any business purely out to make money, in spite of high moral posturing with mission statements and company visions. Does this put off HSPs? Surely, for some of us. Does it intimidate us? Quite possibly, for many of us. Do our collective moral compasses steer us away from being business "savvy," and draw away from the whole proposition of making money? Well if you think about, social Darwinism, an unwritten credo of modern big business, is so non-HSP. I doubt this is how HSPs define winning.

What drives entrepreneurs? Most sources agree that successful entrepreneurs are risk takers, highly confident, and have a love for learning new things.[137] They are also wired for failure resiliency, perhaps aided by an undying passion for their endeavor and a high degree of adaptability and tenacity. In addition, they display great social skills, like networking for results, money management skills, which require an "it's just business" attitude, self-promotion, and charisma.

How does that match up with generalized HSP characteristics? In some places—well. We are creative and innovative thinkers, and as noted, some of us like risk. We love to learn and appreciate the novelty. Where we fall short are those areas where quick decision-making, supreme confidence, the gift of bullshitting our way into someone else's pocketbook without guilt, and a focus on output with an inward drive on self-aggrandizement.

In other words, welcome to ego El Supremo. It's rare to find a consciously aware billionaire, maybe even rarer to find an HSP billionaire.

So are we HSPs doomed to being poor or at least living a frugal life, because of some ineptness or inability to override our moral convictions to make "good" money? Is there an alternative universe that allows for doing the right thing and becoming wealthy as a result? Really, folks, is there something inherently wrong about making money that makes money distasteful and disgusting?

Somehow, we have placed a value judgment on something that in and of itself is neutral. Money is simple energy potential. It's an agreed upon denomination for exchange of goods and services and represents potential energy.

By the age of seven money habits are formed in children that will last them a lifetime.[138] Children learn their attitudes toward money from their parents. Being the sensitive, intuitive, and inquisitive types we are, HSPs no doubt pick up on many subtle cues from our parents that other children might miss. "We can't afford that," "that's too expensive," or "easy come, easy go," might carry extra influence on HSPs because of the added emotional content our deep processing might add.

Because money has so many emotional implications in our lives, we HSPs may grasp significance in terms of lack or abundance depending on how our parents framed money in their lives. In addition to the discomfort of acquiring money, this may help shape HSPs' world view of money in their own lives. Or conversely, HSPs can override these apprehensions about money, in part to an upbringing that emphasized confidence in money acquisition and success. Since money is our cultural barometer of success, an early belief in one's self-worth and confidence makes one more likely to become successful from a monetary standpoint, regardless of personality temperament or makeup.

I keep hearing over and over that HSPs tend to gravitate toward low wage earning jobs. In the end, is this a nature vs. nurture question? Is it our nature to go for easy flow, low paying jobs, or do we tend to move toward work that is part of familial or societal expectations and just gut it out? It appears that many HSPs avoid high profile money jobs because of the stress of it all. It doesn't mean we can't do it, as many of us have.

Maybe HSPs are so laid back that we only prefer low paying jobs and forego the high price of high wage jobs. Perhaps, generally, we tend toward simple life situations, with lots of quiet time, less money, but more personal freedom. If you follow our worries, you will see where our priorities are: ensuring downtime, being close to nature, having time for creativity, and getting personal peace. We then can smugly eschew the greed and selfishness of big profit jobs and business and revel in our low wage art gallery job or counseling job for a non-profit or writing a children's book (*that has sold millions of copies and been made into several blockbuster movies, re: J.K. Rowling*). It can happen.

Some things to ponder:

- Remember, in the end, it is more about balance. Do what you love, and the money will follow (a nod to Marsha Sinetar). It's more about right livelihood than money making anyway. The two can coexist, but let the livelihood call the money. I realize it's an ideal, but an ideal worth striving for and achieving.

- It's time to stretch boundaries and comfort zones. Create a business that benefits people that is sustainable (good business management), offers the best service, and pays attention to detail. Or write a book, make a film, create a song. Start with service in mind; it will eventually lead to money.

- Money is only energy. It's neutral. We as a culture overdramatize the nature of harnessing this energy. We make it seem so out of reach to the common man. It's not always about create labor vs. offer labor. I have always said money is like a river. Learn to carry your bucket to the river and you will drink. There will always be money/energy. There is no need to damn the river to get money; just carry a bigger bucket. I realize this is a simple abstraction, but sometimes you can see the picture before you paint the painting. That's where I'm at. As I sit here writing this book I can see the painting. In the meantime, ponder the metaphor.

- Knowledge is power, not money. Abundance and prosperity are different things than accumulation and hoarding. One is about all that *is*; the other is about all that *isn't*. Wall Street will never understand that distinction. Don't play their game, you will always lose.

Nice Guys Finish Where Exactly?

In America, we tend to see the personality characteristic of kindness (or niceness) as a weakness and not a strength—in men. With our jingoistic fueled capitalistic attitude we praise the notion that humans are basically selfish, self-serving creatures and revere those who make it to the top of the heap, generally stepping over everyone in their way. Altruism, kindness, and niceness are seen as fundamentally weak traits, perhaps meted out once in a while to the less fortunate, but generally not to be prized. It saddens me that over the last twenty years or so, we have adopted this unfortunate attitude, especially with regards to men and their cultural roles.

The reality is that collaboration and kindness are basic survival skills. Without them, humankind would have been disposed of many millennia ago. Without "niceness" or the ability to put others first or the interest of the group ahead of one's own needs, we could not have been able to build the civilization that sustained our species. This key interactive ability became the precursor to "nice." Studies are beginning to bear out this idea that being the aggressive alpha dog is not the most efficient or effective way to succeed, lead, or attract a mate.[139] In the end, in spite of cultural biases against it, niceness is necessary and good.

HSMs are generally considered to be nice guys with our non-aggressive, gentler, kinder nature framed within a masculine exterior. Certainly not all HSMs fit this description, but I think because of our thoughtful, considerate personalities, we tend to be lumped into the nice guy bucket more often than not. But what really is a nice guy?

Niceness is measured on personality scales as agreeableness. The characteristics most associated with niceness are: trust of others, compliant and easy going, unselfish, easily satisfied, modest, and sympathetic.[140] All great qualities. There's also a downside of niceness. Sometimes niceness leads to conflict avoidance and lack of problem-solving skills because of confrontational ideation. It can also lead to self-effacing behaviors in the extreme, low confidence and other self-defeating behaviors.

The joke for years has been that nice guys always finish last. The reference is to dating or romantic prowess, "the nice guy dating effect"; women say they prefer nice guys, but wind up choosing bad boys. The term *nice guy* is often used to describe a male who is gentle, sensitive, compassionate, and vulnerable ... and other pejorative terms in lieu of masculinity.[141]

There are even some negative claims that nice guys are unassertive, dishonest, manipulative and passive-aggressive. In either case, the general rule is that nice guys are weak, ineffective, unattractive, and losers. This extends well beyond dating, into other areas of life. The perception is that niceness equates to submission so that in life the nice guy never gets the prize; whether it's an amour or promotion or being the quarterback, nice guys always lose. Does the research bear this out? The answer is no.

Let's begin with the idea of the Alpha male, the antithesis of the "nice guy." We consider the alpha male to be the top dog of the pack, a dominant, strong, self-centered individual who gets whatever he wants, the dominant player in the group.

Dominance starts at the hormonal level.[142] The hormones influencing dominance are testosterone, cortisol, and oxytocin. Testosterone is the male hormone that influences male behavior in many ways, including physical prowess and aggressiveness. Cortisol is the stress hormone, which kicks in to create active behaviors, and finally oxytocin, the love bonding hormone. Surprised? Studies have shown that most alphas are not the brash talkers and braggarts we expect from alphas, but instead are good listeners and are not always physically intimidating.[143] They are good social connectors and can be mild-mannered as well. They almost sound like closet nice guys with a slight edginess to them.

Most alphas focus on accomplishment and goal fulfillment, which requires a certain degree of "niceness" to get the cooperation of others to deliver desired results. Many accomplished CEOs fall in the nice guy category, such as the founders of Costco, Starbucks, Zappos, the heads of IKEA, Patagonia, Ben and Jerry's, creating great company cultures, leading teams into becoming successful companies, and never losing the nice guy persona.[144] So, nice doesn't have to mean ineffectual or weak or unsuccessful. To the contrary, it may be the only real way to achieve sustainable success via cooperation (nice guy) vs. competitiveness (bad boy).

Alphaism is not gender confined either. Alpha females are prominent in our more egalitarian society. There are indications of the collapse of the old line alpha male strawman that has been the dominant mode for centuries. The economic and societal implications are profound for new roles that men can and should play in society. A lot of talk these days suggests that more and more men are assuming the beta role in the family and the larger society. Now let's be clear, the beta role is not the exact opposite of the alpha.[145] The term for that would be the omega. Omegas are in effect the weak, ineffectual, women-hating male we associate now with betas.

Betas are complementary to alphas. Betas (perhaps uber nice guys) are cooperative, emotionally available, relationship savvy, and conscientious about everything they do. They are good team players and do not abdicate their masculinity by portraying this role.

Alpha, Beta, Omegas—where do HSMs fit in? I suppose HSMs can be any of the above; good, conscientious alphas, cooperative and team-playing betas or even distorted and warped omegas. The environment, upbringing, and genetics all play a role in shaping personality, and like the general population, this individual encoding can enhance or diminish fundamental HSP characteristics.

One of the best strategies for success for men is to adopt some of the best characteristics of the ideal alpha, focusing on what is termed the prestigious male—one who accomplishes goals in a general way.[146] To balance that driving goal-seeking behavior, there is a need to add another component, that of the generous giver. In studies where females rate overall attractiveness of males, the prestigious generous male was seen as the most attractive.[147] What this implies is that being a nice guy can and does work, if coupled with effective goal achieving. I even believe the attractiveness factor can be generalized to the overall population, which can be a new cultural norm. The nice guy alpha, a point of strength and decency. A true leader.

Is this another leadership opportunity for HSMs? Showing the larger male population that characteristics we come by naturally are things men can learn and practice. Perhaps moving forward, a few more studies, more "wins" for this philosophy in business, sports, entertainment, etc., can get some attention on the nice guy personality and demonstrate that nice guys don't always finish last.

Here are some suggestions on what we can do to promote this new male approach:

- Call me old fashioned but being a gentleman never really goes out of style. Practice this not only with women but with family, friends, and strangers. Being a gentleman doesn't have to be in the traditionalist role, which implies a strong protector. But think of the word: gentle man. Gentleness in this sense implies control, control of strength and channeling it for good. Politeness goes a long way, too. One can be direct and truthful and still be tactful and diplomatic. Humans are programmed to search for friends or foes; being nice will make you more friends and being a gentleman will add some dignity and class to your public persona. This is not about degrading the feminine. It is about complimentary behaviors that incorporate niceness and kindness with strength and gratitude.

- Model the new male. There is no weakness in niceness. The perception that being the dominant alpha is always the best way to get things done just doesn't work anymore, not in a broader perspective. Too many old-style alphas and wanna-be alphas make an edgy society. Leadership and dominance are not the same things.

- Quit tacitly—or for that matter, directly—supporting the aggressive alpha personality types. Don't vote for them, don't do business with them and, ladies, don't encourage them. We all deserve better than letting these clowns dominate headlines, politics, sports, and our lives. Finally, don't teach our young boys to grow up to be the old alpha model type of men.

- If you are a leader, lead by example. Show the world your inclusion and diversity attributes, your creativity, and risk-taking, your ethical practices, show your support of work/life balance and deliver gratitude, respect, and recognition to those you lead.

- Let's try to elevate some nice guy heroes. Really, does every hero have to be a badass action figure? Can't decency and kindness against evil and greed win a few of the battles, too? The dramatic tension is so much greater—the underdog versus the top dog. Support film, art, and books that support this notion.

- And, finally, don't be ashamed of being a nice guy. Nice guys can and do finish first. At least you have evolution on your side.

CHAPTER 15:

Relationships and What to Expect

I admit it; I'm a hopeless romantic. But as love lives go, mine has been less than spectacular. As of late, I have come to wonder if there is something innately, hopelessly, and yet ineptly romantic about my approach. Is it my selection of femmes or femme fatales or, at a core level, is it my personality type that drives me recklessly into these failed liaisons?

I appreciate the chase, I enjoy the anticipation of the reward, and love the women, but somehow a string of broken relationships later, two failed marriages, and now a lack of explanation in my choices, I wonder how hopelessly romantic can one get. How does being a highly sensitive male play a role in all of this? Let's see.

Getting What You Want or Getting What You Get

In the pursuit of love, one either gets what one wants or gets what one gets. In other words, how much does fantasy versus reality play into the entire mate-getting game. I have always felt that who we are attracted to is largely an unconscious decision, most of which is a product of our environment, our culture, and perhaps our DNA. Chemistry, as they say, either happens or it doesn't. Love experts say we should be as specific as possible about what we want, but it is what we desire that often drives our decisions. And that, again, is largely deeply buried under the hood. What we want and what we desire are often in opposition.

With that said, how does this affect strategy in the pursuit of love? Well, for most men, especially most non-HSP males, this is simply a law of averages, a zero-sum game. You pursue as many females as possible, and at some point, your mate magically appears in your life. You take your lumps and you move on. Sometimes you get what you want, and sometimes you get what you get.

For HSMs, because of the way we experience love, this strategy has to be balanced a bit differently.

The Rise and Fall of the Romantic Arc

Because HSMs feel emotions more deeply, with deeper expectations—and if things don't work out—deeper heartaches, HSP males must expect that to risk more in love, one understands that the joy, the hurt, and the possible ecstasy will be greater than perhaps any other emotion we feel. This is the romantic arc that we are all bound to but often is more difficult for HSPs, male or female, to deal with in love matters. As Dr. Elaine Aron suggests, it is important to develop some emotional regulation to help moderate the often roller coaster-like ride along the arc of love.[148]

The Female Paradox

Compounding things even more is what I call the female paradox or even the female prerogative. I know this is going to be controversial, but women often state in surveys that what they expect in a mate, especially a male mate, is a sensitive, feeling guy who is honest, passionate, romantic, kind, and with a great sense of humor. Sounds great so far, doesn't it? This description is almost a perfect template for an HSM. But as I've often found out, the hardwiring for the female ideal looks more like a Neanderthal: muscular, confident, aloof, with an arched brow, built for the hunt and dressed in white armor.

The paradox still lives, even in modern times. That leaves HSP males getting to play the role of empathetic brother, rather than champion or lover. I don't fault women for this hardwiring, but recognize that for HSMs looking for female affection, one is going to have to look much longer and be more selective to find a compatible mate—one who gets you.

Looking for Love or Letting Love Look for You

So where does one look for love if you are an HSM? Online dating sites are really popular right now, but rarely are there any sites that can take into account the HSP personality type. Because HSPs are very observant and can ferret out nuances in information, you might expect that we would be good at the selection process on dating sites. However, my experiences have been less than satisfactory.

We HSPs are often drawn to people who are not necessarily good for us. For example, we tend to gravitate toward people with problems; this is part of our empathetic personality type. To compound this, people with problems are drawn to us.[149] Not exactly a recipe for success. This conundrum can be very draining, very frustrating, and a prelude to heartache. Dr. Judith Orloff describes these *emotional vampires* as people who will take advantage of our empathic nature and pretty much suck the life out of us.[150] The odd thing is that we will often allow this to happen, perpetuating the idea that we can somehow change these people. Of course, we can't, and although it makes for good sport, it always ends in some type of epic failure.

Sometimes it's best to let love look for you. Live your life, pursue your passions, hang out with people who make you feel comfortable and appreciated, and at some point, love will find you.

Where HSM Men Go Wrong

As HSMs, we often shoot ourselves in the foot—or as it were—the heart. Things we do wrong are: expecting romantic overtures always to be welcomed (incurable romantic); not fully understanding the male/female dynamic in all of its complexity and paradox; not projecting confidence or shall we say showing our inner Neanderthal; confusing our emotions, and sometimes being too external with them too early in the relationship, which of course, drives women crazy. Again, this requires some self-restraint and self-regulation.

The key is to be aware and mindful of the myriad of emotions you are feeling. Measure them out appropriately and cautiously and only to those who can appreciate your passion, your intuition, and your big heart. And if it does happen—the big rejection—allow yourself to grieve the loss, learn from the mistake, take time to be with yourself and regroup. Let that angst squeeze out of you without depleting you. Of all men, you will recharge again soon enough, more so than most. It is your nature and your life.

In Defense of Great Loves

This is not to say that HSMs are doomed to failed loves. I believe in great loves. We often settle for less, thinking there is no better. And perhaps, for most of the population, this will do. But as an HSM and a hopeless romantic, I am holding out for that great love, regardless of when she shows up in my life. I know she's out there. As one who loves deeply, I will need to find one who also can receive that kind of love, who can handle it. She doesn't have to be an HSP, and frankly, it would be in both of our interests that we are not alike completely. It adds to the edginess of love, the spark, the passion, and bonding of the yin and the yang.

Looking for That Special One

Are HSPs any better or luckier in love than non-HSPs? Because of our affinity to emotion, are we better lovers or more inclined to better, more loving relationships? You would think we'd be all-stars at love—compassionate, caring, and nurturing souls that we are.

The research doesn't seem to support this. According to Dr. Elaine Aron, we tend to be less happy in our romantic relationships. Simply put, we tend to be too idealistic, too caring; too easily focused on the needs of our partners that we often fail to get our own needs met. Since we are typically drawn to people who have problems, these people tend to drag us down into their own insular world, leaving us to abandon our needs in favor of theirs. This deep focusing on pleasing our mates is known as *mate sensitivity* or finding what pleases our love interests and giving them what they need at all costs.[151]

My own experiences, when it comes to love, bear this out. It's not that my selections were all bad; it's that I was badly suited to their needs and them to me. Yet someone in need almost always draws me in.

But what special needs do HSPs have in regard to garnering a fruitful and successful love relationship? For one, it is always best to spend some time determining what your needs are. Take the time and dwell deeply on this.

This process goes way beyond the physical and the initial attraction. Take time to get to know the other person. Know who they are at their core. It's easy to fall prey to the notion that the physical will overcome in some way any of the other components of a person's personality that are not clicking with you. That never works, no matter how good the physical relationship appears.

It's also important to set boundaries early on, on how much you give, how much you take. Locate the perimeters of those boundaries about respect, your privacy, your solitary time. Focus on how you communicate: the style, the intensity, the frequency. Note how sensitive they are to your sensitivity, if they accept your peculiarities, your intuitive ways, your skills of anticipation. Do they exploit your willingness to dive in on their problems; do they begin to focus only on their needs and minimize yours? Stay close to your intuition here. And by all means, get this on the table early.

You need a relationship that will bolster your self-esteem and build you up. If you find yourself creeping around on eggshells, every cracking egg should be a warning to you that the environment for love is not there, not for you.

If the "other" is a vampire, an emotion sucker, run like hell to the nearest exit. Note how you argue/disagree with the person, note how quickly it gets emotional, or worse yet, hysterical and or violent—either physically or verbally. These should all be big red flags. If the conflict becomes attacking and personal, then get out quickly. You *cannot* fix their underlying issues.

Being a hopeless romantic, an erotic idealist, does not make this any easier. The romantic part never prepares you for the practical matters of love. The day-to-day existence, the support when you are down, loving you between the poetic lines, understanding of your deep needs for space, for privacy, for emotional expression is the grind that a long-term relationship brings.

Then there is dealing with the inevitable conflict that living with someone brings. Our HSP penchant for the avoidance of conflict or shying away from blunt-speaking of truth, too often to avoid hurting our partner, will often bring accompanying accusations of lying when withholding our conflicted truth. To be honest or to hurt tumbles around in our heads, two options that typically slay us in our bewildering internal map. Conflict brings a disrobing of our idealized self, often cloaked in secrecy that sometimes reveals dark, deep warts, or exposes tender spots of vulnerability. Sometimes exposing our truth, lying deep within, withheld and festering, there comes a dark moment of realization, looking starkly at the reflection of who we are in the real world of romance.

What we are ideally suited for is the romancing, the conscientious lover part, the creative artistic part of love. We are not practical lovers, more often romantic dreamers who, once confronted with the real world, melt and fade away or leave, looking for that next impassioned high. Perhaps we love too much for our own good, addicted to the biochemical reaction of love, the brain-altering and heart-shaking love of first taste romance. Or we love the endorphin rush, the dopamine bomb, the oxytocin fix we all crave but rarely find.

Can Everywoman understand us enough to live and cope with our highly sensual natures? Does Everywoman match up to our idealistic constructs of the perfect woman? I think maybe we push through the existential pain of unrequited love, of idealized love, that seemingly we all walk through—the deep loneliness that our personality makes for us. Or is it just me?

I wonder if we should search for HSP lovers, those like us, who share our deep caring ways, our deep inner world, unless we cannot stand to be around someone like us. Would too many HSP characteristics slopping around in the tank make the whole engine guck up and freeze?

Finding the ideal lover is unique for all of us. Some will find their mates early on, stick with them, and mate for life. Maybe for others, it's the rebound of a second chance, the opportunity to learn and correct past mistakes. Then there are those who are seekers of experience—drunkards for love. We are intrepid souls who enter others' lives with good intent ("yes, this time, it's right"); we love them like no other and by circumstance or our own making, leave or move on, still yearning, still aching for perfect love.

In the wake of our search are those we touch in our lives, and because we are not heartless bastards, we don't leave them without a glance of what a real caring lover can be. But because of our betrayal, we stab them unintentionally, to loosen us from our bond, so that we, ever seeking, can move on. The life of a gypsy is a lonely one, and along the way, the fences all have barbed wire, leaving trace scars on our hearts.

No, don't date Everywoman, HSP men. You will likely fail unless she is a rare gem. You are not Everyman. You are both better and worse than that. Stephen Stills once said in a song, "If you can't be with the one you love, love the one you're with." I would add … until you find the right one. We are looking for that elusive unicorn of love that always sits at the edge of the horizon, where the sun is setting, silhouetted and motionless, directing you toward them. You need that special lover. They are rare indeed. You will have to look hard, but with diligence and persistence, you will meet your special one. She may be looking for you now. Have faith.

When the Primal Objective Goes Awry

Years ago, when I was working in corporate America, several of my friends and I would talk at lunch about the Primal Objective for men. We were all married or partnered at the time, and being men, sat around the table reminiscing about the days when the Primal Objective was our primary objective. The Primal Objective, of course, is the drive to reproduce and frankly is probably one of the primary drivers in much of male behavior.

For men, the Primal Objective is to mate with as many willing females as possible.[152] Men do the majority of pursuing with the females to satisfy this drive. Everything from improving social standing, increasing income, physical, and mental health, accumulating wealth, grooming, etc., have at their roots the Primal Objective.

The more desirable a mate to females, the likelier the female will select the man. As primitive as this is, this is how nature intended. It reminds me of a quote from Rupert Sheldrake, I think, who said that the human being is the delivery mechanism for DNA. The sum total of what we do is to spread our genetic information. Hence, the gene is responsible for the Primal Objective.

For women, the Primal Objective is the selection of the best possible mate within a group of suitors.[153] Individual preferences, notwithstanding, females select for the ability to aid in the raising of the young and provide assistance in raising said offspring. This may sound primitive, and a bit old fashioned or may not account for modern cultural norms, but at the impulse/drive level this pretty much sums up how it works.

This model does not put the female in a secondary position. As has always been the case, ideally, all mating behavior stems from female choice.[154] Women choose whom they mate with, men compete for selection, and the species continues. By this reckoning, women should own the process.

Men and women have different Primal Objectives, yet both supposedly produce the desired, mutually beneficial outcome. The drive for men to mate with as many partners as possible is so because of the lack of risk and commitment men have to make in reproduction. In an elemental way, they are free to pursue as many mates as they desire.

Yet, somehow, humans have evolved into fairly monogamous creatures—creating pair bonds to ensure success in progeny growth and development. It has worked fairly well for millennia. Not dependent on a single alpha male, lower-ranking males can compete with alphas by offering services to the females in exchange for mating preference and loyalty. It is a complex dance, filled with synchronicity, love, wine, and roses.

This has led through the ages to the current system of mating we experience now. But the fundamentals remain.

All would seem fine except for the fact that this system can go dark. Increasingly we see the exposure of the Primal Objective, especially in men, go uncontrolled and become a runaway and harmful drive. The consequences are a barrage of negative primal urges that create acts of rape, harassment, verbal and physical assault, incest, slavery, and misogyny.

What happens when the Primal Objective goes awry? Unchecked, it leads to enormous psychological and physical damage that perpetuates intergenerationally. Although women and girls are not the only victims, they are by far the largest target group.

A male movement needs to begin that join forces with groups like #Metoo to educate and train men on how to control runaway Primal Objective urges. What is needed is a greater awareness among men and empathy and understanding toward the plight that women share. Men need to learn to respect women and refamiliarize themselves with the way the selection process works. The focus should not be about shaming men for the urges, but rather to teach an appreciation and to understand the larger reproductive cycle, where the ultimate power/choice is with the female. Breaking away from the natural order has dire consequences.

How can HSMs help? HSP males make excellent leaders and inspirational models for other men in many ways. Our natural empathy and ability to process emotions will help us to reach men and show by example how to express feelings out in the open. Part of the problem is the inability to talk about the uncontrollable urges or the control issues many men have. This is not to say that all men are guilty of this behavior or that all HSP males are innocent of wrongdoing. Yet an element of the male community needs to step forward to ally with women to stop these transgressions. HSMs are good candidates because we need to lead the effort to combat toxic masculine destructiveness, not only for our sake but for the sake of all men and boys.

Understand our primal drives are necessary but need to be moderated to have a safe and understanding environment where the Primal Objective and modern romance can follow the natural order.

My Experiences

Just a few side notes on love and HSPs. Elaine Aron notes that for HSPs the issue sometimes comes down to the difference between attachment and love.[155] These two concepts are often confused. Attachment is generally about having certain needs met by another individual, i.e., sex, companionship, a sense of belonging. Attachment can last beyond the end of a relationship and can explain some of the sense of loss when relationships end badly. Love, on the other hand, is more about an attraction and unmistakable bond that creates a longing or desire for closeness, deep connection, and a strong desire to aid or help the individual. The two are often bound to each other, but only with love will you have both. If you are attached to someone, you are not always in love with them.

People tend to attach to HSPs easily. We are so focused on pleasing others, or at the very least meeting their needs, that our amours can easily attach to us because we meet their needs so efficiently. When relationships end with HSPs, there is often guilt and shame, as we often carry the burden of bearing the load of failed relationships. Of course, this is not true, but we are such conscientious lovers, that we see the failure of the relationships as a failure on our part. We love deeply and breaking up is like uprooting a tall pine tree from the fertile ground of deep emotion. We feel responsibility for the object of our affection even if we no longer have the original vibrant love we once shared with them. The root still runs deep, as does our empathy, and we care about the feelings of our partner.

It is true, as research suggests[156] that HSPs are easily bored with relationships and can find that what once was a wonderful love affair no longer interests us. Perhaps the emotional high that some of us thrive on wanes and we lose interest, or maybe more practically, the relationship, which once provided meaning, no longer does and we search elsewhere for that meaning. Meaningfulness for HSPs is very important, and meaningfulness in relationships runs very deep to our core. It isn't about the physical thrill, the visceral rush, the emotional high, which I think we intuitively know won't last; it's the deep connection, the continuing growth offered by a perfectly matched mate who drives our longing.

I can see this in myself and the relationships I've had over the years. I always saw myself as a person who desired a stable long-term situation. I was raised by conservative, Christian parents who did not believe in divorce. My father died when I was seventeen, and my mother, an attractive forty-something woman, was suddenly thrust into the relationship market. In those days, there were no online sites or video dating. She struggled with her widowhood because she believed she would be married to my father for life. That was what I was taught. That is what I aspired to, yet that is not what I practiced.

Dating was hard for me. I was awkward with the new dating reality of the seventies. I wasn't naïve, but I wasn't confident or had the prowess to garner dates easily. I dated for short bursts of time, nothing long-term or serious, then retreated into a cocoon of aloneness. It was almost if dates would just fall out of the sky, I would date them, or they would date me out of curiosity, then move on. I longed for a serious relationship, felt like not managing to achieve one was a fault of mine. This notion reinforced the idea that there was something wrong with me. I could garner initial interest but seemed to falter in keeping them interested. I just felt like I was a complex, mixed-up kid with very few features that generated real interest.

At twenty-seven I met a woman who had been married before and had a child. She and her husband had a turbulent relationship that ended in divorce. I was, in effect, a rebound for her. She showed me great affection, and I ate that up. An HSP getting reciprocal love was a big deal to me. We were really not very compatible, but shortly after we met, she became pregnant, and we married a few months later. It was the right thing to do, but it was with the wrong person. I knew it then, and also knew at some point I was going to have to leave the relationship. We went on to have two more children, and I love them all dearly, including my step-daughter, but I could not bear living in an inauthentic relationship.

About eight or nine years into the relationship, I had an affair with a coworker. To this day, I regret how that all played out. It was so against everything that I was raised to be but found myself longing for a meaningful relationship. This affair cost me the marriage, or should I say provided the out from the marriage. I suppose, as Dr. Aron suggests, like many HSPs, I was bored. It seemed more than that. I was missing something—the deep connection. Divorcing my wife and leaving the kids was the hardest single thing I have done in my life. I tried to reconcile, but it was to no avail. After that, I left for good.

The woman I had the affair with became my second wife. We had an intellectual bond lacking in my first marriage. She was a brilliant woman, fearless and confident. She challenged me in many ways and showed me unbridled love. I felt like we were equals and partners and settled into a long-term relationship.

We were together for twenty-four years. She helped me raise my kids; she allowed me to provide much needed extra income to my former wife above and beyond the court-ordered child support and alimony. In some ways, it was blood money to assuage my guilt and shame for having left the first marriage. My second wife had older children of her own, which often caused rifts between us. We had different parenting styles that often surfaced.

Oddly, we waited for twenty-two years to get married. By then, all the kids were grown, and we had relocated to another state. I assured myself that I was with the woman I would be with the rest of my life. We had gone through so much; I felt like our relationship had been battle-tested.

Two years later, we were divorced. I was struck by how our lives had drifted apart. I left my corporate job to pursue a small business; she stayed at work, continuing to bring home a salary. Our lives were no longer what they once were.

In training for my new business, I met another woman. She seemed to have the characteristics, the personality, and the temperament I was now seeking. She reflected my new status and she struck me. We did not have the affair that many assumed, but I cannot lie that I didn't have feelings for her.

It was the demise of my second marriage. This is the peculiar thing about the similar circumstances ending my relationships. Throughout my relationships, I was not constantly pursuing other women, as some philanderers would do. I reached a breaking point in the relationship, and only then, did something snap in me. Was it the boredom of which Dr. Aron speaks? Was I looking for an impossible ideal, an ideal that could not be real? Did I ignore the ideal when I selected my mates? It would seem my whole life I was looking for that ideal female, a compilation of what I was raised to look for, what culturally and generationally I was programmed to look for (i.e., the intellectual, liberated Playmate). Were my expectations too high?

I found myself alone for the first time in my life. I dated women from online dating sites; the women I fell for always turned out to be the wrong ones as well. I was adrift without a mate. I did this to myself, yet I never gave up on finding my ideal partner.

I thought I found her. She was not what I was expecting. I learned from these life lessons that my ideal was not real. I learned that giving up the ideal and just allowing a relationship to unfold is surprisingly effective, although not always a guarantee of success. Sadly, disappointment occurred again.

I love more deeply and fall sooner than most men. Yet I get bored faster. I seem to avoid love challenges, and that has cost me. If I had taken on more challenging relationships, I would have learned more about myself and my needs earlier in life. The key for us HSMs is to find that woman who pushes the right buttons and knows how to do it in inventive, creative, and novel ways. I believe another key is affection. It's all about balance, even with love.

CHAPTER 16:

Health Concerns – Anxiety, Depression and How they Affect HSMs

Depression in My Genes?

As I wrote this chapter, I experienced an old familiar feeling. It was a lonely, dark feeling, mostly void, but strong enough to register on the emotion scale. It came and went as sadness, like a disappointment, a feeling left behind, though it was not debilitating. I didn't curl up under a table or cry, but I felt it in my body and way deep in my mind. It was hard to express in words; it was mostly a body sensation, like pushing from my eyelids down through my shoulders and cratering in my chest cavity. Is this depression?

Before he died of a massive coronary, my father spent time in the hospital in a dark place. Fearful and absent of hope, he battled his own demons. He was diagnosed with depression. It tormented him and eventually, I believe it caused his death. He struggled with a small business, a growing family, and responsibilities that exceeded his capacities to cope.

I see the same in one of my children, and possibly the early formation in one of my grandchildren. All the individuals mentioned above are or were HSPs. The question is whether depression is more likely in HSPs or if this is simply a particular genetic component that gets passed from one generation to the next.

This Insidious Disease – Is It Just Chemistry or Is It Wayward Thoughts?

Research seems to indicate that depression does have a genetic component, at least a propensity for depression.[157] It's not necessarily a single gene but can be a suite of genes that causes depression. Of course, there are always environmental factors, and it seems that personality influences this as well. Because of the tendency for HSPs to feel things more intensely, it stands to reason that we are more prone to overwhelm with melancholy. On occasion, though, everyone has experienced sadness and disappointment and loss. Yet for the majority of people who experience sadness, recovery is inevitable, and they eventually bounce back.

There appears to be more to it than just incorrect thinking. By now, I think it's pretty clear (watch the commercials on the evening news) there is a chemical deficiency in the brain that can lead to depression. The pharmaceutical industry has stepped in to provide a pharmacopeia of medicines to battle depression and has provided an array of anti-depressant meds to numb and calm and flatten the experience for depressive individuals. I have tried these meds and found that via chemical manipulation, a whole host of other feelings, good and bad, are removed. It's like applying weed killer to your lawn: killing the weeds and your grass as well. I got off the meds as quickly as I could. For an HSP, losing touch with feelings is losing touch with self. Our feelings are how we experience the world.

When Feeling More Deeply Sucks: HSMs and Depression

HSM highs are pretty ecstatic, and our lows are fairly intense. Almost sounds bi-polar. But is depression a natural consequence of experiencing life with more depth, more feeling, and emotion? This might be a hint that HSPs are more likely to become depressed than, say the other 80 percent of the population. Do we swim lower down near the dark waters of loneliness, despair, and emptiness? Is that also caused by some genetic component or a switch that allows us to "paint" with more of the emotional palette humans experience? Maybe we open ourselves more to the darker feelings because we can or because we have no choice. Mix in our natural propensity to overthink situations, and it would be easy to see how this level of intensity could cause depressive episodes in HSPs.

Can Empathy Cause Depression?

Not to pile on here, but add our unusual capacity for empathy to absorb the feelings of others, and you can be certain that at some point overwhelm is lurking just over our shoulders. Even feeling bad about feeling bad, how our sadness affects others can be a cause of concern. Perhaps being too empathetic can lead to some of the characteristics of depression, but I wonder if it can cause depression. Empathy is a survival tool mostly seen in mammals—social creatures—where collective good is paramount to surviving. It seems that nature would not have devised this characteristic if it could be used to undermine the individual's wellbeing. As HSPs, this is one of our greatest assets. Yet if all the ingredients arrive at the same place at the same time—genetics, biochemistry, cognitive distortion, and personality type (i.e., HSP)—you can bake up some serious depression.

Where In Your Body Do *You* Feel It?

I have always gotten this feeling in my body when I'm down and lately I have begun to pay attention to it. It comes and goes, but I always know in my body when it arrives. Some people feel the emotion associated with depression in their chest area; others feel small and compressed; still others feel it in their shoulders, much like a weight, or a burning inside, or emptiness, like the void. I feel it in my chest and throat, a sinking, tingling sensation.

Sometimes it rises from my chest area and then sinks into my solar plexus. It's distinct, like a signal flag in a desert. It can be ephemeral, coming and going without warning. There's something very visceral about depression or feeling sadness.[158] The downing is felt in the body as well as in the head. It blankets you, wraps you tightly and not in a comforting way, filling you with a tight uneasiness. Which is why I think it's so hard to escape it.

Riding Through The Avalanche, Completing the Arc

How do you cope with and deal with depression? As stated previously, this is an insidious and potentially dangerous disease. Weathering the storm can be tricky and trying to remain objective in your head about what's going on is at best a fool's errand. Riding down the avalanche alone can leave you buried alive, slowly suffocating from the weight of forces greater than yourself. There are a myriad of ways of coping, some simple and easy—diet, exercise, relaxation techniques, and taking natural supplements. Others require a great deal of work and connection with someone trained to help—therapy, medicines, and learning new skills designed to help overcome the overwhelm.

Whatever the case, riding down the emotional arc of life requires completion of sorts. Returning to a place that's neutral or even better, a place of peace, will complete the ride. For HSMs, it's all a part of our great adventure. We sample emotions like a truck driver at an all-night buffet. It's easy to get caught up in our own experiences and not realize that most of the world isn't even aware of what we are processing. We've learned that sharing too much can be exposing too much, and so we hide in our world of emotion. This is especially true for negatively branded emotions, the ones men are not supposed to discuss. It's time to be mindful, particularly of those troubling emotions, acknowledge them, share them, and process them. We, too, have to paint with the dark colors sometimes to bring the light colors out on the canvas. It is often our interpretation of that darkness that sheds light for others who suffer likewise but can't express with our depth of processing.

I take comfort in writing this down. I know now in my heart that I will survive the avalanche.

When Not to Be Alone in the Lonely Dark Void

If you are truly alone and are facing the void of depression, reach out and get help. HSMs are just as likely as others when facing difficult depressive states, to think the unthinkable and to lose hope. We are cautious creatures by nature, but in the depth of darkness, release from these oppressive feelings can present in many unsavory forms. Realize help is out there and that you are not alone. Remember, we need all HSMs on deck now. Your life is important.

HSPs and Anxiety, Depression and Health Concerns

In spite of common misconceptions about the propensity for highly sensitive people to be predisposed to anxiety, depression, and somatic illness, there does not appear to be any strong evidence to suggest genetic links to these illnesses for individuals with Sensory Processing Sensitivity.[159] However, characteristics of HSPs, such as overstimulation and overprocessing, may cause avoidance behaviors that seem similar to others who display neurotic behavior or have anxiety and depression. [160] There is some correlation between SPS and Social Anxiety Disorder (SAD). SAD is a persistent fear of one or more social or performance situations in which the person is exposed to unfamiliar and novel people or possible scrutiny by others. [161]

A stronger correlation between SPS and Harm Avoidance appears to highlight the desire by most HSPs to avoid situations or circumstances in which they may become overwhelmed. Harm avoidance is a behavioral inhibition to avoid punishment, novel stimuli, or non-reward situations.[162] Again, this seems to be a common pattern among many SPS individuals. Harm avoidance appears to be triggered by an overly active amygdala, a fear reaction center in the brain, which is something that SPS individuals often display.

HSPs share some characteristics with Bi-Polar Disorder (BPD) individuals. BPD is generally caused by chemical imbalances in the brain and results in severe pendulum-like mood swings from manic to depressive.[163] The common mood swings of SPS personalities may appear to observers to be like BPD, although the source of the mood swings is different and certainly not as severe. One other common attribute shared between BPD and SPS is what is referred to as "Leaky Sensory Gate,"[164] which means there is a low threshold of sensory filters which trigger behavioral and sometimes emotional reactions. SPS individuals are often tracking low below the radar on sensory stimulation and often get bombarded with inputs that non-HSPs rarely perceive. This bombardment and processing of data can lead to overstimulation and withdrawal or avoidance, as noted above.

Because of the sensory inputs and deeper processing, HSPs tend to become more anxious and stressed more often than non-HSPs. A study showed a greater correlation between SPS individuals and greater levels of stress and ill-health.[165] One of the explanations offered is that SPS folks tend to have an ability to discern more somatic information and the awareness of that can be a cause of greater stress.

In other words, with heightened sensory awareness, which includes feedback from the body, HSPs can sense illness perhaps more clearly than others. This is not to say that HSPs are hypochondriacs, but rather the ability to sense somatic minutiae may lead to more worry about body health. This body angst, in turn, leads to stress and anxiety about health issues.

There is some correlation between being HSP and symptoms of neuroticism and displaying a tendency toward health complaints.[166]

HSPs are often assumed to be shy and withdrawn. However, the idea of social avoidance is not always associated with shyness, but rather an attempt to prevent overstimulation by HSPs.[167] The avoidance of crowded rooms, noisy, loud environments, is not necessarily correlated with shyness in HSPs but rather the avoidance of things that overwhelm them. Many HSPs, myself included, are not that shy, but can't keep the social interaction button pressed on continuously—it's just not in our nature. We need some downtime to rejuvenate.

Another study analyzed common features between SPS and Autism Spectrum Disorder (ASD), Post-Traumatic Stress Disorder (PTSD), and Schizophrenia. The conclusion was that although there was some overlap in symptoms displayed, much of which has to do with sensory sensitivity, the reactions beyond the initial sensations are quite different in SPS individuals than in those displaying the other traits/disorders.

What was found was that those with SPS have an innate ability to override aberrant reactions and process the sensory input with greater empathy, more memory capacity (for appropriate reaction), more self-other processing, in a more adaptive package, that makes HSPs more balanced.[168] This adaptive feature makes having SPS individuals useful for survival purposes. This idea is confirmed by Dr. Elaine Aron when she admits that HSPs are more prone to depression, anxiety, and stress, but these innate features give us an enhanced ability to cope and integrate these stimuli given sufficient time and space.[169]

Although it's difficult to make a definitive claim about all HSPs, I think we can assume from the research currently available that although HSPs tend to display characteristics of many other psychological traits and disorders, in fact, it is a unique personality characteristic.

The gist of the trait appears to be the ability to sense information from the environment in greater amounts than non-HSPs. HSPs have a secret weapon in processing this information that many of the disorders discussed do not. It is our ability toward empathy, seeing the other, and ability to process the information that lends us more balance deeply. It is easy to misidentify an HSP man, woman, or child as having a personality disorder, when, in fact, it is merely the lay of the land for SPS. We are not dysfunctional, but our functioning is unique and sometimes puts us at odds with other non-HSPs and the world at large.

This is not to say that HSPs do not have some of the disorders discussed; however, we should not easily batch them up with SPS and create the label game with perfectly functioning HSPs. One key piece of information derived from several studies was the effect of parenting on HSPs. The results suggest that HSPs thrive as adults when they are raised in positive environments, given encouragement and the opportunity to discover on their own and at their own pace the world around them.[170]

Nurturing and love are important to HSPs. The consequences of poor parenting, either overprotection or aloofness, can cause future problems for people with SPS. The outcomes are more likely to be anxiety, stress, and depression. The importance of getting this right requires recognition of sensitivity at an early stage, knowing how to interact with an HSP child clearly, and providing them with love, acceptance, and space to grow into happy, highly functioning adults. HSPs raised in this type of environment thrive as adults. That seems clear.

CHAPTER 17:

HSMs, Gay Men, and Gender Identity

Gay Men, HSMs and Toxic Masculinity

It dawned on me recently that many of the gay men I've met over the years had a certain sensibility about them; a wit and intelligence that suggests an awareness of things, things that are not just physical, but things that are lying beneath the surface in a different realm. I've thought it's intuition or emotional intelligence qualities that they might share with highly sensitive people. Being men, perhaps there was a common link with highly sensitive men that we might share. A quality more developed in HSMs and gay men. Something decidedly non-sexual, like how our brains might be wired for processing emotional content.

Writing about gay men or gay culture and being a straight man has some inherent issues. It's kind of like a white male writer penning a novel from a black male's POV. You can read all you want, do your research, make generalizations, but you will never be sure if you've nailed it because it is not your experience. Nevertheless, pushing on bravely, I have a sense that as a highly sensitive man there may be some characteristics that gay men and HSMs share. And you have to believe there are intersections between the two groups, such as gay men who are also HSMs. Both groups suffer from some of the same issues with the current prevailing paradigm on masculinity. Both groups know there need to be changes made with our culture's definition of masculinity.

As an HSP male, I have found myself sometimes balking at the idea of comparing high sensitivity with being a quality associated with females or gay men. It always hits a core issue on internalizing what masculinity is to me. Not easily fitting into the idealized American masculine model basically means you are either all man and all in, or you are effeminate (acting like a woman) or gay (which *by that* definition is not a real man).

This disregards the notion that sensitivity is a human characteristic and not a sexually derived or gender trait. We, as HSP males, need to recognize that in ourselves. We are part of a toxic masculine culture by proximity that downplays sensitivity in males. This definition is narrow and exclusive. Being something by association is not a true definition and fails to understand the complex nature of human personality, which is so nuanced, so wide-ranging, so infinitely complex that simplistic definitions are beyond utility. Individuals want to be recognized for their uniqueness. And so I say damn the tiny and rigid boundaries of small boxes that small box people want to place people.

Are there perceived characteristics among many straight HSMs that are shared with gay men? The idea that men of different sexual preferences can share other qualities, such as sensitivity, a difficult quality for many men to absorb about themselves, makes comparisons seem problematic— like if we share one thing, we must share all things. This flies in the face of science, which has, over the years, expanded the notions about what the human genome is capable of producing. The diversity of humanity where bits on-bits off, in gene expression, is mind-boggling. For straight men, the notion that being gay is a contagious condition that too close of an association can make you gay by contact is ludicrous, yet it makes the simple discussion about shared characteristics almost taboo for straight men in the larger context of masculinity. This could explain why I have hardly found anything online about this topic.

How is sensitivity in men perceived in the gay community in lieu of the traditional American masculine definition, which includes sensitivity as a primary feminine trait? From a straight male's point of view, I would think it is highly prized, but perhaps, not as much as I imagined.

Traditional masculine values affect how many gay men feel about themselves and their same-sex relationships. These values include: 1) men should not be feminine, 2) men must be respected and admired, 3) men should never show fear, and 4) men should seek out risk and adventure. Also, 5) men should be successful, 6) achieve power and status, 7) compete with other men, 8) restrict their emotions, 9) restrict affectionate behavior with other men and, finally, 10) men should be work and career-driven.[171] Sound familiar?

Since all men raised in our culture are subject to the "boy or man" code, we are all influenced by the biases of this masculine codex. Some gay men embrace these very same masculine values. Therefore, some gay men prefer themselves and their partners to be "manly" men[172], causing some to have biases against potential partners because they display traditional female traits, i.e., sensitivity. This may affect the perception of the character of sensitivity as a pejorative trait for those gay men who are attempting to live up to the same masculine role model that highly sensitive straight men struggle with as well. This might not be true for all gay men, but the effects of these man rules affect at some level all men.

Studies show that men who have issues with living the traditional male role model tend to have insecurities, shame, and psychological issues in interpersonal relationships (gay and straight).[173] Why? Largely, because there is a failure to live up to internalizing this value of masculinity, and most men don't see themselves measuring up. Add in persistence in dysfunctional behaviors because of these masculine values or even worse;

some carry trauma experienced early in life during masculine role social-ization. With these cumulative effects damaging psychological wellbeing; you have the making of our current toxic stew.

Many gay men in these studies hardly found any positive character-istics associated with masculine characteristics but found adverse effects in not living up to the masculine ideals. The subsequent results found that these same men had to "butch" it up to feel adequate.[174] Many gay men feel traditional male role models forced them to objectify their bodies and found a conflict of being masculine enough because of their sexual pref-erences. Imagine being the subject and object of this idealized masculine role model.

To add further complexity, some studies suggest that gay men have many common biological traits with heterosexual women: spatial reason-ing, hearing and voice cadence and tone, finger length (index and ring finger), and other biological markers.[175] Many gay men prefer female-ori-ented occupations (this may include teaching, counseling, fashion, etc.).

Gay men's brains are more like straight women's in that they have common wiring.[176] The anterior commissure is bigger in gay men's brains versus straight men's. This serves as a link between the temporal lobes and with a more active amygdala, produces more intuitive, empathetic, and spiritual natures, not to mention more emotional processing. In addition, gay men and straight women may have more symmetrical shaped brains than straight men and lesbians.

What does this mean? Are gay men masculine versions of the feminine? Of course not. None of this is to suggest that gay men are not masculine or should be perceived to be more feminine. My point is to look at common-alities and shared problems with highly sensitive men who are often seen because of their sensitivity as being more feminine. Frankly, I wonder if the characteristics of sensitivity, truly a non-gender characteristic, may have found more ways to reveal itself in the population through genetic expression. Brain wiring for sensitivity may need to be further explored.

Some of the biological markers gay men share with straight women are flipped in lesbians. Lesbians have more in common with straight men. These biological anomalies are just another example of how nature creates diversity by the expression of utilizing a rich palette of human genes. It should be noted that all HSPs have the characteristic of a hyper-responsive amygdala.[177] Incidentally, no research suggests there are higher incidences of HSMs who are gay than there are in the general population, although it seems there might be. Although I don't know that studies are now available determining the brain differences between HSP males and non-HSP males, it would be interesting to see what, if any, there are in the wiring of the brains.

Some of the highlighted characteristics often associated with women (intuition, empathy, and sensitivity), gay men (in a general sense) and highly sensitive males are quite striking. These are higher levels of emotional processing, greater intuition, higher empathy, and a greater level of spiritual focus.

Granted, none of this is evidenced-based or backed by studies, but I suspect that a population of HSPs, gay men, and straight women, is a significant number of humans sharing these common characteristics of empathy, intuition, compassion, and emotional processing. This is also a group of individuals who have been impacted greatly by the current masculine role models espoused by the U.S. and the U.K.

Why is this significant? We are all subject to and live within the domain of the current toxic masculine milieu that has been tolerated by all the communities mentioned above. At the root of this is the idea of hegemonic masculinity,[178] which legitimizes white male dominance and justifies the subjugation of women and minorities of all stripes. This includes gay and lesbian communities. This has been the role model for centuries with its characteristics of violence and aggression, stoicism, risk-taking, emotional suppression, lack of empathy, competitiveness and subjugation of women, gays, and people of color.

How can gay men and HSP straight males ally to help redefine masculinity in a new way that is relevant to our world? We could start with new boy codes for our young men, one in which we allow them to tell us where they fall on the continuum. No shame, no guilt, no fitting into narrow boxes. Let them grow into what they are. Some will be traditional; others will not. But let them find themselves with wise guidance from parents and responsible feeling adults. By doing this can we aid women and others who have been victimized by this toxic masculinity, by allowing boys and men to choose a more beneficial form of masculinity. By eliminating toxic patriarchal masculinity to free men from a role model that chokes us all allows us as men to be more empathetic, less hung up on dominance, and focus on cooperation and rejuvenation.

In the end, it is all about power. Your power comes from within you. You express it with your life. However, using that power to squelch someone else's power is toxic, not only to them but to you as well. Men, we need to wake up to this. We can brand a new type of masculinity, a masculinity that expresses the male energy (yang), but recognizes and embraces the balancing female energy (yin) within us. It is not weakness, but strength, our innate human strength.

Approaching the Androgynous Zone

One thing we know about HSP males is they typically are more empathetic than most Non-HSP males. With empathy comes more emotion, more feeling, less aggressive behavior, more nurturing—all characteristics typically associated with females. This leads me to think that HSP males or highly sensitive males (HSMs) are more likely to rate higher on the androgynous scale (yes, there is one, more on that later).

When I speak of androgyny, I am referring to a psychological tendency to be neither strongly masculine or feminine,[179] a balance between gender characteristics referring to cultural norms and the balancing between those norms. I am not referring to physical attributes (fashion, appearance) or sexual preferences (transgender, asexual, or bisexual).

Some recent examples culturally of androgynous males appear regularly through rock music history. One of the early trendsetters was Elvis Presley. Later, Jimi Hendrix, David Bowie, and Prince were a few of the artists who presented to the world a mix of both male and female energy on the stage. These men were all considered icons in music, equally attractive to both men and women. In acting, I can think of Brad Pitt and Johnny Depp; both have boyish good looks, seeming as much feminine as masculine. But again, not to dwell on the physical attributes, it is projected energy or emotional processing I want to consider.

In the arts, androgynous behavior is quite prevalent—in fashion, theater, music, and other artistic endeavors. The history of androgyny goes back into ancient times, but I found it remarkable that it was even promoted by early Christian fathers, such as Origen, as a noble, spiritual balance between masculine and feminine.[180] In the middle ages, androgynous individuals were seen as the perfect human configuration, a perfect balance between both male and female characteristics; this balanced identity was seen to be an efficient means to deal with situational issues. By ignoring social convention, adaptability was considered to be paramount to solving a problem.

Dr. Sandra Bem, the developer of the BEM scale of Androgyny,[181] has done quite a bit of research on androgyny. She asserts that androgens are more socially and behaviorally flexible and because of that can be more mentally healthy. In recent years we have seen the rise of the metrosexual, males who embrace their inner peacock, and more men are spending more time on fashion, appearance, and embracing grooming in ways that in years past were seen as effeminate.

This balancing of male/female characteristics reminds me of Carl Jung's dichotomy of the anima (female) and animus (male) within each individual. This no doubt reflects the ancient Taoist ideas of yin and yang, the male and female energy, balanced and in harmony, swirling around inside every male and female.

Bringing this back home to Western, and specifically American culture, what characteristics make a man seem more feminine? We all have heard about the characteristics and roles our society expects from men and women. Most researchers agree norms are a consequence of social rules and values. An individual's disposition on where he or she fits on the cultural spectrum is largely based on genetics, unconscious or conscious identity, and social pressures from external sources.

In the 1950s, Talcott Parsons proposed a model of family roles in which he stated that feminine behavior was summarized by the term expressive (internal), while male behaviors were considered more instrumental (external).[182] His subsequent list of behaviors associated with females and males has long since been refuted and seems archaic and quaint. Everything from education, work, housework, and childcare to decision-making were all delineated by this expressive versus instrumental parameter.

One can easily surmise that internal, expressive roles were code for emotional behavior and external, instrumental roles were code for logical and rational behavior. With women now taking a more active role in work, education, and decision-making, these archaic role models now seem comical. This is both liberating for women, but also presents a liberation possibility for men.

With societal norms being more amorphous and porous these days, the roles that men play in a more generic sense are starting to blend, bend, and balance out of necessity. Through continued socialization, our behaviors become molded via shifting family, spiritual, and school values that in many cases are changing because of increasing economic factors. We are seeing more trends toward less restrictive male/female models.

Yet we still hold on to old masculine modeling in our culture. We still adhere to the age-old characteristics of "me Tarzan, you Jane" in which male physical dominance, hare-brained risk-taking behavior, suppression of emotional response (and I would add, tender emotion), continue to be the norm for our boys and men; where rational and logical thinking stifles intuition, aggressive behaviors are rewarded, and the mindless accumulation of wealth is at the expense of the greater common good. This is the hegemonic masculinity[183] we portray in our movies, novels, and other modeling forms that we illuminate and elevate as our masculine heroes: no weakness allowed here, grasshopper.

That is a helluva a lot to expect from any one person. Although I would never discount the pressures on women, especially single mothers, there is enormous pressure on men to live up to an archaic role model that is literally killing us. The number of males over fifty committing suicide is increasing yearly. We lock men into unrealistic expectations and then give them no outlet to release this pressure. I still believe that a boy called a "sissy" is under incrementally more pressure than a girl labeled a "tomboy."

I'm not saying it's always easier for females displaying male characteristics, but the pressure for boys to conform, which is mighty, comes smackdown on their little heads to drop their gentle ways and man up. Often this comes from the father, typically the stern disciplinarian in the family, who expects the son to live up to his own manly definitions of what a boy is supposed to be. For girls, I argue that their tomboyish ways are considered a passing phase and seem to be more tolerated. Hence, the pressures start early for boys and lay between our conscious awareness and buried deep in our unconscious.

If we are seeing more androgynous behavior, is this tendency toward moving to the middle (balanced characteristics) within an individual's personality a genetic trait? Do HSMs have by nature that trait, by our gentler, more empathetic ways? Is it a bits on-bits off configuration in our genes that make us seem more androgynous?

At the core of our personalities are HSMs, a combination of both male and female attributes that allow us to be more empathetic, more nurturing, more emotionally driven. If so, is that a good thing or a bad thing? Does it make us more vulnerable? Or, we can argue, as Bem said, we are more flexible and stronger because of it.

As HSMs, we can see ourselves as the new model for males in a society that is changing for both male and females. The rapid technological changes in our society must be moderated by human adaptations that continue to emphasize the human characteristics that focus on sensitivity and empathy. Culturally we need to show clear sensitivity to our effects on the environment, on society, on perpetuating the population, and emphasizing equality.

I would argue there is a shift in energy going on now. A world too dominated by yang energy is breaking down to allow the yin energy to bring in balance. This may seem troublesome for some men, but HSM men will lead this effort and embrace the change. We are perfectly suited to this task, although we need to recognize opportunities when we see them.

As I say this, ironically, I find that as I get older, I seem to become more anchored in masculine energy. I don't know if it's a function of age, resignation, or just my comfort level with more balance in my personality, which allows more of my masculine side to come through. Nevertheless, I embrace the changes ahead as I imagine the yin/yang fish endlessly chasing each other's tails, striving for perfect balance, that constant motion, melting into perfect harmony.

Personal Experiences

If you were born sensitive and are a male, the first thing that comes to mind to most people is that you are effeminate. If you are effeminate and male, the next thing that comes to mind is that you must be gay. A leap and an assumption if there ever was one. This, as if both being effeminate and being gay are bad things.

I see sexual identity as being a continuum, may even be fluid, as it is for some individuals. However, this should never be confused with sensitivity. Sensitive men have a range of emotion and sensation, and I dare say the perception that eludes most men. Women are traditionally much better at this, but HSP males possess some of this superpower. Growing up, because of my sensitivity, I never assumed I was effeminate or even gay. It just never crossed my mind. I knew what my sexual identity was pretty early on in life. I didn't even know about gender identity, so that topic never came up. I wanted to be a man and always tried to fit the good ol' Southern male role model.

That model has been somehow locked into time. It reflects a day when men had hegemony, and females were seen as weak and inferior. They needed protection and security. That's what men provided. That's what I aspired to; even as I watched the feminist movement unfold and begin dismantling this archaic model of masculinity. The problem has always been toxic masculinity; it damages females and males of all ages. All men suffer from the heavy yoke of this distortion. We will not crush it in one fell swoop. It will not disappear overnight. And women will need the aid of men to rein in its destruction.

We must start by teaching our young boys another way. Part of the noxious nature of hegemonic masculinity is in the devaluing of women and feminine qualities. Men place women in an inferior status by implying that women are inherently weak and fragile. In light of scientific evidence that claim seems beyond ludicrous. The endurance of women is legendary, their strength should be a source of inspiration, yet it is denied by toxic masculinity. The feminine side of all humans should be valued. A man showing feminine tendencies is not denying his sex or betraying his manhood; he is fully expressing his humanity.

This balance in men has become unhinged. We now even expect women who are in the halls and places that men have traditionally frequented to project this masculine persona.

If we do not abrogate this imbalance in males, our society is doomed to implode with the destructive power of imbalanced and unbalanced masculinity. This is to say that the destructive nature of unbridled masculinity, not balanced by female energy, will lead us to a place of no return. Witness the destruction of war, of pollution, of greed, of lust for power, of sexual abuse, and the corruption of morals, and you see the destructive side of masculine energy.

This is not about a single man or the gender of a man; it is the flowing power within our society fueled by toxic masculinity. It is letting loose the firehose of testosterone-laden manhood and applying a scorched earth policy on the planet and its inhabitants. It will take us all down, poisoning humanity.

As I get older, I am learning to be comfortable with my sensitive male nature. I now frame it in my mind as a gift. I prize my uniqueness and the rarity of my personality type. I seek to encourage it in all young boys/men I meet who are HSP, many just opening up their eyes to their gift to explore this trait.

We men can only change toxic masculinity by modeling and promoting another way. Not all men will be like us, but we are a buffer from testosterone laden warrior types; we are the wise counselors, the gentle priests, the deep and passionate thinkers who write the poetry, produce iconic imagery, and speak of peace and harmony, and yes, when necessary defend the species. We are not cowards; we are not afraid. We see the other way, the big picture.

We are fluid and express both our divine sides, masculine and feminine. We are not amorphous or androgynous or transgender. We are spiritual journeyers, listening, watching, waiting, teaching, and learning. We express those natures because we can and we should.

CHAPTER 18:

Can't Find My Way Home

I have been on a physical journey and a spiritual quest for the better part of ten years. I left a good corporate job, a good secure marriage, and a comfortable life to pursue the elusive unicorn of happiness, right livelihood, and to fulfill what destiny I had left in life. It has been full of painful lessons, foolish turns, odd shifts of fate, and serendipity, with long pauses of loneliness and seemingly empty space.

A few years back I took a vacation to Eastern Oregon. Part of the trip was to climb a very narrow, wash-boarded dirt road up a sheer hillside. Driving it was scary, hardly room for two cars to pass and in some places only room for one car. Even in a four-wheel-drive vehicle, the sheer drop-offs were intimidating and nerve-wracking. The first few miles were filled with anxious caution, and I knew without turnouts that there was no turning back.

Once we leveled out on the plateau above, the road widened, making the remainder of the journey a wonderful excursion. At the summit, we were just over a mile above the meandering Snake River far down below. It was a beautiful and awe-inspiring sight, well worth the heart-pounding ascent.

Such is life. Tolkien once remarked in his *Lord of the Rings* trilogy, "not all those who wander are lost." I hold this thought close to me when all seems murky and unclear. Sometimes it's not about finding the path, but rather allowing the path to find you.

No trail taken is ever wasted, even those that lead us on dead ends. There is truth in every turn. Just like small trail flowers along the way, easy to overlook or step down with heavy beating feet, but each a small bundle of beauty to behold and a valued treasure if one examines closely. One need only look up and around to grasp a view so beautiful that it hurts to leave, once seen is then sealed in the heart forever.

However, any trail can be a trial. As an HSP male, I have often wondered how well suited I am for this journey. Is it harder for me because of my inherent HSP characteristics? Am I just prone to taking these side treks or does life have to force me into these non-linear loops?

Being sensitive and a gypsy seems odd cohabitants in my personality, yet maybe it makes me well suited for this journey. With positive HSP qualities such as awareness, creativity, empathy, appreciation, intuition, and passion, I think it makes me a better observer and chronicler of all that I take in. The real test is how well I can integrate, process, and assimilate the lessons of the trip.

We HSPs are complex creatures. Our life journeys often test our strength and courage. We are strong but strong like water, not like rock. Our strength is pliable, amorphous, and fluid, and what seems soft is powerfully persistent. A knife can scratch a rock, yet does nothing to the water. Water, given time, can erode even the hardest, most immobile and immutable rock. So, which is the stronger? The silent rock edifice standing on the shore or the crashing, relentless wave?

Finding the nuggets on our journey is what makes life worthwhile. We are both sensitive and highly sensing, which makes these shiny chunks easier to spot, but harder to process. Emotionally charged events can leave the heart heavy with doubt, remorse, or sorrow. Key stressors for us on the journey are crazy zigs and zags in life when our journey deviates from the plan and our expectations falter. Challenges tax us, and having to handle less than desired outcomes when we make personal wrong turns add to our rumination. We then ride the tidal waves of immense highs and lows. Finding the secret treasures in our journey can rejuvenate and enlighten us, especially when we need that lift.

Allowing that mash-up of good and bad to mix and ferment can make the sum of the journey something to savor, a deep reflective lesson, one for growth.

We do this with complex emotions, crammed life lessons, solitary journeys, all without the ability to see far down the road. We still need to step forward, one foot leading the other, not always knowing where the trail leads, bending around a broad tree, descending into a deep, dark glen. We never know for sure. The existence of the trail is a testament to the fact that others have preceded us. We must trust the instincts and history of the trail, relishing every moment, fighting back the doubt, knowing that the trail is not always the destination, but the path wherein the journey lies. As Lao-Tzu, the Chinese philosopher expressed, "What is beyond, is also here."

As for me, faith, trust, and anticipation of my destination keep me boot-bound to the ground ahead of me. The power to imagine getting back home to familiar faces and longed-for places is what sustains me. Wasted and tired, beat down but inspired, I keep looking to find my way home again. No longer the same man who left. Soon, I will know, as Forrest Gump said, *"I'm tired now. I think I'll go home."*

Endnotes

1   https://en.wikipedia.org/wiki/Sensory_processing_sensitivity

2   Ibid

3   https://www.ncbi.nlm.nih.gov/pmc/articles/PMC3409988/

4   https://www.ncbi.nlm.nih.gov/pmc/articles/PMC5832686/

5   https://www.ncbi.nlm.nih.gov/pmc/articles/PMC3409988/

6   https://www.ncbi.nlm.nih.gov/pmc/articles/PMC5832686/

7   http://hsperson.com/about-dr-elaine-aron/

8   https://en.wikipedia.org/wiki/Labeling_theory

9   https://www.psychologytoday.com/blog/alternative-truths/201005/why-its-dangerous-label-people

10 https://www.psychologytoday.com/blog/meditation-modern-life/201604/identifying-the-no-self

11 https://www.psychologytoday.com/blog/authentic-engagement/201309/authenticity-and-identity

12 https://www.dictionary.com/browse/eccentric

13 http://psychology.wikia.com/wiki/Eccentric_behavior

14 http://www.genconnect.com/albert-einstein-nicole-kidman-jim-hallowes-list-of-famous-highly-sensitive-people/

15 https://hsperson.com/faq/evidence-for-does/

16 Ibid.

17 Ibid

18 Ibid.

19 https://en.wikipedia.org/wiki/Sensory_processing_sensitivity

20 https://scottbarrykaufman.com/wp-content/uploads/2013/08/Pers-Soc-Psychol-Rev-2012-Aron-1088868311434213.pdf

21 https://en.wikipedia.org/wiki/Sensory_processing_sensitivity

22 https://reader.elsevier.com/reader/sd/pii/S0149763418306250?token=4B
    B1776515ACDA4CC0506CE58BA16249C7D772B9A427B7342BFC4FF8
    F5B258BB385ED918DDB46C5C6176F9086AEE984A

23 https://scottbarrykaufman.com/wp-content/uploads/2013/08/Pers-Soc-
    Psychol-Rev-2012-Aron-1088868311434213.pdf

24 https://scottbarrykaufman.com/wp-content/uploads/2013/08/Pers-Soc-
    Psychol-Rev-2012-Aron-1088868311434213.pdf

25 Ibid.

26 Reference?

27 https://hsperson.com/faq/evidence-for-does/

28 https://www.hsperson.com/pages/1Aug05.htm

29 https://www.aconsciousrethink.com/5304/10-traits-deep-thinker/

30 https://www.simplypsychology.org/levelsofprocessing.html

31 http://psychology.wikia.com/wiki/Levels-of-processing_effect

32 https://academic.oup.com/brain/article/124/2/399/402300

33 https://www.ncbi.nlm.nih.gov/pmc/articles/PMC3385676/

34 https://www.psychologytoday.com/us/blog/what-mentally-strong-
    people-dont-do/201602/6-tips-stop-overthinking

35 Ibid.

36 https://www.inc.com/amy-morin/science-says-this-is-what-happens-
    when-you-overthink-things.html

37 https://en.wikipedia.org/wiki/Passive-aggressive_behavior

38 http://www.apa.org/monitor/mar03/angeracross.aspx

39 http://www.hsperson.com/pages/2May07.htm

40 https://www.psychologytoday.com/blog/passive-aggressive-
    diaries/201403/7-reasons-why-people-use-passive-aggressive-behavior

41 http://hsperson.com/pages/2Feb13.htm

42 http://executivereasoning.com/peptides/

43 http://reclaimyourtrueemotions.com/how-do-you-know-if-you-are-
    addicted-to-your-emotions/

44 http://executivereasoning.com/peptides/

45 https://drtracycooper.wordpress.com/2015/05/04/the-sensation-seeking-
    highly-sensitive-male/

46 http://www.menshealth.com/health/3-signs-you-started-as-a-girl

47 http://psychology.wikia.com/wiki/Positive_Disintegration

48 Ibid.

49 http://psychology.wikia.com/wiki/Autism

50 http://psychology.wikia.com/wiki/Sensory_processing_disorder

51 https://www.psychologytoday.com/blog/smashing-the-brainblocks/201511/7-things-you-need-know-about-fear

52 https://www.psychologytoday.com/blog/insight-therapy/201009/overcoming-fear-the-only-way-out-is-through

53 https://www.psychologytoday.com/blog/smashing-the-brainblocks/201511/7-things-you-need-know-about-fear

54 http://www.hsperson.com/pages/1Nov04.htm

55 http://www.huffingtonpost.com/dr-jim-taylor/kids-and-technology_b_2422535.html

56 http://www.butte.edu/departments/cas/tipsheets/thinking/reasoning.html

57 https://www.mindtools.com/pages/article/managing-perfectionists.htm

58 https://www.hsperson.com/pages/2May07.htm

59 https://www.goodtherapy.org/learn-about-therapy/issues/sensitivity

60 https://www.psychologytoday.com/us/blog/anger-in-the-age-entitlement/201404/whats-wrong-criticism

61 https://www.goodtherapy.org/learn-about-therapy/issues/sensitivity

62 https://www.psychologicalscience.org/publications/observer/obsonline/people-sensitive-to-criticism-may-be-biased-toward-focusing-on-the-negative-2.html

63 https://www.mybrainsolutions.com/library/2014/04/breaking-down-the-feeling-of-overwhelmed/

64 https://www.psychologytoday.com/us/blog/body-sense/201204/emotional-and-physical-pain-activate-similar-brain-regions

65 ibid

66 https://quietmooncounseling.com/2017/12/04/part-2-how-to-handle-overwhelm-hsp/

   https://www.goodtherapy.org/blog/conflict-resolution-four-myers-briggs-temperaments-040814

67 https://www.mbtionline.com/

68 https://hsperson.com/emotional-regulation-and-hsps/

69 https://www.apa.org/action/resources/research-in-action/protect.aspx

70   http://communication.oxfordre.com/view/10.1093/
acrefore/9780190228613.001.0001/acrefore-9780190228613-e-1

71   http://mediasmarts.ca/digital-media-literacy/media-issues/violence/
what-do-we-know-about-media-violence

72   http://pediatrics.aappublications.org/content/124/5/1495

73   https://drtracycooper.wordpress.com/2015/05/04/the-sensation-seeking-
highly-sensitive-male/

74   http://www.hsperson.com/pages/1May06.htm

75   https://drtracycooper.wordpress.com/2015/04/01/the-sensation-seeking-
highly-sensitive-person-hsp/

76   http://psychology.wikia.com/wiki/Impulsiveness

77   https://www.truity.com/personality-type/INFJ

78   http://www.myersbriggs.org/my-mbti-personality-type/mbti-basics/

79   http://www.teamtechnology.co.uk/tt/t-articl/mb-simpl.htm

80   http://personalityjunkie.com/the-infj/

81   https://en.wikipedia.org/wiki/INFJ

82   https://www.truity.com/personality-type/INFJ

83   http://psychology.wikia.com/wiki/Extraversion_and_introversion

84   https://hsperson.com/introversion-extroversion-and-the-highly-sensitive-
person/

85   Ibid.

86   http://jamesclear.com/junk-food-science

87   https://en.wikipedia.org/wiki/Insulin_resistance

88   https://www.ucsf.edu/news/2011/12/11089/comfort-food-may-be-self-
medication-stress-dialing-down-stress-response

89   http://articles.mercola.com/sites/articles/archive/2014/01/02/food-
affects-mood.aspx

90   https://www.forbes.com/sites/jennifercohen/2012/10/02/what-your-
junk-food-choices-say-about-you/#57db0f836ab5

91

92   https://www.psychologytoday.com/us/blog/the-highly-sensitive-
person/201805/introversion-extroversion-and-the-highly-sensitive-person

93   https://www.psychologytoday.com/us/blog/tech-support/201403/5-
pitfalls-positive-thinking

94   https://en.wikipedia.org/wiki/Idealist_temperament

95   https://psychology.wikia.org/wiki/Hypochondria

96 https://www.ncbi.nlm.nih.gov/pmc/articles/PMC3449016/

97 http://www.hsperson.com/pages/1Feb12.htm

98 https://pdfs.semanticscholar.org/2b8b/573d4c7a0e78b6b16d085d1fb85f8
61ed8fd.pdf

99 https://www.psychologytoday.com/us/blog/the-human-
experience/201304/how-stop-playing-the-victim-game

100 https://www.ncbi.nlm.nih.gov/pmc/articles/PMC4396524/

101 https://www.psychologytoday.com/blog/the-introverts-corner/200912/
introverts-and-parties-just-add-alcohol

102 https://www.ncbi.nlm.nih.gov/pmc/articles/PMC4012703/

103 https://psychology.wikia.org/wiki/Self-medication

104 https://psychology.wikia.org/wiki/Psychoactive_drug

105 https://en.wikipedia.org/wiki/Set_and_setting

106 https://www.psychologytoday.com/us/blog/sense-and-sensitivity/201111/
high-sensitivity-low-self-esteem

107 http://psychology.wikia.com/wiki/Emotional_security

108 http://psychology.wikia.com/wiki/Self_confidence

109 https://www.psychologytoday.com/us/blog/me-we/201312/10-sources-
low-self-esteem

110 Ibid

111 http://psychology.wikia.com/wiki/Unconscious_mind

112 https://en.wiktionary.org/wiki/appel_du_vide

113 https://en.wikipedia.org/wiki/Suicidal_ideation

114 http://psychology.wikia.com/wiki/Existential_crises

115 https://hsperson.com/faq/evidence-for-does/

116 ibid

117 http://psychology.wikia.com/wiki/Learned_helplessness

118 https://www.psychologytoday.com/us/blog/how-everyone-became-
depressed/201406/sad-worthless-hopeless

119 https://www.atrainceu.com/course-module-short-view/1473440-82_
depression-gender-matters-module-3

120 https://en.wikipedia.org/wiki/Suicide_in_the_United_States

121 http://psychology.wikia.com/wiki/Causes_of_suicide

122 https://drtracycooper.wordpress.com/2017/05/23/why-men-commit-
suicide-the-three-warning-signs-most-people-miss/

123 Ibid

124 https://hsperson.com/suicide-and-high-sensitivity/

125 https://www.atrainceu.com/course-module-short-view/1473440-82_depression-gender-matters-module-3

126 https://www.scientificamerican.com/article/how-lewy-body-dementia-gripped-robin-williams1/

127 https://deadline.com/2018/06/rose-mcgowan-anthony-bourdain-suicide-statement-depression-1202407718/

128 http://www.huffingtonpost.com/2015/01/30/sports-fan-mental-health-benefits_n_6565314.html

129 https://www.ukessays.com/essays/psychology/effects-of-violence-in-sports-psychology-essay.php

130 http://www.wbur.org/cognoscenti/2014/03/18/sports-violence-psychology-leonard-l-glass

131 http://www.huffingtonpost.com/douglas-labier/americas-continuing-empat_b_637718.html

132 https://www.theatlantic.com/politics/archive/2014/09/liberals-care-more-about-empathy-than-conservatives/380404/

133 http://articles.chicagotribune.com/2011-06-22/health/sc-health-0622-movies-impact-on-body-20110622_1_horror-films-intense-movies-birgit-wolz

134 http://www.scpr.org/news/2014/12/04/48457/what-watching-movies-can-tell-us-about-how-our-bra/

135 https://phys.org/news/2015-05-psychological-effects-music.html

136 http://www.telegraph.co.uk/culture/film/film-news/8647544/Men-and-women-should-never-watch-films-together-research-shows.html

137 https://www.entrepreneur.com/article/243792

138 http://www.telegraph.co.uk/finance/personalfinance/10075722/Money-habits-are-formed-by-age-seven.html

139 https://www.psychologytoday.com/blog/extreme-fear/201010/wholl-be-the-alpha-male-ask-the-hormones

140 https://en.wikipedia.org/wiki/Nice_guy

141 Ibid.

142 https://www.psychologytoday.com/blog/extreme-fear/201010/wholl-be-the-alpha-male-ask-the-hormones

143 http://www.artofmanliness.com/2014/07/07/the-myth-of-the-alpha-male/

144 http://ask.metafilter.com/299843/Who-Are-the-Successful-Nice-CEOs-Out-There

145 https://www.psychologytoday.com/blog/our-gender-ourselves/201108/is-the-end-the-alpha-male

146 http://www.artofmanliness.com/2014/07/07/the-myth-of-the-alpha-male/

147 Ibid.

148 http://hsperson.com/alanis-morissette/

149 https://www.psychologytoday.com/blog/sense-and-sensitivity/201509/looking-love-hsp

150 http://www.drjudithorloff.com/_blog/Dr_Judith_Orloff's_Blog/post/celebrating-the-highly-sensitive-man

151 https://www.psychologytoday.com/us/blog/sense-and-sensitivity/201802/the-hsp-relationship-dilemma

152 https://en.wikipedia.org/wiki/Human_mating_strategies

153 Ibid.

154 http://thematinggrounds.com/how-mating-works/

155 http://www.hsperson.com/pages/1Aug10.htm

156 http://www.hsperson.com/pages/1Nov10.htm

157 https://www.ncbi.nlm.nih.gov/pmc/articles/PMC3077049/

158 http://www.huffingtonpost.com/2014/08/21/what-depression-feels-like_n_5696227.html

159 http://reseauconceptuel.umontreal.ca/rid=1MWJVHXB3-1CJ056D-1GF/SPD_Sensory%20processing%20sensitivity%20and%20its%20relation%20to%20parental%20bonding,%20anxiety,%20and%20depression.pdf

160 Ibid.

161 https://www.ncbi.nlm.nih.gov/pmc/articles/PMC2174907/

162 Ibid.

163 https://www.psychologytoday.com/us/blog/sense-and-sensitivity/201707/are-you-highly-sensitive-and-bipolar

164 Ibid.

165 https://s3.amazonaws.com/academia.edu.documents/2003053/2006_Benham_-HSP_-stress_and_physical_symptom_reports.pdf?AWSAccessKeyId=AKIAIWOWYYGZ2Y53UL3A&Expires=1558111728&Signature=RLUMk7KgG75hj297JfZbYh3GF18%3D&response-content-disposition=inline%3B%20filename%3DThe_Highly_Sensitive_Person_

Stress_and_P.pdf

166 https://journals.sagepub.com/doi/pdf/10.1177/2165222816660077

167 Ibid/

168 https://www.ncbi.nlm.nih.gov/pmc/articles/PMC5832686/

169 http://www.hsperson.com/pages/2Feb10.htm

170 http://reseauconceptuel.umontreal.ca/rid=1MWJVHXB3-1CJ056D-1GF/SPD_Sensory%20processing%20sensitivity%20and%20its%20relation%20to%20parental%20bonding,%20anxiety,%20and%20depression.pdf

171 https://www.ncbi.nlm.nih.gov/pmc/articles/PMC5442596/

172 Ibid.

173 Ibid.

174 Ibid.

175 http://nymag.com/news/features/33520/index6.html#print

176 http://www.washingtonpost.com/wp-dyn/content/article/2008/06/22/AR2008062201994_pf.htm

177 https://www.psychologytoday.com/us/blog/love-and-sex-in-the-digital-age/201710/metoo-meet-imperfectmen

178 https://en.wikipedia.org/wiki/Hegemonic_masculinity

179 https://en.wikipedia.org/wiki/Androgyny

180 Ibid.

181 https://en.wikipedia.org/wiki/Bem_Sex-Role_Inventory

182 http://psychology.wikia.com/wiki/Androgyny

183 http://psychology.wikia.com/wiki/Sex_roles